Dedicated to the children and families whose
lives have been, are being, and will be transformed and
enriched through Boys Town's compassionate care.

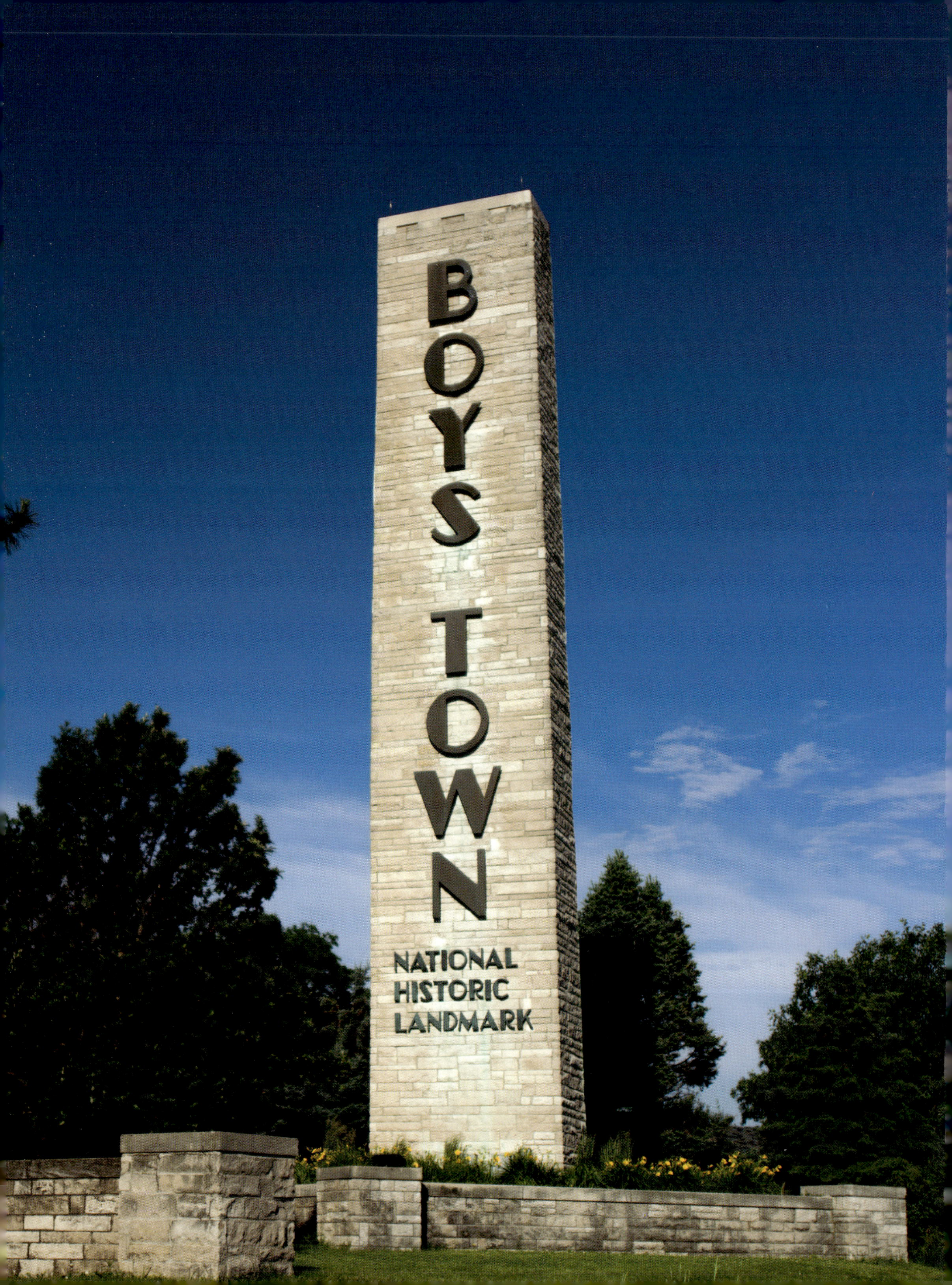
BOYS TOWN
NATIONAL
HISTORIC
LANDMARK

A Century of Service, A History of Healing

The Boys Town Story

By Thomas Lynch and Terry Hyland

THE
DONNING COMPANY
PUBLISHERS

The Donning Company Publishers
184 Business Park Drive, Suite 206
Virginia Beach, VA 23462

Lex Cavanah, General Manager
Nathan Stufflebean, Production Supervisor
Anne Burns, Editor
Terry Epps, Graphic Designer
Katie Gardner, Project Research Coordinator/Marketing and Project Coordinator
Monika Ebertz, Imaging Artist

Barry Haire, Project Director

Library of Congress Cataloging-in-Publication Data

Names: Lynch, Thomas J. (Thomas Joseph), author. | Hyland, Terry, author.
Title: A century of service, a history of healing : the Boys Town story / by
   Thomas Lynch and Terry Hyland.
Description: Virginia Beach, VA : Donning Company Publishers, [2016] |
   Includes bibliographical references and index.
Identifiers: LCCN 2016017553 | ISBN 9781681840543 (soft cover); ISBN 9781681840536 (hard cover)
Subjects: LCSH: Father Flanagan's Boys' Home--History. | Flanagan, Edward
   Joseph, 1886-1948. | Orphans--Nebraska--Boys Town. | Problem
   children--Institutional care--Nebraska--Boys Town. | Problem
   children--Behavior modification--Nebraska--Boys Town. | Social work with
   children--Nebraska--Boys Town. | Boys Town (Neb.)
Classification: LCC HV876.F4 L96 2016 | DDC 362.73/2--dc23
LC record available at https://lccn.loc.gov/2016017553

Printed in the United States of America at Walsworth

Table of Contents

Foreword

By Sarah Mohn

 *Sarah was a citizen of Boys Town for three years, graduating in 1992. In 1991, her fellow citizens elected her as the first female mayor in Boys Town's history. Sarah has served as the director of the Boys Town National Alumni Association, and for the past seven years, has worked with struggling families as a family consultant with Boys Town's In-Home Family Services program in Nebraska and Iowa.*

Father Flanagan's dream became a part of my reality when I arrived at Boys Town in 1989. While most Boys Town kids take weeks, months, and even years to realize what a good place they're in, I knew, within thirty short seconds, I was HOME.

Granted, there were good times as well as challenging times as I learned to live in a family while learning to love myself and others. I thank my Family-Teachers, my peers, my teachers and coaches, and Father Val Peter for teaching me I was valuable and worthy of respect. Boys Town gave me the opportunities to grow as a person and a leader and to eventually become a productive member of society.

As a sixteen-year-old, I felt a calling in my heart to give back to the HOME that saved my life. After graduation and college, Boys Town gave me that opportunity by hiring me as an Assistant Family-Teacher and later as a family consultant.

For nearly two decades, I have dedicated my life to keeping Father Flanagan's dream alive. Every day, it is my goal to keep his mission, his vision, and his values first and foremost in the work I do with children and their families. I am proud to be part of Boys Town's history and mission, and I will continue to serve as long as my mind, body, and soul allows, helping others in need in the same way Boys Town so compassionately helped me.

Foreword

By Tony Jones

Tony came to Boys Town with his brother Tyrone in 1983. After graduating in 1988, he attended the University of Nebraska-Omaha and later earned his bachelor's degree in human and social services from Bellevue University. He and his wife, Simone, have been Boys Town Family-Teachers since 1996. (Tyrone graduated from Boys Town in 1987, served in the U.S. Army, and now lives and works in Seattle.)

With only the clothes on our backs and a single pair of socks to share, my brother Tyrone and I stood ankle deep in the snow on a blustery winter day, wondering what would happen to us.

Our beloved great-grandmother, who cared for us all of our childhood, had lost her battle with cancer. Now we were orphaned and alone on the streets of Detroit, fighting for our lives and looking for the strength to reach out to her church for help. A kind priest at St. Elizabeth's, Father John Markham, contacted Boys Town in Nebraska on our behalf, and we soon were accepted into the residential program there.

When Boys Town opened its doors to my brother and me, we began to open our hearts to the spirit of its founder, Father Edward J. Flanagan. His dream was to give disadvantaged and underprivileged youth an opportunity to reach their full potential—physically, mentally, and spiritually.

At Boys Town, I learned how to triumph over adversity, achieve my goals, and let others love me. Boys Town gave me the love and guidance only a family can provide. But as I reflect on my life there as a youth, I recall a time when I was lonely and full of despair. I found myself struggling with what my future might hold after I left the Home. Having no one to turn to, I prayed to God to give me the strength to persevere. Then I started to realize I could positively influence the lives of others in the same fashion Father Flanagan had helped so many in his lifetime.

At Boys Town, I learned the true meaning of the phrase, "I am my brother's keeper." It means to walk in the footsteps of Father Flanagan and fulfill his dream by carrying on the work he started. It was this spirit of help, hope, and healing that had saved my brother and me.

My prayers were answered years later when I became a Boys Town Family-Teacher along with my lovely wife, Simone. For over twenty years, we have carried on Father Flanagan's mission by caring for nearly two hundred at-risk, hurting boys in our Family Home at Boys Town. Our work has been a living confirmation of one of Father Flanagan's most powerful and inspirational sayings: "The work will continue, you see, whether I am there or not, because it is God's work, not mine."

From the streets of Detroit to the streets of the Village of Boys Town, I have realized his dream and mine.

Acknowledgments

Boys Town's first century of service to America's most vulnerable citizens was authored by countless people who, over distinct eras and passages of time and complex, overlapping periods of social change, were united in a common mission to make the world a better place for children and families.

Similarly, chronicling Boys Town's incredible history of service and healing required the efforts of many talented and creative contributors—historians, archivists, designers, photographers, writers and editors, and reviewers. We acknowledge and thank the following Boys Town staff members for their invaluable contributions to this commemorative volume:

Sarah Mohn and Tony Jones for writing the book's forewords and sharing their perspectives as former Boys Town youth who now carry on our mission as Boys Town employees.

Tom Lynch, Benjamin Clark, Katherine Ehrig-Page, and other Boys Town Hall of History employees and volunteers for their meticulous work in identifying, locating, and preparing archival photographs and historical materials and ensuring accuracy in the storytelling.

Father Steven Boes, John Arch, Dan Daly (PhD), Laura Tatten, Kimm Dilocker, Marsha Johns, and other Boys Town administrators for their day-to-day leadership of Boys Town and providing their keen insight to ensure our centennial story was comprehensive and inclusive.

Michael Buckley for taking and compiling most of the modern color photographs that appear in the book, and Eli Hernandez and Anne Hughes for helping to coordinate overall photography needs and providing advice on design and layout issues.

Stan Graeve, Brent Robinson, and Michael Sterba for developing and writing stories about youth, families, and others whose lives have been changed and improved by Boys Town.

All Boys Town employees and volunteers—past and present—for bringing their own unique talents to the mission, being part of a team that always puts children and families first, and answering a calling whose rewards transcend those of any "normal" job.

Donning Publishing Company for its expert editing, design work, and direction in bringing the book's many different elements together to produce a truly remarkable keepsake of Boys Town's milestone anniversary.

Finally, Boys Town thanks all of its supporters—past, present, and future—for believing every child deserves to be loved, happy, healthy, and valued by society and every family should be strong and stable. Without our supporters' commitment and dedication, none of what Boys Town has accomplished over the past one hundred years would have been possible. Because of them, Father Flanagan's vision has come to fruition and HIS DREAM LIVES ON!

Introduction

It was a chilly day in early December 1917. Passersby hurried along the streets of downtown Omaha, Nebraska, their thoughts perhaps on Christmas, only two weeks away, and the preparations they still needed to make. Or, maybe they were wondering how the holidays would be different this year, with America now involved in the Great War being waged on the battlefields of Europe. In all the hustle and bustle, no one paid much attention to the tall, bespectacled priest who was shepherding several ragamuffin boys along the sidewalk.

When the little group reached a somewhat run-down Victorian-style mansion, the priest confidently strode to the front door, unlocked it, and bade his young charges to enter. Once inside, he turned to the cluster of expectant faces and welcomed the boys to their new home.

There was no ribbon-cutting ceremony. No parade with marching bands. No speech by the mayor.

When most people looked at Father Edward Flanagan's first home for boys, they perhaps only saw it as one man's "nice" gesture to give some poor street kids a bed, three square meals a day, and a roof over their heads. The young priest's act of kindness didn't register much on the landscape of current events; it was, after all, just another small effort to "do something" about the problem of hungry, homeless orphans and back-alley ruffians.

But Father Flanagan saw things much differently. In fact, even before more and more boys began showing up at his doorstep, looking for refuge and understanding, he was already envisioning a grand new future for childcare in America. On that ordinary day in that ordinary place, only he recognized an extraordinary revolution had begun.

And Father Flanagan knew exactly where he wanted the revolution to lead.

He dreamed of a community of family-style homes and schools, overseen by dedicated childcare professionals, where troubled children of all races, religions, and cultural backgrounds could find a second chance and start rebuilding their lives. He saw these communities being established across the country, along with other complementary programs that could help children and families grow stronger. He also saw a system of care that helped families create a more loving, nurturing home and solve problems that might otherwise separate kids from their parents. The end result, in Father Flanagan's mind, was an America—perhaps a world—where children were valued, respected, loved, cared for, educated, and guided so they could become good people, productive workers, involved citizens, and the caring, responsible parents of generations of children to come.

In the days, weeks, and years following that chilly December day in Omaha, a movement slowly gathered momentum. With courage and faith, Father Flanagan preached his principles of child and family care to government leaders, community decision makers, childcare advocates, and anyone and everyone who would listen, striking a nerve in the public's collective conscience and slowly recruiting a small army of supporters and believers.

Far ahead of his time, the good priest took childcare into uncharted territory, breaking down barriers and challenging the status quo, which, until then, often meant ignoring the needs of children and denying their God-given right to be happy, healthy, and hopeful about their future.

Today's Boys Town kids may look different from their "brothers" of the Home's early days, but they all have one thing in common: At Boys Town, they found a home where they could grow, learn, take control of their lives, and look toward to the future with hope and confidence. Saving children and healing families has always been the Boys Town way—then, now, and for the next hundred years.

Until the day he died in 1948 at age sixty-one, Father Flanagan devoted his life to the plight of children who needed someone to believe in them. Now, a century later, Father Flanagan's vision has proven to be 20/20 and his mission has grown to the epic proportions he imagined a century ago.

The story of Boys Town is the great American success story, with a significant difference.

Rather than being measured only in terms of its growth from a humble home for wayward boys to a national leader in the care of children and families, Boys Town's success also has been magnified and personified by the millions of people whose lives have been altered, redirected, and transformed through Boys Town's intercession. In many ways, Boys Town is a reflection of America and the American dream. Only here could a once-frail immigrant priest, armed only with an abundance of faith and an endless supply of hope, launch the idea that children are the nation's greatest asset and create something, one hundred years later, as a shining model for effective, compassionate child and family care, both at home and abroad. And while Father Flanagan ignited a revolution and established Boys Town as the gold standard for quality childcare, those who followed him as the Home's leaders mirrored his passion and determination in nurturing the dream.

Monsignor Nicholas Wegner took on the daunting challenge of succeeding Father Flanagan at his untimely death and brought financial stability to the Home, ensuring Boys Town could grow and help even more troubled children.

Monsignor Robert Hupp, Boys Town's third national executive director, brought seismic changes to the Home, recognizing the need for a new treatment approach and implementing a residential care model that remains one of Boys Town's flagship programs. In 1979, Boys Town began admitting girls, ensuring all children could have the opportunity to find hope and experience healing at the Home. Health care, especially research and treatment focused on helping boys and girls with hearing, speech, and other communication disorders, also became a priority as Boys Town National Research Hospital opened and grew to be internationally recognized for its work and leadership.

Father Valentine Peter, the fourth national executive director, elevated Boys Town from a local child and family care organization to one national in scope, both in its physical presence at more than a dozen sites across the country and in its impact in changing the way America cares for children and families.

Father Steven Boes, the current national executive director, introduced an enhanced Integrated Continuum of Care, emphasizing services that enabled Boys Town to help more children and families in their own homes while still providing quality out-of-home care for kids with greater needs. Under Father Boes, Boys Town also has pursued community initiatives, collaborating with local leaders and schools to concentrate services where they are needed most and giving families greater access to valuable resources. Boys Town also has expanded its research capabilities, studying the connection between biology and children's problem behaviors in order to develop new, groundbreaking treatment approaches.

Today's Boys Town is a reflection of Father Flanagan's vision as a multifaceted haven of hope and healing that touches the lives of more than two million people across the country every year. What began as an immigrant priest's revolutionary idea to change how America cared for children is now one of the country's largest nonprofit child and family organizations.

Boys Town has always enthusiastically accepted its leadership role in reshaping and reforming child and family care. **In essence, Boys Town has been America's conscience, exposing practices and policies that hurt children and championing reforms and changes that help children.** Boys Town's obligation has always been to help fix what is broken, to improve what works well, and to share expertise, experience, and knowledge so more children and families can benefit. That's why Boys Town continues to evolve and grow. And as the needs of children and families have changed and become more complex, Boys Town has responded by developing new ways to make a positive difference in their lives.

The story of Boys Town is an adventure spanning ten decades of modern American history. It's the story of a living, breathing organism, born through a mixture of faith and determination, nurtured to maturity through equal parts of hope and confidence, and thriving today because a simple dream of caring for children with love, respect, and dignity has been embraced and carried on by millions.

Through words and photos, this book chronicles Boys Town's incredible journey through a century of life-changing and history-altering service. Its pages carry the words and images of many of the people who built and supported Boys Town over the decades and, most importantly, the stories and reflections of those who were rescued by Boys Town. The volume is a touchstone to Boys Town's past as well as a model for understanding its future.

As Boys Town moves into its second century, it will continue to shine as a beacon of hope for all of America—for every child, every family, and every community—ignited by faith, dedication, and love, sustained through knowledge, research, and experience, and forever burning brightly because so many believe every boy and girl deserves a happy, healthy, productive life. For today's young people and for those of generations to come, the mission continues!

In its one hundred-year history, Boys Town has had only five national executive directors. Following the tradition of Boys Town's founder, Father Edward Flanagan, all have been Catholic priests. All five brought unique talents, perspectives, knowledge, and insights to this formidable position, helming the nonsectarian, nondenominational organization through times of peace, war, social upheaval, and historical, financial, and philosophical changes and challenges.

Tracing the tenures of these five national executive directors traces the history of Boys Town. And while each man's leadership made an indelible mark on the Home, none was ever bigger than the organization and the profound impact it had on the lives of countless youth and families and how America cares for its most vulnerable citizens.

A REVOLUTION IN CHILDCARE

In 1915, Omaha seemed to be flooded with homeless, jobless, and hungry men. A poor farm economy had sent thousands of men to the city in search of steady employment. Many got off the train in Omaha and wandered the streets seeking work and food. When they found no jobs, no shelter, little food, and even less hope, hundreds beseeched local churches for help. Many churches would provide a meal, but none had the resources to help so many men in need for a prolonged period of time.

CHAPTER ONE

The Visionary
Father Edward J. Flanagan
1917–1948

OPPOSITE: Father Edward J. Flanagan, founder of Boys Town. *(Portrait artist: Boys Town alumnus Paul Otero)*

Father Edward Flanagan had spent a short time with a parish in northeastern Nebraska shortly after celebrating his first Mass as a priest in Omaha. Returning to the city after being assigned to St. Patrick's Church, he witnessed firsthand the escalating plight of these homeless and unemployed men. Enlisting the aid of the St. Vincent dePaul Society, he was able to lease a vacant hotel as a temporary residence where he could provide meals, lodging, and work for at least some of the itinerant population.

The forty cots in Father Flanagan's Workingmen's Hotel were filled almost immediately after opening day in January 1916, and the list of those waiting to get in grew daily. As he would do many times later, Father Flanagan appealed to the public to help him help others. A generous outpouring resulted in sixty more cots, as well as clothing and shoes for the hotel's residents. Only six weeks after opening, twenty men had landed full-time jobs while others had garnered temporary work.

When the success of Father Flanagan's efforts came to the attention of Archbishop Jeremiah Harty, the archbishop transferred the priest to a different parish so he could devote more time to the hotel, which had since moved to a more spacious location. The new hotel had three hundred beds and an "employment agency" that by the end of 1917 had secured 1,500 jobs for its residents and former residents.

ABOVE: The Workingmen's Hotel at 11th and Mason Streets in downtown Omaha, Nebraska. In 1913, Father Flanagan opened this shelter for poor homeless men who were trying to find a job and bring stability to their lives.

LEFT: Father Flanagan stands in the doorway of a second Workingmen's Hotel at 209 North 13th Street in Omaha. Called the Livesy Flats, this second shelter offered apartments rented by homeless men with jobs.

But while this effort kept thousands of men off the streets of Omaha, it sometimes meant only a temporary respite in their lives. Many men had become so entrenched in their transient way of life, they were unable to make lasting changes. Discouraged, Father Flanagan wrote:

> I knew . . . that my life's work lay in the rehabilitation of these men. And yet, my methods were so basically wrong . . . In talking with the men, I learned that they had been orphaned in childhood . . . Or, they were members of large families where income was not sufficient to care for them . . . Or, again, they (came) from families broken by divorce. Invariably they were homeless and abandoned . . . They veered here, were shoved there throughout their formative years and, reaching a man's estate, were only shells of men . . . I knew that my work was not with shells of men, but with the embryo men—the homeless waifs who (had) nowhere to turn, no one to guide them.

A revolution was about to begin.

Father Flanagan at age twenty-seven, when he began working with Omaha's homeless men. Despite his youth, Father Flanagan was using innovative and sometimes unconventional methods to make a positive difference in the lives of others.

A Home for Boys

As serious as the problem with transient men was in Omaha in 1917, there was an even greater need when it came to the delinquent and homeless boys who roamed the city's streets. Some were orphaned, some were runaways, and others just had the sad misfortune of being born into poor families that could not feed or care for them. Desperate and hungry, many a youngster had resorted to stealing a loaf of bread, an apple, or money from an area merchant and had ended up in jail. The courts couldn't care for the many boys who were constantly shuffling through the system, and most ended up back on the street, bitter and bound to repeat their offenses.

In early December, Archbishop Harty relieved Father Flanagan of his parish duties so he could concentrate fully on his plan to operate a home for these wayward boys. Father Flanagan borrowed $90 from a trusted friend and put down the first month's rent for a large house near 25th and Dodge Streets in downtown Omaha. (For many years, the priest kept his promise not to reveal the name of this supporter, a prominent Jewish attorney named Henry Monsky. Monsky, who would be a lifelong supporter of Father Flanagan's work, shared the priest's concern for the youngsters who were caught in the court system with no real hope of permanent care.)

With a borrowed $90, Father Flanagan rented this Victorian-style boarding house at 25th and Dodge Streets in Omaha as his first Home for Boys. The first boys, gathered by Father Flanagan from the juvenile courts and the streets, moved into the Home on December 12, 1917.

EARLY LIFE PORTENDED VIRTUOUS DESTINY

Family, faith, and frailty shaped Edward Joseph Flanagan's future from his earliest days. Born near the village of Ballymoe, County Galway, Ireland, on July 13, 1886, Edward was plagued by poor health from infancy. Unable to work or play as hard as his three brothers and seven sisters, the frail youngster became a reader and an observer. John and Honora Flanagan—people of modest means and deep faith— hoped their son would one day become a Catholic priest, so they made every effort to educate him in the best schools. In time, Edward did feel the calling to enter the priesthood.

The Village of Ballymoe, County Galway, Ireland, the birthplace of Father Flanagan, as it looked around 1904, the year he left for America.

In the summer of 1904, Edward boarded a liner bound for America, where he hoped to enter the seminary and begin his life of service to God. He earned an undergraduate degree in two years from Mount St. Mary's College in Maryland and then moved to St. Joseph's Seminary in New York City. But challenges and obstacles soon interfered with his goals. A St. Joseph's staff member described Edward in 1907 as a "nice little gentleman, but delicate in health . . . just fair in talents." A bout with double pneumonia kept him out of classes for months, and the weakened state of his lungs convinced seminary officials he could not handle the rigors of another term.

Edward's parents had emigrated to America in 1906 and were living in New York City at the time. They and Edward decided to move to Omaha, Nebraska, where older son, Patrick, was a parish priest. The local bishop, upon meeting Edward through Patrick, saw much promise in the young aspiring priest and the diocese gave Edward an opportunity to study at Gregorian University in Rome. A cold, wet winter in Rome, however, brought on a reoccurrence of respiratory illness, and by February 1908, Edward was forced to return to Omaha to recuperate.

Eighteen-year-old Edward Flanagan (front, center) and his older brother Father Patrick Flanagan (front, right) gather with other Irish immigrants upon their arrival at New York's Ellis Island in 1904.

For more than a year, the dispirited young man struggled to regain his health, working in the accounting department of a meat-packing company. In 1909, the bishop of Omaha again sent Edward overseas, this time to the dry mountain air of Innsbruck, Austria. There, Edward resumed his quest to become a priest in the theology department of the city's famous university.

On July 26, 1912, the Feast of St. Anne, Edward was ordained a priest in Innsbruck. Scarcely a month later, Father Flanagan returned to the United States where John and Honora watched with joy as their son celebrated his first Solemn High Mass at Holy Angels Church in Omaha. The young priest was soon assigned to a church in O'Neill, Nebraska.

For John and Honora, their dream was complete. For Father Flanagan, his was just beginning.

ABOVE: In this photo from around 1908, John and Honora Flanagan pose with eight of their eleven children, including (front row, from left) Edward, Michael, Patrick, (back row, from left) Delia, Theresa, James, Nellie, and Susan. For many years, Nellie was Father Flanagan's housekeeper at Boys Town.

LEFT: Father Flanagan (left) enjoys a mountain-climbing expedition with other seminarians in Austria around 1911. He attended a seminary in Austria because the fresh mountain air helped him cope with his respiratory health problems.

"...we were happy and determined to make a success of our small institution."

On December 12, Father Flanagan welcomed his first group of boys to their new home on Dodge Street. They had come from the courts, the streets, and from referrals by sympathetic citizens. Things were bleak in the beginning. The boys had a roof over their heads (at least for a month) but not much else. Between scarcities created by World War I and an overall lack of funding, the priest was hard pressed to provide enough food and clothing for his boys. It helped that Archbishop Harty had arranged for two nuns and a novice from the School Sisters of Notre Dame to help cook, clean, sew, and care for the boys. But as Christmas approached, it looked to be anything but a happy holiday season.

By the morning of Christmas Eve, twenty-five boys were living in the house. Father Flanagan had nothing to give the nuns to cook for Christmas dinner, and it looked like the holiday would be just another day of uncertainty.

But as would be the case time and time again, someone stepped in to help just when things seemed hopeless. An Omaha merchant delivered a barrel of sauerkraut on Christmas Eve. It wasn't the fattened goose, but it let Father Flanagan and the boys know someone cared. "It was a rather humble festival," Father Flanagan said. "But we were happy and determined to make a success of our small institution."

These five boys were among the first residents of Father Flanagan's Home for Boys. By early 1918, more than seventy boys were living at the Home.

A Move to Larger Quarters

As word of Father Flanagan's Home for Boys began to spread, donations from friends and supporters began to make life a little easier for the residents. Food was more plentiful, the boys had clean clothes and shoes, and a horse and wagon was rented to take the boys to school and church.

By the spring of 1918, Father Flanagan was taking care of one hundred boys. And as the population of the Home grew, so did its popularity. Capitalizing on that momentum, the priest organized the Home's first benefit dinner. It was a smashing success, with four thousand people in attendance and $5,300 raised.

The event was an early indicator of Father Flanagan's extraordinary talent for connecting with the public in order to raise awareness and financial support for the plight of children in need. With working-class people, especially those who were parents, he was able to appeal to their compassionate nature and their desire to help children who couldn't help themselves. With businessmen and community leaders, his common sense argument that taking boys off the street and teaching them positive values would reduce crime and save society money was practical and convincing.

Not quite two years after the Home's opening, the growing number of boys and the tight quarters in the original house necessitated a move. Father Flanagan had a larger budget because of the successful benefit dinner, and he was able to inexpensively rent a building called the German-American Home on Omaha's south side. The new building was more than suitable for the growing "family." It was spacious and featured a playground, a bowling alley, and pool tables. These were important considerations in Father Flanagan's search for a new home. While completing their homework and chores was a top priority, Father Flanagan believed the boys should always have time for play. "Some of the finest people in the world go through life under a handicap because they never learned how to play when they were children," he said.

By mid-1918, there were so many boys living in his original Home that Father Flanagan had to look for a larger building. The move to the German-American Home in south Omaha allowed Father Flanagan to take in even more boys and provided additional space for education and recreation.

A MOTHER'S TOUCH

From the beginning, the good deeds of others have been crucial to Boys Town's survival and success. In the early days, perhaps no group's contributions were more important than those of the Mothers' Guild.

The Mothers' Guild began as a group of dedicated women first organized around 1920 by Honora Flanagan, Father Flanagan's mother. Originally, the women would meet at the Home for Boys on Thursday afternoons to sew quilts and mend clothing for the boys. Eventually the group took a more organized form under the leadership of Cassie Riley, meeting under the name of "The Mothers' Guild." Thursdays became known as "Mother's Day" at the Home.

The women of the guild were described in the *Boys' Home Journal* as "noble-hearted creatures of God, leaving their own flock like the divine Master and coming down and spreading sunshine in the lives of the poor boys who have been deprived of their own dear mothers." Once officially recognized in November 1920, the group not only continued to sew but also collected weekly dues of twenty-five cents. Over the years, the guild used the money it raised to purchase Boy Scout uniforms and fill Christmas stockings.

Honora Flanagan, Father Flanagan's mother, organized the original Mothers' Guild to make quilts and comforters and sew and mend clothing for the boys. By the end of the 1920s, there were Mothers' Guilds throughout the Midwest and as far away as New York City.

Of the guild's work Father Flanagan said: "There is such peace and happiness here because these wonderful women are spending themselves in the service of God, doing His humble work with these boys."

Although the group was formed out of compassion for Father Flanagan's boys, the women also enjoyed the social aspect of their club. "Sometimes they just have an afternoon party, have lunch and play cards or talk about their daily life, have a generally jolly time, collect the little fee charged and this money is sent to us by the secretary or treasurer," the *Journal* reported.

As news of the guild spread, Father Flanagan began receiving letters from women all over the country who wished to form their own clubs. The Mothers' Guild eventually expanded to more than a dozen states, with groups formed as far away as New York.

The guild continued its good works until World War II, when Father Flanagan decided the women's skills should be directed toward the war effort. Unfortunately, the start of the war meant the end of the guild—and the handmade quilts for the boys.

However, in 2005, the guild was revived in Omaha and new members again began creating quilts —"hugs" made of cloth and thread—for the boys and girls of Boys Town. In recent years, a new generation of Mothers' Guild members, made up mostly of Omaha Quilting Guild members and Boys Town employees, has stepped up to carry on the storied quilting tradition.

Recently, the group created quilts and other handmade items for fundraising auctions and provided quilts for events to recognize Boys Town staff and schoolteachers. Their quilts also decorate beds in the historic Father Flanagan House, a favorite stop for tourists in the Village of Boys Town.

One of the guild's goals is to create a quilt for every Boys Town High School graduate every year. These quilts serve as a lasting, tangible connection to Boys Town for each future alumnus.

In recent years, the Mothers' Guild was revived at the Village of Boys Town, meeting regularly for sewing bees to make quilts and Christmas stockings for every Boys Town citizen.

Once settled in, the boys planted a vegetable garden and Father Flanagan began asking for livestock—a milk cow or some pigs—so the home could be more self-sufficient. Most of those requests were made in the monthly publication the priest had started in 1918. *Father Flanagan's Boys' Home Journal®* became the primary means of informing the public about the boys' activities and needs and served as the Home's primary fundraising tool between major events.

As the Home grew, one major need was a larger staff. Father Flanagan was able to hire a few staff members at a very low wage, but his own family, including his mother, his sister Nellie, and Patrick and Lenora Norton (a nephew and niece), shouldered much of the day-to-day workload, along with nuns from several different orders.

Besides food, clothing, and a warm bed, Father Flanagan counted education as a necessity for his boys. Some boys were not accepted into the public schools because of their backgrounds and delinquent pasts. But more often, they had trouble keeping up in their studies because most of them had never regularly attended school before. Recognizing their needs were different from those of most children, Father Flanagan devised his own school system. With the help of the nuns, family members, and a few other staff, he transformed the parlors of the Home into classrooms, and the nuns added teaching to their already-long list of duties. Father Flanagan also taught classes. When an Omaha music teacher volunteered his services, the Home assembled its first band, with the boys playing donated instruments.

Education was an important part of each boy's daily life at the German-American Home. Early classes were taught by lay volunteer teachers as well as the Sisters of Notre Dame.

Father Flanagan taught some school classes himself. Ensuring the boys received a good education was part of his holistic childcare philosophy, which emphasized developing a plan for each boy that set individual goals and outcomes and ways to achieve them.

One of Father Flanagan's greatest desires was to help every one of his boys grow up to be an honest citizen. This meant teaching them a trade at which they could earn a decent living. If the boys received an education and learned a trade, Father Flanagan was convinced they would leave the Home with at least "two strikes in their favor." To support this notion, a trade school was started in the basement of the German-American Home.

The trade school grew quickly. A retired shoemaker was brought in to teach the boys the fine art of shoemaking and repair. In 1919, the Home created the Sanitary Products Company, which produced soaps and disinfectants that were sold to help make ends meet. Father Flanagan continued to hire more staff to teach a wide variety of trades, all of which gave the boys valuable skills while benefiting the Home. The shoe repair shop mended old shoes donated for the boys; a bakery, which opened later, supplied bread and baked goods; and agricultural students raised vegetables and some livestock for the Home's food supply.

But as hard as they worked, Father Flanagan, his boys, and their caregivers couldn't do enough. More boys showed up at the doorstep every day, and the priest soon had no choice but to turn some away because there simply wasn't enough room or enough food. It was a task Father Flanagan hated, and it strengthened his resolve to put the Home on solid financial footing.

With nearly two hundred youngsters to care for, and with limited funding, space, and help, Father Flanagan faced a daunting challenge as the era known as the "Roaring Twenties" got underway.

As he would prove time and time again, it was a challenge he was born to conquer.

ALL RACES AND RELIGIONS

In Father Flanagan's eyes, all boys who sought refuge at his Home were equal—equally hungry; equally in need of a warm, safe place to sleep; equally deserving of hope for a better life. From the beginning of his Home for Boys, the priest accepted boys regardless of their religion or race. "When the idea of a boys' home grew in my mind, I never thought anything remarkable about taking in all of the races and all of the creeds," Father Flanagan said. "To me, they are all God's children. They are my brothers. They are children of God. I must protect them to the best of my ability."

This approach was unheard of at a time when separation and inequality were the norm, racial bigotry was rampant, and anything that disrupted the status quo was considered radical and suspicious, at the least. In fact, only two years after Father Flanagan started his Home for Boys, a black man being held in the courthouse jail in downtown Omaha was seized by a mob, hanged from a light pole, and shot more than one hundred times.

But Father Flanagan's stance was firm, again illustrating just how revolutionary and progressive his ideas about childcare were. He was not afraid to fight against unfair practices and prejudiced thinking, especially when they interfered with a child's opportunities to receive proper care and an education. As an immigrant himself, Father Flanagan fervently believed the American ideals of freedom, equality, and justice were to be lived, not just preached. "I see no disaster threatening us because of any particular race, creed, or color," he said. But he did see "danger for all in an ideology which discriminates against anyone politically or economically" because he was born into a different race or worshiped at a different altar.

Unfortunately, Father Flanagan's boys were no strangers to intolerance, at home or elsewhere. They were teased and shunned at the public schools they attended because they dressed shabbily and lacked manners. Many boys, especially those who had been abandoned by their parents, struggled in school because they had stopped going to classes.

From the very beginning, Father Flanagan accepted boys of all races, religions, and cultural backgrounds into his Home for Boys, something unheard of in the early 1900s. This group of youngsters was photographed outside the German-American Home around 1920.

A group of boys gather for a photo in the summer of 1922 before leaving with the Boys Town traveling road show. The boys journeyed across the state of Nebraska in horse-drawn wagons, entertaining in communities along the way to raise funds for and awareness of Boys Town's mission. Oftentimes, the troupe would pick up homeless boys who needed a place to live and bring them back to Boys Town. The boys' uniforms were modified versions of those worn by U.S. soldiers in World War I.

The situation was even more dangerous when the boys traveled to other communities across the Midwest to garner support for the Home. Father Flanagan had organized an interracial group of boys to spread the message of the Home and raise funds through entertainment. "The World's Greatest Juvenile Entertainers" performed two-hour shows, pleasing their audiences with songs, skits, jokes, and speeches. At first, the troupe traveled to their engagements in bright red, second-hand circus wagons. Later, they would ride in their own special Pullman train car.

Father Flanagan's nephew, Patrick Norton, chaperoned the boys while an agent booked as many shows as the boys could travel to on weekends and during the summer. Most communities were eager to see the boys and welcomed them. But not every town was filled with supportive admirers of a group of young men of different races who mixed freely and entertained together, as a family.

Norton would vividly remember one incident in which a minister who had joined the Ku Klux Klan told the Boys Town group if they tried to put on a show in his community, he would tar and feather all of them. Through the next few decades, there also were a number of hotels in places like Miami, Baltimore, and Washington, D.C., that invited the well-known Boys Town musicians and athletes to visit, only to rescind the invitation when they discovered the group was racially mixed.

In the face of such bigotry and narrow-mindedness, Father Flanagan never backed down from his principles of treating each boy with dignity, equality, and respect.

A Starting Place for Greater Good

Conditions for homeless and abandoned children in turn-of-the-century America were appalling. Father Flanagan knew that in Omaha, and in cities and towns across the country, many of the boys who were without a family or in trouble with the law because they had turned to a life of crime to survive ended up in reformatories, orphanages, or workhouses. In the early 1900s, these were terrible places for children; the boys who lived in them often were abused, mistreated, forced to labor for long hours; sometimes they starved. Father Flanagan felt this was a shameful way for society to care for its most helpless and vulnerable citizens. He had seen firsthand the brokenness and hopelessness these children carried with them into adulthood in the destitute men he worked with at the Workingmen's Hotel.

So when he opened his Home for Boys, it was more than just a building where individual youngsters could find safety, three meals a day, and a bed of their own. More important, it was an early model and a public symbol for what he believed childcare should look like, in Omaha, in the Midwest, and across America. From the very start of his work with wayward boys, his intentions were to change not only the course of individual lives but to also reform the whole system of care for children, a reform that included doing away with the reformatories, orphanages, and the workhouses that represented the current system's greatest failures.

While the Home remained non-denominational, Father Flanagan turned to the teachings of his Catholic faith for guidance and inspiration in his work. He had been taught that despite the influence of Original Sin, people were still basically good inside and could cooperate with God's grace to find redemption. The prevailing secular social theory at the time was "Eugenics," which stated there were two types of people: white Western European people who were capable of becoming good citizens and all others, who were not (this included all non-white races, Poles, Czechs, Italians, Irish, and others). Father Flanagan rejected this secular model, declaring, "There are no bad boys; only bad environment, bad training, bad example."

Father Flanagan also kept up with the newest developments in education, sociology, and psychology. Far ahead of his time in the use of research practices, he had begun using surveys and other methods with the destitute men he had worked with to measure whether their lives were improving due to the help they received. He would continue to use this type of research to measure the impact of the care the boys were receiving at the Home.

Father Flanagan also formed what is known today as an Individual Education Plan for each boy and incorporated the ideas of pioneering psychologists into his model of care. The following is an excerpt from a speech Father Flanagan would make later in his life that embodied the common message he conveyed:

> We must agree, I think, that we do not build schools, either public or private, for the purpose of turning out diplomas, but rather for the purpose of turning out young men and women shaped for life. This calls for more than a knowledge of physics or grammar; it calls for a philosophy of life, for a religious faith, if you please; it calls for appreciation of values that are not alien to the cosmic order and for the acceptance of those values as relevant and significant; it calls for the recognition of the individual as a child of God.

Testing New Approaches

As his Home for Boys grew, Father Flanagan used it as a testing ground, a place where he could develop and try out new theories and concepts for childcare. Much of what he learned came from his relationships with the boys in his care. Father Flanagan knew he did not have all the answers, so he began to do his own research on the types of backgrounds each boy came from and the individual problems they brought with them to the Home. (This research also involved tracking his boys after they left the Home to provide evidence they had become good citizens.) This revolutionary approach—basing the care of a child on his experiences and needs—eventually began to catch the attention of others who could bring much-needed support to the Home and its mission and set the stage for greater exposure and acceptance of Father Flanagan's methodology in the future.

Gradually, Father Flanagan was becoming a well-known champion of children and their causes and a vocal proponent of the need for wholesale changes in America's system of childcare.

On to Overlook

Father Flanagan abhorred the heartbreaking task of telling boys he could not take them in when the Home had reached its capacity. The Home's needs were clear: more space and housing, a larger staff, an abundant supply of food and other necessities, and a budget that would make all of these things possible, today and tomorrow.

Father Flanagan began to envision a place outside Omaha—a large, open, and natural area—where there was room to grow and where he and his boys could distance themselves from the neighbors who had become uneasy with the priest's growing troupe of young residents—ill-clothed, struggling educationally, and most controversial of all, racially and religiously mixed. The search for a new home, and the prayers, began.

Ten miles west of the city lay a 160-acre piece of land called Overlook Farm. When Father Flanagan first inquired about it, he learned it wasn't for sale. Convinced the farm was the place he was looking for, Father Flanagan insisted on talking with the owners, Anne and David Baum, and their daughter, Margaret. The family was so moved by Father Flanagan's story they agreed to sell.

Again, money was an issue. But while he did not have the funding to purchase the farm outright, Father Flanagan had an abundance of faith. The Baums accepted a forty-acre farm Father Flanagan had bought earlier in trade and a small down payment. Arrangements were made for full payment later.

The purchase of Overlook Farm was just the beginning. Next came the monumental task of transforming a fertile piece of land where crops were once raised into a community where boys could grow into men. Construction plans called for housing two hundred boys, as well as an administration building, a chapel, schoolrooms, a dining hall, and plenty of room for recreation and play. Father Flanagan estimated the cost of constructing the administration building alone at $300,000, and he organized a fundraising committee headed by J. E. Davidson, vice president of Nebraska Power Company. Until the money was raised and the new building and housing were completed, Father Flanagan and his boys would live and study in renovated barns and chicken coops and in temporary buildings that were hastily constructed by local workmen and the older boys.

In 1921, Father Flanagan purchased Overlook Farm west of Omaha to create a permanent home and community for his ever-growing family of boys. Weary youngsters who traveled long distances to begin a new life at the Home knew they had reached their destination when they saw this original entrance.

HE AIN'T HEAVY...
HE'S M' BROTHER

Besides being far ahead of his time in his approach to caring for children, Father Flanagan also had a talent for telling Boys Town's story to the public and inspiring their compassion and support for his boys.

During the Home's early days, Father Flanagan used a photo of a young boy with his arms outstretched to symbolize the "homeless boy" in his *Home Journal*, in mail appeals for funds, and on the first Boys Town seal. Louis R. Bostwick, a well-known Omaha photographer, had taken the photograph of the boy.

Bostwick also had taken another photograph in 1921 of two other boys. The photo captured Reuben Granger carrying Howard Loomis on his back. Granger had come to the German-American Home when he was thirteen; a woman presumed to be his mother dropped him off and never returned. Loomis wore leg braces because he'd had polio. He sometimes had trouble getting around, so the older boys would take turns carrying him.

Years later, Father Flanagan saw an illustration of two boys in a pose similar to Bostwick's photo of Granger and Loomis. The illustration was in a 1941 Louis Allis Company publication, the *Messenger*, and carried the inscription, "He ain't heavy, Mr., he's m' brother." The illustration apparently reminded the priest of the Loomis and Granger photo, and he requested the company's permission to adapt the illustration and phrase for Boys Town's use.

Inspiration for Boys Town's famous "Two Brothers" symbol may date as far back as this August 16, 1921, photograph of one of the Home's residents, Howard Loomis, being carried by another boy, Reuben Granger. The photo was taken during an outing for the boys at Omaha's Krug Park.

Thereafter, the trademarked "Two Brothers" and "He ain't heavy, Father . . . he's m' brother" became universally recognized symbols of Boys Town. And since 1949, millions of Americans have received Two Brothers seals from Boys Town and used them on their Christmas holiday mail.

In the 2000s, a variation of the Two Brothers symbol—this time with a boy carrying a younger girl—was created to represent how Boys Town cares for both boys and girls through its life-changing programs. That new symbol, inspired by the iconic photo of decades ago, remains part of the Boys Town logo today.

One thing the construction plans didn't include was a fence. "This is a home," Father Flanagan explained to doubters who thought delinquent boys should be contained. "You do not wall in members of your family."

Less than ten days after moving to Overlook in the fall of 1921, Father Flanagan began inviting the public to see the boys' new home. Each day, he welcomed a local group—the Kiwanis, the Omaha Women's Club, the Rotary Club—for lunch at the farm. The boys gave their visitors tours as Father Flanagan explained how new construction would enable him to care for as many as five hundred boys. As some boys served the meal, others entertained their guests by singing and playing musical selections on their second-hand instruments. Visitors came away charmed by their young hosts and agreeing the priest had a wonderful effect on those in his care. Most importantly, they were moved to support Father Flanagan's passion to help change the lives of hundreds more.

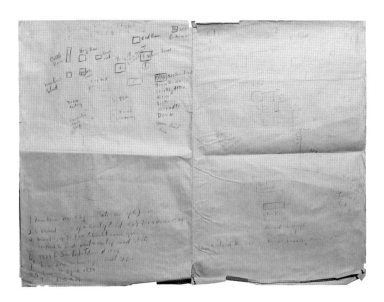

A sketch of Father Flanagan's plans for the future expansion of the Home at Overlook Farm.

The younger boys got to ride in a truck (Father Flanagan could only afford to rent one) to their new home at Overlook Farm on moving day in October 1921. The older boys, carrying suitcases holding their possessions, marched out of Omaha and covered the nearly twenty miles on foot.

ABOVE: Jewish attorney Henry Monsky (seated at right) was not only a good friend of Father Flanagan's, but also was instrumental in helping him start his Home for Boys. Monsky shared the priest's philosophy that children needed proper care and nurturance, and he loaned him $90 to rent the first Home in 1917. For thirty years, until his death in 1947, Monsky served as an advisor and legal counsel to Father Flanagan.

BELOW: At the height of the Great Depression and the Dust Bowl droughts in the early 1930s, Father Flanagan made desperate appeals for public support to keep Boys Town open with headlines like this one in the *Boys' Home Journal*.

Because of the drought, we have had no harvest---
Our Cupboard Is Nearly Empty

200 HUNGRY GROWING BOYS ARE ASKING FOR YOUR AID.

A good part of our food supply has always come from our gardens and our fields. Last spring we planted more than 15 acres of gardens, 19 acres of potatoes and 110 acres of small grain. But an exceptionally dry summer caused us a complete loss of many thousands of dollars of potential food produce. About 100 acres of corn resulted in partial loss.

Because we have no harvest, what our Home will use this year must be purchased. This means we must have money—money which must come from our friends, for we get no help from church, city, state, federal relief or community chest. As the picture shows, we have already bought some food supplies with money which generous friends have sent us. May we count on you for help?

Please Send Your Contribution to---
Father Flanagan's Boys' Home
Omaha, Nebr.

Desperate Times

The move to Overlook Farm was a major step in Father Flanagan's plan to create what would soon become known as the small community of "Boys Town®." But even the promise of a newer, bigger home and the initial good will generated with the public couldn't stave off the harsh realities of bills due and an ever-growing population of needy boys. Although the funding campaign launched in the fall of 1921 by Henry Monsky and other prominent Omaha businessmen had raised $200,000 for the construction of the main five-story building at Overlook, there were still monthly mortgage payments, escalating maintenance fees, and the rising costs of food and clothing as more boys arrived every week.

Father Flanagan's vision remained steadfast and clear. He would keep his "City of Little Men" going, regardless of the cost. "Father was a dreamer. He could sit and tell you what he was going to do two years from now, and it got done somehow," said Al Witcofski, one of those boy residents during the 1920s. Compounding the money problems the Home faced in the late 1920s and early 1930s was the Great Depression and a long period of drought, both of which had the entire country mired in unemployment, hunger, fear, and uncertainty.

During this dark period, Father Flanagan struggled, sometimes day to day, to keep his boys fed and clothed and to keep the Home open. Traveling to countless speaking engagements, pleading with citizens, organizing campaigns, and managing the Home's staff and finances, all the while making time for the boys, eventually took its toll on the priest. In August 1931, he was admitted to a Denver hospital specializing in respiratory problems. Even this threat to his health didn't deter him. From his hospital bed, he made phone calls and wrote letters to friends and strangers asking for help in paying the Home's debts. "Never in my life have I thought I would write such a letter as this," his letters read. "The Boys' Home for which I have worked so hard and for so many years, must be closed unless the necessary money is raised immediately . . . If the Home closes it will break my heart. That won't matter much. But it will break the hearts of these two hundred boys and deprive a chance in life to thousands of boys in the years to come . . ."

"...If the Home closes it will break my heart. That won't matter much. But it will break the hearts of these two hundred boys and deprive a chance in life to thousands of boys..."

Headlines in the *Boys' Home Journal* carried the same sad theme: "$87,500 Must Be Raised at Once"; "Shall We Return These Homeless Boys to the Streets and Alleys?"; "We Ask You Only for Financial Assistance in Order to Keep Our Doors Open." In 1934, there was an even direr headline: "Our Cupboard Is Almost Empty." The accompanying article explained how drought had kept the boys from growing and raising their own food, forcing the Home to buy what it needed. "Because we have no harvest, what our Home will use this year must be purchased," the article said. "This means we must have money—money which must come from our friends, for we get no help from church, city, state, federal relief, or community chest."

Boys Town made every effort to be self-sufficient, raising its own crops and animals for food. The boys also learned work skills from farming and tending the animals. The Dust Bowl days of the late 1920s and early 1930s dealt a severe blow to Boys Town's ability to keep food on the table for its citizens.

Thousands of dollars did not pour in overnight, and at times the Home came perilously close to shutting its doors. Father Flanagan even had to make the heartbreaking decision to place some boys with farm families temporarily and have others move to foster homes.

But through prayer and the sacrifices of supporters, there always seemed to be just enough donations of money, food, clothing, and livestock to provide proper care for the remaining boys and pay the mortgage. Slowly, just as the country was making its own recovery from the Great Depression, the Home began to regain its financial footing, allowing former boys to return and new boys to be admitted. By 1936, the Home was stable enough to be officially incorporated as the Village of Boys Town by the State of Nebraska.

A few years later, Father Flanagan made the first deposit in a foundation fund he had dreamed of starting for more than ten years. This perpetual fund would be built from public donations and eventually would be large enough to support the operation of the Home. This would ensure Boys Town would be there to help needy children far into the future. (Again, Father Flanagan's vision was extraordinary; today, the Father Flanagan Fund for Needy Children is worth $900 million and supplements donations from supporters to cover Boys Town's annual budget of more than $400 million.)

For the first time since its founding, it looked like Boys Town was here to stay.

LEFT: Boys Town maintained its own dairy herd and milking the cows was a daily chore for the boys.

BELOW: Two boys check the progress of hot bed garden plants being grown in wooden enclosures.

From a Hollywood Hit, Worldwide Fame

By the late 1930s, Boys Town's resurgence and continued efforts to court public support had made it the subject of many newspaper and magazine articles. It was inevitable that this human-interest phenomenon would catch the attention of a Hollywood movie studio.

In 1938, producers from MGM Studios traveled to Boys Town to discuss the prospects of a movie about the Home. Father Flanagan was at first reluctant to have the story of Boys Town told Hollywood-style, fearful the portrayal of his boys and his mission would not be accurate. MGM Studios President Louis B. Mayer assured the priest that MGM was planning a true-to-life film, finally convincing Father Flanagan to agree to the project.

A few months later, Spencer Tracy and Mickey Rooney, two of the biggest stars of the day, and a sixty-one-member crew arrived at Boys Town to begin ten days of on-location filming. Director Norman Taurog included many Boys Town boys as extras in scenes, and the boys prepared a huge farewell barbecue for the cast and crew when shooting wrapped up.

In the sweltering summer of 1938, film crews from MGM Studios began shooting on location for the movie *Boys Town*. Director Norman Taurog (seated, wearing a pith helmet) and his crews spent ten days filming in the Village of Boys Town, using many citizens as extras. Father Flanagan reviewed the movie's script daily to ensure the Home was being portrayed in an accurate, positive light.

ABOVE: Huge crowds gathered to welcome the stars of the *Boys Town* movie upon their arrival at Omaha's Union Station. More than 30,000 people filled the streets for the movie's premiere. Some climbed light poles for a better vantage point.

RIGHT: Father Flanagan shares a humorous moment with Spencer Tracy (left) and Mickey Rooney, the stars of the movie *Boys Town* during the film's premiere in Omaha in September 1938. Both Tracy and Rooney would remain lifelong supporters of Boys Town.

The film was finished quickly, but then was shelved for a month because Mayer was convinced, "It will never sell; there's no sex." Urged by the cast and crew to release the movie, Mayer eventually agreed to an Omaha premiere on September 7, 1938. One hundred fifty lucky residents received tickets for the showing, but a crowd of 30,000 jammed the streets outside the Omaha Theatre—some peering from rooftops and telephone poles—to catch a glimpse of Tracy, Rooney, and the other Hollywood stars in attendance.

Omaha's reaction was only a glimpse of what was to come. Once released nationally, *Boys Town* became a phenomenal hit. Newspapers across the country reported people standing in line for hours to see the film. They emerged from the theaters sobbing, only to get back in line to see the second showing.

Boys Town won two Academy Awards. Dore Schary and Eleanore Griffin were honored for writing the Best Original Screenplay and Spencer Tracy won the Best Actor award (his second in a row) for his portrayal of a kind but firm Father Flanagan. Mirroring the spirit of Father Flanagan, Tracy graciously accepted the Oscar and promptly gave it to Boys Town, where it remains on display today.

Father Flanagan, sick in bed, admires the Best Actor Oscar won by Spencer Tracy for his portrayal of the priest in the movie *Boys Town*. Tracy accepted the award in honor of Father Flanagan and later presented the statuette to him. The Oscar remains on display today in the Boys Town Hall of History.

HIS BOYS ALWAYS CAME FIRST

Father Flanagan often felt he had the weight of the world on his shoulders. Keeping Boys Town open and caring for kids was a constant and draining demand. Traveling the country to advocate for children's rights and to fundraise for the Home took its toll physically and emotionally.

But Father Flanagan always had time for his boys.

When a new boy arrived at Boys Town, the priest made sure he had a good meal before finding him a bed. If a boy needed a warm coat or some new clothes, Father Flanagan made sure he got it. If one of the youngsters just needed to talk, he was there with a kind and caring ear.

A wonderful example of the love and respect the boys had for Father Flanagan was the Christmas gift they gave him in 1939. For months, the boys labored in secret on their surprise, a large desk constructed from 250,000 pieces of inlaid wood. Father Flanagan used the desk in his study and it became one of his most prized possessions.

Even decades after living at Boys Town former boys cherished vivid memories of Father Flanagan. During a visit in 2007, Joe Ortega, who graduated at Boys Town in 1947, and Everett Littlefield, a 1944 graduate, talked about the impact Father Flanagan had on their lives when he cared for them as young boys.

"Our prayers are that the church will recognize Father Flanagan as a saint, because to us, he is a saint," said Ortega, sitting a few feet from the priest's tomb. He recalled Father Flanagan was far ahead of his time in terms of treating people of all races and religions equally, and he tried to instill values of brotherhood and fairness in all of his boys. "That was a lesson I learned, and I tried to live up to it," Ortega said, tears welling in his eyes.

Ortega, who was ten when he came to Boys Town, remembered the kindly priest got his attention and put him at ease by giving him some Christmas candy from his office desk. He also remembered having Father Flanagan hear his confession. "Father Flanagan had a way of dragging out every sin you had," he said. "By the time I got out of there, if I had died, I would have gone right to heaven."

Littlefield said he regrets that today's youth were not able to know Father Flanagan and benefit from all the good things he taught the boys of Littlefield's era. Although Father Flanagan traveled a lot in the 1940s, often to speak at war bond rallies, he was most at home with his Boys Town family. "If he was here, he was among the boys," Littlefield said.

A beautiful, handcrafted desk made of thousands of inlaid pieces of wood was the boys' surprise Christmas present to Father Flanagan in 1939. It was placed in Father Flanagan's study and became one of his most prized possessions. The desk was a testament to how much the boys admired and loved their mentor and friend.

Every boy at Boys Town knew he had a friend in Father Flanagan. No matter how busy he was, the priest always found the time to welcome a new boy to the Home, help a youngster who was going through a rough time, or just have a talk with the boys about school or their hobbies.

Growing Popularity for a Growing Home

Years before the *Boys Town* movie, famous visitors like Franklin Roosevelt, Lou Gehrig, Babe Ruth, and Tom Mix made stops at the Village of Boys Town. The Home's popularity and recognition only increased with the movie's release, and Boys Town, Father Flanagan, and his famous phrase, "There is no such thing as a bad boy," became part of the popular culture of the day.

A steady parade of entertainers, sports figures, and politicians who were inspired by the movie also were welcomed at the Home. Visits by Bing Crosby, Bob Hope, George Burns and Gracie Allen, and many others proved to be not only exciting for the boys but sometimes profitable.

RIGHT: In 1940, the husband-wife act of Gracie Allen and George Burns put on a thirty-minute show for the boys while touring the Home. Gracie was named honorary mayor of Boys Town and George was made an honorary citizen.

BELOW: Lou Gehrig and Babe Ruth, fresh off their 1927 World Series championship season with the New York Yankees, paid a visit to Boys Town at Father Flanagan's invitation. Gehrig and Ruth, who grew up an orphan, both became lifetime supporters of the Home.

The Boys Town baseball team received new uniforms after comedians Bud Abbott and Lou Costello visited the Home in 1942. During their time with the boys, the comedy duo noticed how tattered the team's old uniforms were and later donated new ones.

"We didn't have any baseball uniforms then," said former resident Al Witcofski. "We played in our overalls. Until two comedians came—Bud Abbott and Lou Costello. They bought the uniforms. That's the way we got pretty near everything. Somebody would always come through."

Father Flanagan believed children had rights and should be protected. These rights and this protection covered everything from basic necessities like nutritious food, clean clothes, and a bed to sleep in to child labor laws that prohibited employers from forcing children to work in dangerous conditions for unfair pay. Father Flanagan also sought to close reformatories and other juvenile facilities where children were abused and literally held prisoner.

In the 1930s and 1940s, civic clubs and leaders from around the country clamored to have Father Flanagan share his advice and views on childcare in speeches and at events. Father Flanagan accepted as many speaking engagements as he could, but requests came from all over the country. The hundreds of speeches he gave to organizations—from local clubs to the U.S. Senate —often carried titles like "Juvenile Delinquency," "Need for Christian Love in Dealing with Young People," and, perhaps his most famous, "There's No Such Thing as a Bad Boy." (Floyd Starr of Starr Commonwealth Schools coined this famous phrase, but it was so popularized by Father Flanagan it became known as his own.) In addition to live speaking tours, Father Flanagan also spoke frequently on radio programs broadcast across the nation.

Father Flanagan's approach to and ideas for improving childcare were so innovative that his knowledge and expertise were much sought after by government leaders and childcare advocates. In 1941, the governor of California and a judge called on him to devise a new program for Whittier State School, where two young residents had committed suicide and there were reported incidents of severe abuse of children. Father Flanagan implemented the Boys Town approach to childcare at the school, throwing out the prevailing (and mistaken) attitude of the school staff that the fate and future of a child was predetermined by the situation he was born into. Reformed, the school continued to successfully help children for many decades.

As before, the tremendous scope and breakneck pace of Father Flanagan's schedule proved to be detrimental to his health. His ever-present respiratory problems flared several times, sending him to hospitals. Each time, he continued his work with renewed fervor once he felt reasonably healthy again.

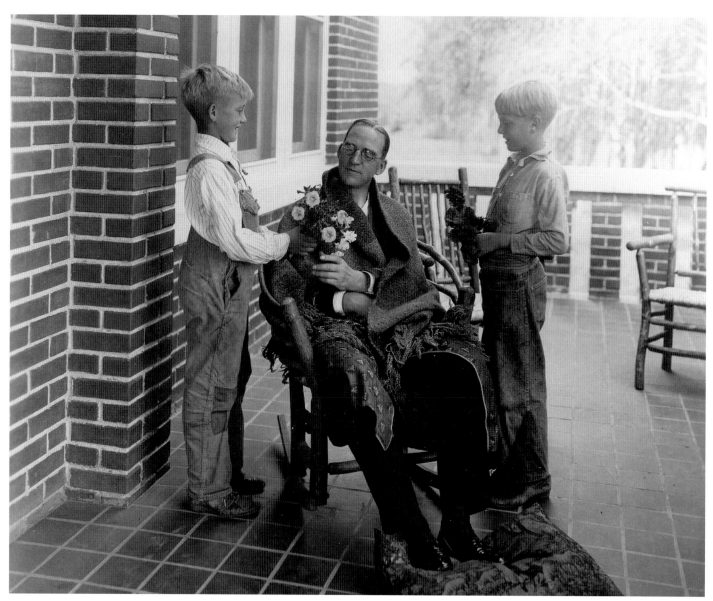

Father Flanagan receives flowers from two of his boys while recovering from an illness in 1931. Poor health and the tremendous pressures and demands of running Boys Town would eventually take their toll on the priest in his later years.

World War II brought another crisis to the lives of many youth across the country, a crisis Father Flanagan recognized and spoke to often. The war had called thousands of fathers away from their families, and many children were suffering in these now single-parent homes. Some youngsters had to quit school in order to help their mothers support large families. Some went hungry; others were forced to leave home and move in with family friends or relatives so they could receive proper care. Father Flanagan spoke to groups frequently about the plight of these children. He also went on war bond tours, selling $3 million in bonds in 1942.

Hundreds of former Boys Town residents, and a number of current residents who were old enough, enlisted in the armed forces when the United States entered the war after the Japanese attack on Pearl Harbor in December 1941. (Three former Boys Town boys were killed in the attack, the first residents to die in military combat.) Father Flanagan, who was named "America's No. 1 War Dad," had instilled a tremendous sense of patriotism and love of country in his boys, and they embodied those ideals through their exemplary service. (See page 222 for more on the military service of Boys Town residents.)

Hundreds of former Boys Town citizens served in the armed forces during World War II. In 1945, Father Flanagan received a special flag from the City of Baltimore commemorating the eight hundred former Boys Town boys who were in uniform and the thirty-five "Gold Star" boys who had been killed in combat.

Servicemen surround Father Flanagan during his visit to a military base in Sioux Falls, South Dakota, in May 1944. Lee O'Hern, the jeep driver, was a former Boys Town citizen. Father Flanagan toured U.S. bases around the world during World War II to boost morale and sell war bonds.

After the war's end, U.S. Secretary of War Robert Patterson and General Douglas MacArthur asked Father Flanagan to examine the conditions of war orphans in Japan and Korea in 1947. He made the trip and reported his recommendations for their care to President Harry S. Truman.

In 1948, again at the request of the War Department, Father Flanagan traveled to Europe to observe the conditions of war orphans. When he said good-bye to his boys to go on that trip, neither he nor they could have known it would be their last moments together.

LEFT: General Douglas MacArthur and Father Flanagan leave a meeting during which the priest reported on his 1947 trip to Japan to review the living conditions of children there and across Asia. Many government and military leaders turned to Father Flanagan for advice on how to care for children left parentless during World War II.

BELOW: Austrian children gather around Father Flanagan during his fact-finding mission to Europe in 1948. Father Flanagan was in Europe to assess the plight of war orphans. Nine days after this photo was taken, he would pass away in Berlin, Germany.

"The work will continue, you see, whether I am there or not, for it is God's work, not mine."

Losing a Friend and a Father Figure

On May 15, 1948, Father Flanagan suffered a heart attack in Berlin, Germany.

A priest and a doctor, along with Father Flanagan's nephew, Patrick Norton, who had made the trip with him, were called to his bedside. Norton recalled: "While Father (Emmitt) Walsh (an Army chaplain) said the prayers for the dead, Father, in his characteristic manner, stroked his bushy eyebrow. As the prayers were finished, Father Flanagan himself concluded the prayer with 'Amen.' It was his last word. Father Flanagan was dead. It was a beautiful death, if death can be called beautiful."

Father Flanagan was sixty-one years old.

Back at the Home, his boys were listening to a radio program when the shocking news was announced. "We interrupt this program to bring you a bulletin from Berlin, Germany. Father Flanagan, founder and director of the famed Boys Town, Nebraska, died suddenly this morning." Within minutes of the broadcast, the boys solemnly filled Dowd Memorial Chapel of the Immaculate Conception, the Catholic church built in the Village in 1941 thanks to a donation from long-time Boys Town supporter Marie Dowd of New York City. Amid their tears and prayers, they wondered who would care for them now.

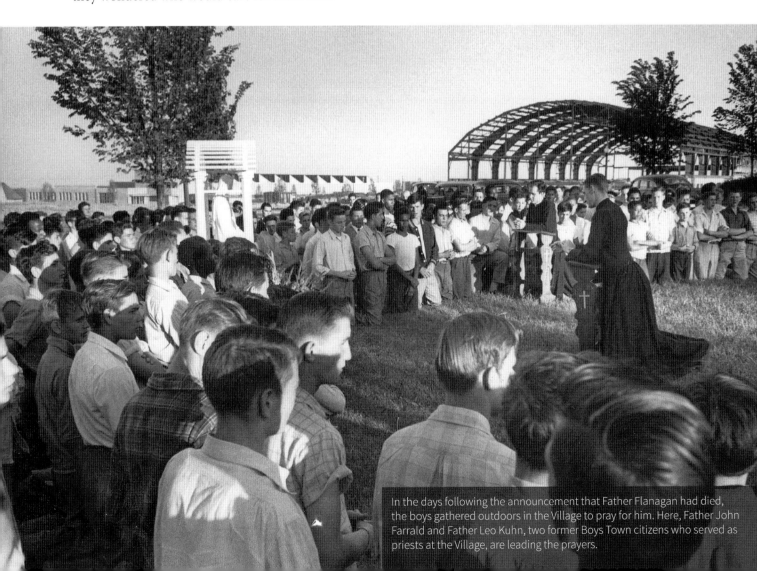

In the days following the announcement that Father Flanagan had died, the boys gathered outdoors in the Village to pray for him. Here, Father John Farrald and Father Leo Kuhn, two former Boys Town citizens who served as priests at the Village, are leading the prayers.

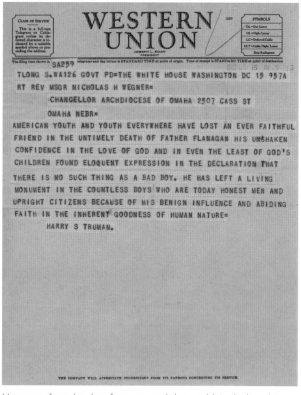

Messages from leaders from around the world, including this telegram from President Harry Truman, expressed condolences at the loss of Father Flanagan and his leadership in childcare.

Telegrams poured in from all over the world. President Truman, FBI Director J. Edgar Hoover, Spencer Tracy, Norman Taurog, and hundreds of others expressed their sorrow and sense of loss.

President Truman wired: "American youth and youth everywhere have lost an ever faithful friend in the untimely death of Father Flanagan. His unshaken confidence in the love of God and in even the least of God's children found eloquent expression in the declaration that there is no such thing as a bad boy. He has left a living monument in the countless boys who are today honest men and upright citizens because of his benign influence and abiding faith in the inherent goodness of human nature."

Perhaps the finest public tribute to Father Flanagan and his work came from radio commentator Drew Person in a May 16 broadcast: "All over this land there are graduates of Boys Town who owe their place in society to Father Flanagan. His hand was extended to any boy who needed him, regardless of color or creed. No matter how forsaken or discouraged or defiant a boy, Father Flanagan could reach him. His Boys Town was a workshop where he molded character, bolstered self-confidence, distilled new hope for the future. The world is poorer for the loss of Father Flanagan, but we are all richer for having felt the influence of a man who by living democracy made democracy live."

Three days after his death, Father Flanagan's mortal remains were returned to his beloved Boys Town. A crowd of 1,500 met the military aircraft at Omaha's airport, and everyone stood silent as Boys Town Band member Frank Lyons played "Taps."

The Village newspaper, *The Boys Town Times*, reported an estimated 30,000 people viewed Father Flanagan's body as it lay in state two days before burial. Among them were current and former residents of Boys Town who loved their teacher, mentor, and "father" so much, just as he loved them.

On May 21, 1948, Father Edmond C. Walsh was the celebrant for the first funeral Mass held for citizens of Boys Town, alumni, relatives, and staff members. Three other priests, all Boys Town graduates, participated in the service. A public Solemn Mass of Requiem followed, with Father Flanagan's brother, Father Patrick A. Flanagan, as the celebrant. City and county government offices and many businesses suspended activities the morning of the funeral.

Father Flanagan was laid to his final rest in the baptistry of Dowd Memorial Chapel. The simple marble slab that sealed the sarcophagus read:

Father Flanagan, Founder of Boys Town, Lover of Christ and Man.
July 13, 1886 – May 15, 1948

An era had ended. But while the dreamer was gone, the dream lived on.

ABOVE: Former Boys Town citizens escorted Father Flanagan's casket when it arrived in Omaha on May 20, 1948, several days after his untimely death in Germany.

RIGHT: Thousands of well-wishers, including former and current Boys Town boys who said tearful good-byes to their friend and mentor, filed past Father Flanagan's casket prior to his funeral Mass.

Father Flanagan + Founder of Boys Town +
+ Lover of + Christ + and man +
July 13 1886 + May 15 1948

1917–1948
DAILY LIFE FOR THE BOYS

Whether they were among the youngsters Father Flanagan took in after he opened his first Home in downtown Omaha or those who came following the move to Overlook Farm, Boys Town's earliest citizens knew they could count on several certainties.

They were safe. They had enough to eat and a warm bed to sleep in. They were going to school. They were learning a trade. And Father Flanagan and their "brothers" were their family. "I shall be forever thankful that Father Flanagan took me in," one of the boys said in 1920. "He has given me the confidence that the world is not against me and other unfortunate boys." Before he was ten, this boy had lost his father and watched his mother lose her struggle to support the family on her own. He eventually ended up at Father Flanagan's Home for Boys, where he heard of even worse tragedies from the other boys. "I thought I was the poorest boy in the world until I came to the Home and heard from the others boys' lips of the hardships they had endured," he said.

Father Flanagan gets a salute from a line of his boys outside the German-American Home.

Headlines in newspapers across the country told the shocking stories of America's wayward and orphaned children. Father Flanagan would include these headlines in his *Boy's Home Journal* to drum up public support for Boys Town.

Hardship, loneliness, and despair were the common denominators for most of the boys who showed up on Father Flanagan's doorstep in those first thirty years of the Home's existence. They were the victims described in the newspaper headlines of the day, headlines that spoke of cruel treatment, lack of care, and abandonment happening not just in Omaha but across America: "Poor Fear Cold, Give Tots Away"; "Parent Pawns Boys and Girl for $300"; "Hungry Children Faint in Schools"; "Children Found Living with Pigs"; "Broken Homes Blamed for Erring Children"; "Nine Babies Abandoned Each Day in New York City."

No matter how children were suffering, their basic needs were the same. Father Flanagan knew if left on the streets, boys like these would grow up to find themselves in jail—or worse. Most of the boys who had criminal records started by stealing food or snatching handbags to get money for food, a pair of shoes, or a coat for the winter. Soon it became a way of life for them, a life Father Flanagan felt it was his destiny to change. "The youth who makes a mistake may be compared to a plant growing in depleted soil and deprived of health-giving sunshine," he said. "He hasn't got a chance."

Father Flanagan used images like these to bring attention to the appalling living conditions of homeless children and to spark public support for Boys Town and its mission to provide youngsters with a good home and education.

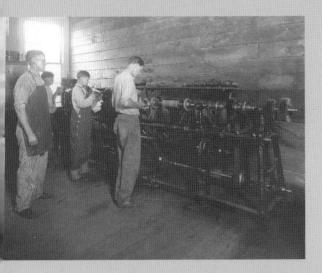

As soon as a boy reached the front steps of the Home—whether he was dropped off there with a tag that said "Boys Town" pinned to his clothes, wandered in on his own, or was sent by the courts—he fell into a daily routine all the boys followed. To start the day, he was awakened at 6:30 a.m. so he had time to make his bed and wash up before breakfast.

Father Flanagan believed idleness was a principle cause of delinquency, so schoolwork and vocational training filled most of the boys' days. But the priest also made sure they had free time to play or enjoy hobbies like stamp collecting or model building. The boys played baseball and basketball, but their favorite game was marbles.

ABOVE: An instructor oversees several youth as they work in the Boys Town machine shop. Father Flanagan believed learning a trade was one of the best ways the boys could prepare themselves to get a job and live on their own after they left Boys Town.

RIGHT: Boys congregated in this play room every day to read books, play games, and have fun. In the cold weather months, the boys often wore their coats inside because there wasn't always enough money to run the furnace during the daytime hours.

BELOW: Marbles was a favorite sport of the boys under Father Flanagan's care. Father Flanagan believed play was an important part of every boy's upbringing and development. Here, a large group of boys prepare to release their "shooters" at the marble circle.

Working on the Boys Town farm was an essential part of daily life for the boys. During the Dust Bowl days of the Great Depression, the boys depended on horse-drawn water tanks and bucket brigades to get water to thirsty crops and vegetable gardens.

The boys were responsible for keeping their living quarters neat and clean and caring for the garden crops and livestock. (After the move to Overlook in 1921, the older boys even helped complete some of the new buildings there.) The boys earned an allowance of twenty-five to forty cents for their chores. Most spent their money on candy, apples, or new marbles.

In the 1920s, Boys Town continued to grow into a community, both in size and population. New buildings continued to go up and the farming operation expanded. By the late 1930s, life for the boys was more stable and routine, and they had even more opportunities to learn, work, and play.

After the move to Overlook Farm in 1921, many new buildings went up to accommodate the growing number of boys who were seeking refuge at Boys Town. The Omaha Building housed the main living quarters, including dormitories like this where every boy had his own bed.

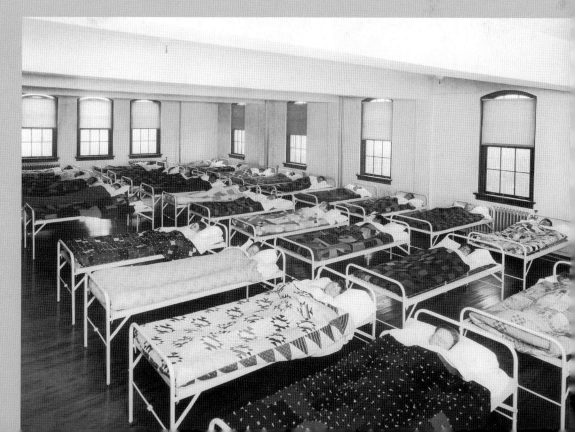

The boys ate all their meals together in a large dining hall, shared holiday celebrations, and were occasionally treated to plays and musicals in Omaha. A big highlight was a weekly movie, usually on Sunday nights. A former employee remembered those events: "We would have dinner at five and the movie started at seven. They didn't want the little guys in the movie house early because they would get to jumping around. They were kind of a rambunctious group. So they would stand outside and as soon as those (auditorium) doors would open, there would be a hundred little guys running across the field, just a like herd of buffalo."

Daily meals were served family-style in a large dining room in the Omaha Building. Much of the food the boys ate was grown on the Boys Town farm (following Father Flanagan's efforts to make the Home as self-sufficient as possible) or was donated by supporters.

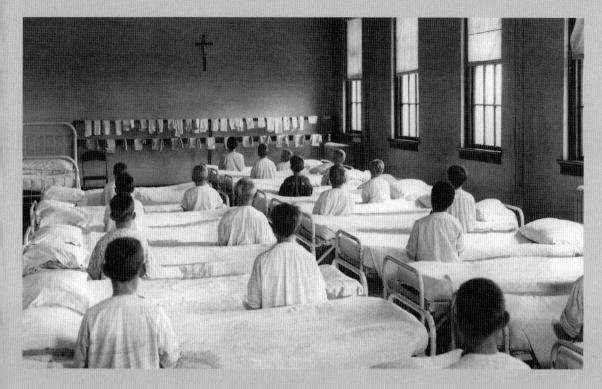

Bedtime prayers were a nightly ritual for the boys in their dormitories. Father Flanagan believed, "Every boy must learn to pray; how he prays is up to him," so each boy could pray the prayers of his chosen faith.

Father Flanagan also insisted the boys say their nightly prayers together. But decisions about formal worship were always left to the boys. "Every boy must learn to pray," Father Flanagan said. "How he prays is up to him." Boys of all creeds and some with no religious foundation at all lived at the Home. They were encouraged to continue practicing whatever faith they had learned before arriving. Catholic and Protestant services were held in the Village, and Jewish boys were driven to synagogues in Omaha. The boys who had not received any religious guidance were allowed to choose what faith they wanted to practice. And they were constantly encouraged to pray. "For prayer can work miracles," Father Flanagan taught. "A true religious training for children is most essential if we are to expect to develop them into good men and good women—worthy citizens of our great country."

Another component to shaping his boys into worthy citizens was teaching them about the law and government. Unfortunately, many boys knew too much about the wrong side of the law. Father Flanagan helped the boys learn about government through a hands-on approach—they held elections for a mayor, a municipal court of students, and a council of commissioners, all of whom were actively involved in making and enforcing the rules of the Home.

Father Flanagan started mayoral elections at Boys Town in the 1930s to teach his boys the concepts of citizenship and democracy. The boy who was elected mayor ran the Village, along with his council of commissioners. These youngsters were lining up to vote for their favorite candidate. Every boy could vote, regardless of his age or race.

With more boys to care for, the Home's staff also increased. Father Flanagan now employed farm workers, telephone operators, secretaries, cooks, and housekeepers. A doctor stopped by daily for the boys' medical needs, and Creighton University dental students assisted an Omaha dentist once a week in providing quality dental care for the boys. Father Flanagan had always handled admission applications to the Home himself, but with the number of inquiries now taking so much of his time, a Welfare Department was formed.

ABOVE: In Boys Town's early years, Father Flanagan depended on dedicated volunteers to help staff the Home and care for the boys. Here, he joins a group of local men and women who organized and put on a summer picnic for Boys Town residents.

RIGHT: From the opening of the Home until the late 1960s, various orders of nuns helped teach, nurse, cook, clean, and care for the boys. These nuns accompanied a group of boys for an outing to Krug Park in Omaha.

ABOVE: In the family Father Flanagan created at Boys Town, the boys learned to trust and depend on each other as brothers who shared the common experience of needing a home and a direction in life. As much as possible, Father Flanagan tried to make Boys Town an uplifting and happy place where the boys could forget their past sadness and thrive. The boys in these photos bear out Father Flanagan's success.

LEFT: Several boys show off their armloads of Christmas presents sometime in the 1940s. Father Flanagan knew many of the boys in his care had never had a happy Christmas, so he made sure every one of them received gifts as well as treats like fruit, nuts, and candy.

Even with its daily challenges, Boys Town was running as smoothly as a community made up of and responsible for hundreds of boys of all ages could be expected to operate. And as busy as they were every day, the boys were still able to just be kids and enjoy growing up. One of the Home's many visitors commented: "I expected to see boys dressed alike and living under some sort of military discipline. I came here and found boys living in the atmosphere of a home, wearing clothes that they have brought with them or which have been supplied them, playing with their own tops or marbles, using baseball equipment that is community property, and laughing with a laughter that proves only one thing—happiness."

By the time of Father Flanagan's death in 1948, daily life for the boys in the Village was a beneficial mix of school, work, play, and family togetherness. The "City of Little Men" was thriving and so were its young citizens.

A CENTURY OF SERVICE, A HISTORY OF HEALING

PASSING THE TORCH

Father Flanagan's unexpected death dealt an emotional blow to the young residents of Boys Town and left a tremendous void in the leadership of the Home. For thirty-one years, Father Flanagan had served as the charismatic voice, face, and decision maker of Boys Town. Now he was gone. The boys asked, "Who will care for us now?" Staff members wondered how anyone could take Father Flanagan's place and whether the Home would be able to carry on.

The transition would happen. But it would be anything but smooth.

CHAPTER TWO
Growth and Financial Stability
Monsignor Nicholas H. Wegner
1948–1973

OPPOSITE: Monsignor Nicholas Wegner, Boys Town's second national executive director.

Two years before Father Flanagan's passing, a priest in his early thirties from south Omaha was assigned by Omaha Archbishop James Hugh Ryan to work at Boys Town. Father Edmond Walsh, a U.S. Navy chaplain during World War II, developed a close relationship with Father Flanagan. Perhaps with some premonition, Father Flanagan mentioned publicly just before leaving on his fateful trip to Germany that Father Walsh was his choice to succeed him as executive director of Boys Town.

In fact, Father Walsh was named acting director immediately after Father Flanagan's death.

But Archbishop Ryan had died several months before Father Flanagan. In the summer and early fall of 1948, circumstances in the archbishop's office caused events at Boys Town to take a different direction. In September, the new archbishop, Gerald T. Bergan, named Monsignor Nicholas H. Wegner as Boys Town's second executive director. No public reason was ever given for the decision. However, it is likely Archbishop Bergan wished to name his own man as diocesan chancellor, a post Monsignor Wegner had held since 1939, and appointing Wegner to the Boys Town position allowed him to do that.

A NEBRASKA NATIVE SON

Nicholas H. Wegner was born in 1898 near Humphrey, Nebraska, the eleventh of twelve children in a farm family. As a teenager, Wegner showed great talent as a baseball pitcher and played semi-professional baseball for several teams. He saved the $50 to $100 he earned from each game and used the money to cover his tuition at St. Joseph's Seminary in Illinois, eventually turning down several offers to play at the Major League level. He went on to study in Rome and was ordained there on May 25, 1925. Returning to Omaha, Monsignor Wegner's first assignment was as an assistant pastor at St. Cecelia's Cathedral. In 1929, he was appointed assistant chancellor and, as an able administrator, began his steady rise through the ranks of the Omaha diocese.

Under Monsignor Wegner's watchful care, Boys Town doubled its youth population; expanded educational, vocational, athletic, and arts opportunities for its residents; established a solid financial footing; and spread its ideas on youth care around the globe. He earned the respect and love of the boys, staff, and alumni and ably handled his many roles as Boys Town's leader. Young citizens told a local newspaper Monsignor Wegner was "an all-around good fellow" and he "talked to us just the way a father would."

With the help of God and the prayer of our friends, the good work so ably begun by Father Flanagan and carried to such glorious heights will continue to prosper and meet with success.

—Monsignor Wegner

LEFT: A highly touted Major League prospect, Monsignor Wegner traded a baseball uniform for a priest's collar and eventually became the second national executive director of Boys Town.

ABOVE: Monsignor Wegner was ordained on May 25, 1925, after studying in Rome.

"...the good work so ably begun by Father Flanagan and carried to such glorious heights will continue to prosper and meet with success..."

Whatever Archbishop Bergan's reason was for Wegner's assignment to lead Boys Town, the surprise appointment, Monsignor Wegner's initial reluctance to accept it, and Father Walsh's crushing disappointment made for an uneasy transfer of leadership. Once in place, though, Monsignor Wegner reassured the staff and the public that he had closely followed and supported Father Flanagan's work. He quickly tried to calm those who feared radical change at the Home: "In the administration of Boys Town, I will try in every way possible to follow in the footsteps of its founder. And while I look with a great deal of fear and trepidation to the task that lies before me, I feel that with the help and cooperation of the very able staff of Boys Town and the help of God and the prayer of our friends, the good work so ably begun by Father Flanagan and carried to such glorious heights will continue to prosper and meet with success . . ."

True to his word, Monsignor Wegner did follow Father Flanagan's philosophy in running the Home. When Boys Town's tolerance for racial and religious differences was challenged, Monsignor Wegner responded to critics by simply stating, "Admission to Boys Town is based primarily upon the boy's need for a home." Later, under attack for allowing boys of different religions to live together, he wrote: "Although Father Flanagan's Boys' Home was founded by a Catholic priest, please be advised that we accept boys regardless of their creed or color . . . No boy under our care is obligated in any way, shape, or form to become a Catholic, and we have a Protestant minister who conducts Protestant services for the boys of various Protestant affiliations."

Before entering the priesthood, Monsignor Wegner was an excellent baseball player who had offers from several teams to play in the Major League. Here, umpiring a game for the boys at Boys Town, he holds up three fingers on his right hand, where strikes are usually signaled, to show he believed every boy deserved an extra chance to change his life for the better.

Growth and Financial Security

It was clear Monsignor Wegner would be a staunch defender of Father Flanagan's principles and would maintain the Home's existing programs. But he wanted to do more—much more.

Monsignor Wegner aspired to continue with his predecessor's expansion plans, double Boys Town's population, and attain financial security for the Home in keeping with Father Flanagan's intentions. Father Flanagan had set his campus expansion plans in motion before his death, and the plan he had developed in 1946 was completed during Monsignor Wegner's first year as executive director. A high school, a dining hall, a 1,200-seat music hall, a vocational career center, a field house for athletics, and twenty-five new cottages quickly sprang up across the Village landscape. In addition to the construction called for in the plan, a Protestant chapel, a forty-bed hospital and clinic, an orientation center, and, later, a middle school were built on the burgeoning campus.

LEFT: The new Boys Town High School officially opened in 1948, providing academic classes for the Village's older citizens. The building has been renovated over the years, but still serves as the Home's main learning center.

BELOW: The new high school dining hall, known as the Great Hall, gave the boys a modern, spacious gathering place for daily meals and special events and celebrations. In this photo, boys working as dining hall staff await the arrival of their fellow residents for lunch.

The boys enjoy a stage show in the newly constructed Boys Town Music Hall. The hall became a gathering place for movies, holiday activities, welcoming visiting celebrities, and other events.

A major part of Boys Town's physical expansion in the late 1940s and early 1950s was the 138,000-square-foot athletic field house, which featured an indoor track, a full gymnasium, and an Olympic-size swimming pool.

THE MAN WHO BUILT CHAMPIONS

His legacy as a coach, teacher, and mentor is as big as the cavernous athletic field house that today bears his name in the Village of Boys Town, Nebraska.

From 1943 to 1972, Maurice "Skip" Palrang demanded and received the best from his players on football fields, basketball courts, and baseball diamonds across Nebraska and the United States. His leadership lifted boys out of their troubled pasts and helped them reach goals, both as athletes and people, they never thought were possible.

The achievements of his teams speak for themselves:

- **As Boys Town's football coach, Palrang led the Boys Town Cowboys to 201 wins and twelve ties against only sixty-six losses.** Boys Town won two Nebraska state championships and established itself as a national gridiron powerhouse, traveling across the country to play teams from much larger schools before huge crowds and usually coming out on top.
- **In basketball, Palrang's teams compiled a 240–94 record and won three state championships.**
- **In baseball, Palrang's teams won two state championships and further cemented Boys Town's reputation as a dominant athletic program.**
- In 1949, after a 9–1 football season at Boys Town, **Palrang was named the national Pop Warner Coach of the Year.** Other awards included being named Nebraska Coach of the Year in 1965 by the *Omaha World-Herald* and the 1967 Rockne Club citation. He was head coach of the victorious South team in Nebraska's inaugural Shrine Bowl in 1959.
- **Palrang was inducted into the Nebraska High School Sports Hall of Fame in 1994.**

Besides being a great coach, Palrang was a top-flight classroom instructor. He taught chemistry, Spanish, English, and math. He held a bachelor's degree from Regis College in Denver and a master's degree from Creighton University in Omaha. Many of Palrang's students went on to successful careers in a variety of areas, including law, business, education, government, and childcare. They all would attribute their success to the care they received at Boys Town and the drive to succeed they acquired playing for the coach they admired.

Palrang died in 1978 at the age of seventy-one. Boys Town's indoor athletic facility was renamed the Palrang Memorial Field House that same year.

(To read more about Boys Town athletics and competitive activities, see page 200.)

Winning became a way of life for Boys Town student-athletes over the nearly thirty-year career of coaching legend Maurice "Skip" Palrang. Palrang coached a number of sports, winning state championships in football, basketball, and baseball. The Boys Town Field House was named in his honor after his death in 1978.

From a waiting list of three thousand boys, Monsignor Wegner took in about fifty boys each month. (The best records available indicate the Home's population peaked at 880 in the 1960s.) Monsignor Wegner's goal of attaining financial security created the greatest challenge. Father Flanagan's expansion plans carried a $6 million price tag, plunging the Home even further in debt. When Father Flanagan had been asked years earlier how he would pay off that huge amount, the priest had responded, "Divine Providence will take care of that . . ."

Fortunately, Father Flanagan proved to be as much a visionary in his pioneering fundraising techniques as he had been in the care of abandoned and troubled boys. In the late 1930s, the Home had added national mass mailings to what previously had been its regional fundraising efforts. Father Flanagan had hired a financial director and Boys Town began purchasing mailing lists and sending appeal letters to potential donors nationwide at Christmas and Easter. Father Flanagan's popularity had grown to be worldwide by this time, and even after his death, more and more people continued to generously support his boys and the Home. Monsignor Wegner would capitalize on this strong foundation of public trust and support to pay down Boys Town's debt and build up the endowment fund so the need to appeal for outside donations could be greatly reduced.

ABOVE: The Boys Town pylon was designed by Father Flanagan and constructed near the Home's original main entrance after his death in 1948. In the early years, many boys made their way to Boys Town on foot or by train and Father Flanagan wanted to provide a landmark they could see from miles away to let them know they were nearing their destination. Many older former residents still remember the thrill of seeing the large limestone pylon for the first time.

RIGHT: Monsignor Wegner donned a cowboy hat to greet one of the Home's supporters during a western-themed fundraising event in the 1950s. Monsignor Wegner's ongoing efforts helped Boys Town establish financial stability by paying down its large debt and building up its endowment fund so more boys could receive help in the future.

STAYING CLOSE TO 'HOME'

On June 4, 1951, thirty-nine Boys Town citizens together with sixty-seven Boys Town High School seniors who would soon be alumni gathered in the Boys Town High School library at the invitation of Monsignor Wegner to form the Boys Town Alumni Association. The association set these goals: to keep alive among the alumni bonds of friendship formed at Boys Town; to assist brother alumni whenever possible; to maintain closer contacts with, manifest interest in, and foster genuine loyalty toward the Home and school; and to promote the general good and welfare of Father Flanagan's Boys' Home® by good works, example, and words.

Most importantly, the association provided a way for former boys to stay connected to their "home" and to provide support for the children who followed them. In 1952, the association held its first national convention. The next convention was in 1953, and since then, alumni have followed a tradition of gathering for their reunion every two years.

Approximately three thousand former Boys Town boys and girls are members of the alumni association today. The association publishes a quarterly newsletter, provides scholarships for Boys Town High School graduates, and has its own Hall of Fame and Sports Hall of Fame. (Read more about Boys Town alumni on page 234.)

Boys Town alumni and their spouses gathered at the Home in 1952 for the inaugural national convention of the Boys Town National Alumni Association®. The next convention was in 1953, and since then, the association has presented the reunions every two years, drawing hundreds of former Boys Town citizens who return "home" to renew friendships, reminisce, and tour the Village.

New, Unfamiliar Challenges

In late 1959, Monsignor Wegner checked into the Mayo Clinic in Rochester, Minnesota, for stomach surgery. After the procedure, he developed an infection that required six months of recovery. Monsignor Wegner returned to work part-time in April 1960, but over the next fifteen years he underwent more than a dozen surgeries for various ailments.

At the same time Boys Town's leader was struggling with health problems, Boys Town was facing new, unfamiliar challenges in its ability to care for boys who were being admitted to the Home. The turbulent events of the 1960s—the Vietnam War, the civil rights movement, protests and marches in the streets, the assassinations of key leaders, and a greater questioning of authority (especially by young people)—led to major cultural and societal changes. This upheaval helped fuel youth problems that had not been seen, at least on a large scale, in earlier times. Boys started to arrive at Boys Town with histories of suicide attempts, physical battering, and sexual abuse. For too many children, what was hailed as the age of peace and love was also an era of drug and alcohol addiction. Boys also were coming from families broken by divorce. Father Flanagan's tried-and-true treatment methods of providing love, shelter, and vocational training were still valuable, but often were not enough to deal with these problems. And Boys Town wasn't alone. Across the country, childcare organizations were struggling to find answers for dealing with this new generation of at-risk and troubled children.

During the years of social and cultural upheaval that were changing America in the 1960s, many boys started arriving at Boys Town with new problems the Home had not seen in earlier years. As it evolved to meet their needs, Boys Town remained a place where lost youth could find a family and hope for the future.

Though they were living in a unique place, Boys Town youth still had many opportunities to enjoy the fun experiences that were part of just being kids. Here, a group of older boys pick up their orders during an outing to a pizza restaurant.

Innovative treatment strategies were needed to help youngsters overcome the devastating effects of drugs and alcohol, abuse, and the gradual deterioration of the family unit. Boys Town was at a crossroads. It could stick with its familiar, traditional methods of the past that now didn't seem to work with children whose problems required more specialized help. Or, it could take the major risk of re-inventing itself in order to really change the negative behaviors of children who were on a path of dependence and failure.

Solving this dilemma became even more urgent in light of an unexpected event on Boys Town's horizon.

Disclosure and a New Direction

The task of establishing and maintaining the financial stability of Boys Town had presented an ongoing and difficult challenge since Father Flanagan first opened his Home.

As he assumed leadership duties, Monsignor Wegner had been up to the task, working in a deliberate and conservative manner to perpetuate the work his predecessor had started. He had successfully solicited funds both for operations and to build up the endowment fund. And as a private institution, Boys Town had never been required to report publicly on the size of its fund. Through most of Monsignor Wegner's tenure that was the standard practice: private institutions remained private, especially regarding their finances.

But by the early 1970s, there was a different outlook. Many believed private institutions that offered public services should be subject to public scrutiny of their financial situation. On March 30, 1972, the *Omaha Sun* newspaper published a story on Boys Town's finances. The story was played as an exposé, under big headlines, and reported Boys Town's Foundation Fund was worth more than $150 million and the organization's net worth, adding the value of buildings and grounds, was over $200 million. Wire services spread the story from coast to coast.

Sun Newspapers of Omaha

March 30, 1972

SPECIAL REPORT

All contents of Section C Copyright Sun Newspapers of Omaha, 1972

BOYS TOWN AMERICA'S WEALTHIEST CITY?

'Give an account of thy stewardship...'
Luke, 16

* * *

THIS IS AN ACCOUNT of the stewardship that Father Flanagan's Boy's Home, internationally renowned as Boys Town, has given to hundreds of millions of dollars donated by the American public in the 55 years of its existence.

Never in those years has Boys Town felt constrained to report to its millions of donors how the money was used. Unlike most major institutions which rely on public financial support, Boys Town has drawn deeper into secrecy—indeed has flatly refused questions about finances from donors and newsmen.

This is why the Sun late last year decided to take an in-depth look at the affairs of the institution, perhaps the best-known privately-supported child-care home in America. The Sun dug through public records, talked to persons now and formerly acquainted with Boys Town's operations, and finally confronted Boys Town's leadership with the facts. The facts are that:

—Boys Town now has net worth of at least 209 million dollars, and perhaps much more.

—Boys Town has a money machine that brings in some $25 million a year from public donations and investment income.

—Boys Town increases its net worth by 16 to 18 million dollars a year. This is three to four times as much as it spends to take good care of its boys.

—Boys Town still continues to send out some 33 million letters a year telling Americans it needs their money ("$1, $2, $5 or any amount you care to give") to keep the wolf from the door.

In short, Boys Town has more money than it knows what to do with. It may be the richest city in America. Based on 1970 census figures (993 persons, and 1970 financial reports ($191.4 million net worth), it had net worth of over $190,000 per person. It had net income—after all expenses and after insignificant taxes—of $16,500 per person, man, woman and child.

* * *

EQUALLY UNSETTLING, Boys Town finds itself out of step with the times. Its boy population is falling, and it is being reluctantly forced to accept some boys it wouldn't have taken a few years ago. Indeed, its whole concept—the large "custodial" institution—is under question if not direct attack by many nationally respected agencies and theorists in the child-care field.

It is a dilemma that the almost-sainted Monsignor Edward J. Flanagan, founder of Boys Town, never had to think about. He was on thin financial ice most of his 30 years at Boys Town. When he died in 1948, the money had begun to come in, and he had it pledged to pay off a major plant expansion. The administration since that time, headed by Msgr. Nicholas H. Wegner, has concentrated on fundraising and on preserving the concepts of 1948. Now Boys Town is stuck with all that money and wedded to an almost frighteningly successful money-raising program without a plan for spending the money.

This is one reason why the board of directors of the nonprofit Boy's Home Corporation (Archbishop Daniel E. Sheehan, Msgr. Wegner and 15 prominent Omaha laymen selected by them) this month decided for the first time to instruct the administration of Boys Town to seek professional counsel "to survey the total institution and to make recommendations as to the future of Boys Town . . . "

Over the mild protests of Msgr. Wegner, the nine directors attending the annual meeting March 8 voted unanimous support of the motion made by Leo A. Daly and seconded by Dr. Claude Organ. Archbishop Sheehan promptly appointed a committee—Daly (chairman), Organ, Attorney William Grodinsky and Banker Arthur W. Knapp—to advise Msgr. Wegner in his search for professional consultants.

* * *

BROAD AND GENERAL though the resolution was, it was by far the boldest policy move Boys Town's directors have made in the 24 years since Father Flanagan's death. For most of those years Boys Town has become more and more a mystery to Omahans, while becoming the No. 1 tourist attraction of the Omaha area. Close to half a million cross-country travelers swarm its broad green campus each year.

Boy's Town's landmark—a 50-foot stone pylon on the south side of West Dodge Road a quarter-mile west of 132nd Street—is the entrance to 1,300 acres of contiguous land which the institution has acquired in the 51 years since Father Flanagan first mortgaged all of his and several benefactors' credit to acquire the original 160-acre "Overlook Farm." This land alone now is worth about $8 million, though it's carried on Boys Town's books at less than $2,000,000 (See top story on Page 7-C).

This is not the only land Boys Town owns. There is a detached 120-acre parcel near 144th and Pacific Streets; there is a summer camp at Lake Okoboji, Iowa; there is some ranch land in Wyoming; and there are a couple of buildings in downtown Omaha, one of which houses some 125 employes and four floors of typewriting and mailing equipment to dispatch the some 34 million pieces of fund-soliciting mail that go out under the postmark of the Boys Town postoffice in a typical year. (See story on Page 3-C.)

Still, the West Dodge campus and farm (itself a tidily profitable operation) is the "home place," the source of Boys Town's heartstring appeal, the place where the boys live, work and go to school. It is a showcase for the 1940s architecture of the late Leo A. Daly, father of the man who made the motion at the March 8 meeting and who now heads the international architectural firm which bears the family name.

(Continued on Page 2-C.)

A 1972 *Omaha Sun* newspaper story revealed Boys Town's net worth was in excess of $200 million. The story was played as an exposé, saying Boys Town had continued raising funds from the public even as its foundation fund grew through investments. But Boys Town supporters and other media outlets defended Boys Town, saying the Home was doing what any large organization would do to ensure it could continue to provide services to children far into the future.

"Boys Town will be here for years to come, binding up the hurts of children and teenage youth and setting them on the road to good citizenship..."

On the surface, the disclosure of the fund's amount and the fact Boys Town had continued fundraising efforts even though it had such a large amount of money in reserve indicated the Home had somehow deceived the public or done something wrong. As more details of the story became known, however, another viewpoint emerged and a number of defenders came forward. A columnist for *The New York Times* commented, "There is no scandal in the Boys Town operation; they are just successful at what they do, and the money is going to good use."

Boys Town officials explained that nearly all other institutions such as schools, universities, libraries, and hospitals "almost from necessity" create endowment programs to augment their income from tuition, fees, and contributions. Many also conduct frequent capital fundraising campaigns. Most of the money in the Boys Town endowment fund had come from private memorials from wills and estates, not from the mail appeals whose donations were used to pay annual operating costs. The Boys Town Board of Trustees acknowledged the Home had made emotional direct mail appeals for money while not disclosing the size of the foundation fund. And they decided to cancel the 1972 Christmas mail appeal.

But given the Home's often tenuous financial situation since its founding, having a substantial endowment fund made perfect sense. "There were times in the early days when this Home was on the point of closing because of lack of funds," Monsignor Wegner said. Because of its endowment fund, "Boys Town will be here for years to come, binding up the hurts of children and teenage youth and setting them on the road to good citizenship . . ."

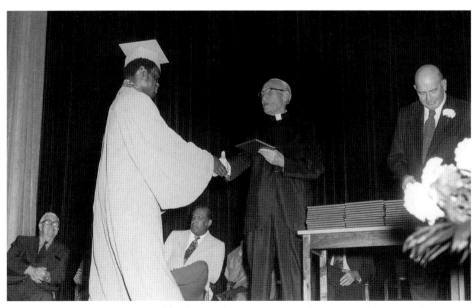

Despite the controversy generated by the *Omaha Sun* coverage of Boys Town's finances, the Home continued its day-to-day mission of caring for the boys. Here, Monsignor Wegner congratulates a graduate during commencement exercises for the Boys Town Class of 1972.

Board member Arthur W. Knapp further bolstered Monsignor Wegner's stance. "You have to keep perpetuating yourself," he said. "(Boys Town) is something that has caught hold of the average man, who wants to feel he is part of helping something that is really great."

Even before the *Omaha Sun* article was published, the board of trustees had decided to hire a consulting firm to conduct a major evaluation of the Home's youth care program and financial situation. The firm Booz, Allen, & Hamilton Inc. completed a multi-volume study that recommended Boys Town expand its programs and services into new areas while continuing to raise funds. The study also outlined the societal changes that made providing group care of the boys in dormitory settings outdated and ineffective and proposed several approaches that offered more individualized care for children.

In 1972, Patrick Brookhouser, MD, (left) and John Bordley, MD, (right) presented to the Boys Town Board of Trustees the concept of an institute for the study and treatment of communication disorders in children. The board approved the $30 million project, and five years later the institute began providing services to boys and girls from across the country. Dr. Brookhouser would become the director of the institute, which was later renamed Boys Town National Research Hospital.

Another outcome of the consultants' recommendations was the Home's announcement in June 1972 that the board of trustees had approved the development of the Boys Town Institute for Communication Disorders in Children at a cost of $30 million. The approval came after a presentation to the board on the concept of an institute dedicated to human communication disorders by Patrick E. Brookhouser, MD, and John E. Bordley, MD. (Dr. Brookhouser would later be named the director of the institute, which would eventually be renamed Boys Town National Research Hospital®.) A few months later, the board also gave preliminary approval to a $40 million research program for the study of youth development. In addition, the Home began a practice of releasing and publishing its financial information in an annual report made available to donors, the public, and the media every spring.

Decades later, the *Sun*'s revelations, which at the time had seemed to be a stain on Boys Town's reputation, would be viewed as another fortuitous event that spurred the Home's evolution into a more effective, impactful, and innovative childcare leader.

An official groundbreaking ceremony for the Boys Town Institute for Communication Disorders in Children was held in 1975. Honored guests included Louise Tracy, widow of actor Spencer Tracy who portrayed Father Flanagan in the 1938 movie *Boys Town*. Mrs. Tracy is seen here with Dr. Patrick Brookhouser (left) and Monsignor Robert Hupp (far left), who had succeeded Monsignor Wegner as Boys Town's national executive director.

Another Change of the Guard

Even with the improvements the Home was making, there was still the issue of how to provide the best and most effective care for the boys who were already at Boys Town and those who would follow. Again, these were children plagued by drug and alcohol addictions, divorce, suicide attempts, neglect, and physical and sexual abuse. The current program was neither changing the behavior of these children nor helping them (or their families) cope with these extraordinary problems.

Searching for and implementing a new childcare technology would require hard work, energy, and persistence. Unfortunately, the board felt this would be too demanding for Monsignor Wegner, who was now seventy-five and in poor health. Monsignor Wegner did not want to leave the helm at Boys Town after twenty-five years of service, but on September 15, 1973, against his wishes, the first successor to Father Flanagan retired. He continued to reside at Boys Town in living quarters at the clinic until a series of strokes in 1975 sent him to St. Catherine's Hospital Center for Continuing Care. There, on March 18, 1976, he passed away. His funeral services were held in the Dowd Memorial Chapel at Boys Town, attended by the countless boys who had turned to him for guidance and direction during his twenty-five years

The elementary school boys presented Monsignor Wegner with a congratulatory gift during his retirement party in late 1973.

of committed service. (In 1977, the Boys Town Middle School was fittingly named Wegner Middle School in his honor.)

The *Omaha World-Herald* provided a fitting tribute: "He had to take the mantle of Father Flanagan as the shepherd of Boys Town. It was a tough act to follow. It didn't take long to find out Boys Town was in good hands. What Father Flanagan planted, Monsignor Wegner brought to full flower. Boys Town today, in its security and continuity, is as much a monument to Monsignor Wegner's dedication and singleness of purpose as it is to Father Flanagan's vision."

For only the second time in almost sixty years, Boys Town needed a new leader.

High school boys surround Monsignor Wegner outside the Boys Town Great Hall following his retirement dinner in 1973.

DAILY LIFE FOR THE BOYS

Throughout Monsignor Wegner's tenure, Boys Town residents and their caregivers continued to live in smaller cottages (for older youth) or large dormitories (for younger residents). More than five hundred boys lived at Boys Town at any one time, and each cottage was home to twenty youth. A supervisor and an assistant were in charge of each dorm, keeping order and making sure the boys had everything they needed in terms of clothing, bedding, and personal effects. Each boy had his own bed and each cottage had bathrooms and showers.

The boys ate meals together in a large mess hall. Later, a large building called the Great Hall was constructed and it became the primary gathering place for breakfast, lunch, dinner, and meals for special events.

At home in their cottages, the older boys had equal responsibilities for chores and schoolwork. All the boys were allowed time to listen to the radio, play games, and watch television when their schoolwork was done. And each boy was valued and accepted as a member of the Boys Town "family."

Like any large family, all of the boys were expected to pitch in on projects and chores at the Home, including canning vegetables gathered from the fall harvest. Father Flanagan believed doing even the small chores helped teach the boys responsibility and a strong work ethic.

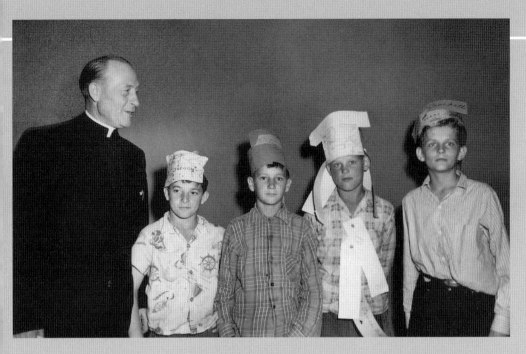

Boys Town's schools combined learning and fun whenever possible. Monsignor Wegner admires the hats worn by several boys for a school program about the different states.

On a typical day, the boys would rise early, get dressed, eat breakfast, and head for school. After classes, there were chores to do before the boys could relax with a hobby or play outside. Members of sports teams practiced right after school, and other various clubs and activities had meetings during that time. The boys gathered for supper together before heading to their cottages to do homework. Then it was time to settle down for the evening and go to bed.

ABOVE: A group of boys enjoy free time reading and playing games in their dormitory.

RIGHT: Each Boys Town dorm had a craft room where the boys could work on hobbies. These youngsters proudly showed off the model airplanes they had built.

ABOVE: Like "brothers" everywhere, the Boys Town boys liked to roughhouse and have fun. While good behavior was expected, a friendly wrestling match was a common occurrence in the dorms.

RIGHT: Pets were an important part of the Boys Town family. Each cottage where the older boys lived had one or two dogs the boys cared for and played with as they grew up at the Home.

BELOW: Sledding was a favorite winter activity for the boys. Here, several line up for a downhill race near their residence.

On Sundays, the boys would walk to Boys Town's Protestant or Catholic churches for worship services or be driven to a local synagogue if they were of the Jewish faith. There were also movie nights, games, sports contests, radio and television, and other activities for the boys.

During this time, Boys Town continued the tradition of "Twelfth Night," a Christmas celebration that began under Father Flanagan where the boys enjoyed a holiday-related activity on each of the twelve consecutive nights from Christmas Day to January 6, the Feast of Epiphany. Many boys had never enjoyed a Christmas celebration as part of a family before coming to Boys Town, and Twelfth Night would remain a lasting memory for nearly every citizen who lived at the Home during the 1940s, 1950s, and 1960s. (See more about Boys Town holiday and special event celebrations on page 204.)

Every Christmas, candy companies would send each Boys Town resident a box of candy bars to enjoy for weeks after the holidays. Here, a group of older boys—representing their home states of Missouri, New Jersey, Iowa, and Kansas—display their Christmas loot. Many boys fondly remember poker games where candy bars were used as betting chips.

ABOVE: Monsignor Wegner crowns a boy King Stephen as his court looks on, one of the many traditions of Boys Town's Twelfth Night celebration at Christmastime. The lucky boy who was chosen as king could order all the other boys around during his one-day reign. However, once the king's reign ended, he had to run a gauntlet of snowballs playfully thrown by his former "subjects."

BELOW: On Christmas morning, Monsignor Wegner would visit each cottage and dormitory to watch as the boys gleefully opened their Christmas gifts.

The growth of Boys Town under Monsignor Wegner's leadership also opened new doors of opportunities for the boys, ensuring that the lives of the Home's young citizens were being shaped and guided by positive social, educational, spiritual, and extracurricular experiences. Monsignor Wegner made sure their priorities remained focused on school, church, and home. He also tried to make sure each boy left the Home well-prepared for

adulthood and life as a productive citizen. The Boys Town Vocational Career Center offered courses in trades like tailoring, barbering, auto mechanics, ceramics, and industrial arts. The boys were responsible for their own student bank accounts. The Home also established a scholarship fund so students who wished to enroll in a university or post-secondary training school would have that opportunity.

Boys Town prided itself on having a state-of-the-art training center for teaching the boys trades and vocational careers. The Vocational Career Center offered at least twenty trade courses, including an automotive repair shop. Here, students describe the parts of an engine to Monsignor Wegner and some visitors.

Monsignor Wegner believed regardless of their religious background or affiliation, children needed to learn the lessons of worship, reverence, and moral responsibility that a faith life could teach. He encouraged personal and social religious habits in the boys, such as prayer and regular church or synagogue attendance. Above all, Monsignor Wegner instilled in the hearts of his boys the importance of being their "brother's keeper."

The boys also were involved in a variety of activities that taught them valuable life lessons, prepared them for life after Boys Town, and continued to prove to the public that the Home was helping to mold productive citizens. The Boys Town "Aggies" 4-H Club produced Grand National Champion livestock and often entered them in fairs and expositions. In 1949, the club began hosting the Boys Town Royal Livestock Show at the field house every August for 4-H clubs from throughout the Midwest.

A boy displays his prize 4-H calf at the Boys Town farm. The boys often entered the animals they raised in competitions. Such projects helped teach responsibility and taking pride in a job well done.

ABOVE: Under the direction of Father Francis Schmitt, the Boys Town Choir became known nationwide. The choir was heard on the radio, and later on television, and made annual tours to cities across the United States, Japan, Canada, and Cuba. Carnegie Hall, President Truman, Ed Sullivan, and Disney World all hosted the famous choral group over the years. The Boys Town Choir would also record albums of Christmas music with such stars as the Everly Brothers and Gordon MacRae (opposite page).

RIGHT: Radio and television brought Midnight Mass from Boys Town's Dowd Chapel to millions of American homes during the Christmas season from the 1940s through the 1960s. Music provided by the Boys Town Choir was the centerpiece of this holiday celebration.

Long-time Boys Town Choir Director Father Francis Schmitt and several members of his choir map out their next tour across the United States. The choir traveled extensively by train, performing dozens of shows during the year. On trips during the school year, tutors and teachers accompanied the boys to make sure they kept up with their studies.

Monsignor Wegner's tenure also saw the development of many outstanding athletic traditions and success in sports. A baseball pitcher throughout his college years who turned down two Major League contracts to become a priest, Monsignor Wegner was an avid sportsman. In 1943, Boys Town hired Coach Maurice "Skip" Palrang, who together with Monsignor Wegner launched one of the most successful eras of athletics in Boys Town history. Boys Town teams chalked up victory after victory, winning several state championships in football, swimming, basketball, track, baseball, and wrestling. Many of Boys Town's outstanding student-athletes later made their mark in amateur and professional sports after graduation.

Before joining the Omaha Metropolitan League in 1964, the Boys Town Cowboys football team played exhibition games in twenty-one states and the District of Columbia before crowds of as many as 40,000 spectators. The team traveled across the country in the "Flex," the team bus nicknamed by the boys. The "Flex" became part of the Home's great athletic tradition as it carried team after championship team to opponents' schools for twenty-one years. Team members often demanded the driver travel certain highway routes to guarantee victory and not "jinx" a winning streak.

Boys Town football teams enjoyed tremendous success on the local and national stage in the 1950s and 1960s, sometimes traveling across the country to play larger schools before crowds of 40,000 or more spectators. For closer games, the team traveled on a bus they affectionately called the "Flex." Even against the bigger schools, the Boys Town Cowboys proved to be a tough opponent.

During Monsignor Wegner's tenure, thousands of boys who entered Boys Town as shy, uncertain children left the Home as well-rounded, ready-for-the-world young men because of the lessons they learned. The needs of the youth may have changed, but Monsignor Wegner's commitment to the principles and mission of the Home remained constant and unwavering.

During Monsignor Wegner's tenure, boys came to Boys Town alone and lost, but they left as part of a family of "brothers," aspiring to a common goal of living their lives as productive citizens.

A CENTURY OF SERVICE, A HISTORY OF HEALING

BOYS TOWN REMADE

With the passing of Monsignor Wegner and the uncertainty surrounding how Boys Town would meet the changing needs of children in the future, the Home faced yet another crucial leadership decision. The new executive director would not only have to understand the unique troubles of the boys who were now coming to Boys Town, but also find and implement a program combining the compassionate care of the past with new strategies that could help youth change their negative, harmful behaviors.

CHAPTER THREE
Innovation and a Bold New Direction
Monsignor Robert P. Hupp
1973–1985

The board of trustees found that leader in Monsignor Robert P. Hupp, another native Nebraskan who had risen through the ranks to become vicar general of the Archdiocese of Omaha. On October 11, 1973, Monsignor Hupp was named the third national executive director of Boys Town. Monsignor Hupp inherited a population of boys he called "social orphans." These were children whose family lives had been damaged by abuse, poverty, drugs, alcoholism, divorce, and other social ills. Now they were at Boys Town, trying to deal with the severe emotional and behavioral fallout of these traumatic experiences. Helping these boys beyond providing for their daily care would require Boys Town to act boldly and confidently.

OPPOSITE: Monsignor Robert Hupp, Boys Town's third national executive director.

RIGHT: A large banner welcoming Monsignor Hupp on his first day on the job goes up near Boys Town's main entrance on Dodge Street.

As youth with new and more serious problems continued to seek refuge at Boys Town in the early 1970s, the Home's leadership faced the difficult task of changing the way it provided care in order to meet the changing needs of America's at-risk kids.

Fortunately, there was already a blueprint for the future. And Monsignor Hupp was firm in his resolve to pioneer new methods and directions of care and give programs and ideas a chance to succeed, all for the good of the children. "We must never be content to stand still when children are at risk," he said.

One of the key elements identified in the earlier Booz, Allen, & Hamilton study had been the need to provide care for children in a family-style setting. This meshed nicely with Father Flanagan's long-term vision for Boys Town, and now the Home was poised to make his dream a reality. Monsignor Hupp and a screening committee from the board began a national search for a program that would bring a true "family concept" to the treatment Boys Town provided for its citizens. The search would prove to be long and arduous, marked by false starts, disappointing results, successes and failures, and new beginnings. And always hanging in the balance were the lives of youngsters who desperately needed help.

"We must never be content to stand still when children are at risk."

FROM SERVICE TO COUNTRY TO SERVICE TO YOUTH

Robert P. Hupp was born in Clearwater, Nebraska, in 1915, the oldest of nine children. Once he decided to enter the priesthood, he left his native Nebraska to study at St. Louis Preparatory Seminary and Kenrick Seminary. At Kenrick, he was known as "The Clipper" because he cut his classmates' hair to earn tuition money.

After being ordained at St. Cecilia's Cathedral in Omaha in 1940, he served at two Omaha parishes before joining the U.S. Navy and serving as a chaplain during World War II. Later, Monsignor Hupp founded Christ the King Catholic Church parish in Omaha and became the vicar general of the Archdiocese of Omaha.

After serving as the third national executive director of Boys Town for more than a dozen years, he retired and continued to live at Boys Town for several years before health problems eventually forced him to move to an assisted living facility. He passed away on August 29, 2003, and was buried in Omaha.

We see far . . . when we stand on the shoulders of giants. It was the charismatic program innovator, Father Flanagan, complemented by the administrative executive, Monsignor Wegner, who provided the frame for me to climb.
—Monsignor Hupp

ABOVE: Monsignor Hupp served as a chaplain in the U.S. Navy during World War II. Here, he addresses the crew of the USS *Kyne* in 1944.

LEFT: One of Monsignor Hupp's favorite activities was riding his bike around the Boys Town campus. He often drew a crowd of young companions.

Eventually, the journey led Boys Town to the Teaching-Family Model developed at Achievement Place at the University of Kansas in Lawrence. The Teaching-Family Model had grown out of a research/funding collaboration between the Bureau of Child Research in Lawrence and the National Institute of Mental Health's Center for Crime and Delinquency.

The primary objectives of the Teaching-Family Model were to develop a community-based, family-style, skill-oriented group home treatment for disadvantaged and delinquent youth. The model was intended to be effective, economical, beneficial to its consumers, and replicable by other programs. But as attractive as it seemed, proponents thought it would be impossible to put in place in a large community like Boys Town. Some even argued the Village should be abandoned and homes for youth that used the Teaching-Family Model should be located right in the community.

Monsignor Hupp and his administrators courageously insisted that Boys Town was the perfect place to adopt the model. To that end, the Home hired a number of professionals, including Achievement Place staff members, to refine the program for as many as fifty homes on the home campus.

In late 1974, Boys Town hired its first "Family-Teachers®," a married couple who would begin caring for a small group of youth in a former cottage being converted into a "Family Home®." Three other couples were hired soon after, and that core group worked with other staff members to develop formal training materials for the Family-Teachers who were being recruited. As new couples were trained, they moved into the remaining converted cottages and sixteen newly built homes. By the end of 1975, the last of the dormitories was closed and the transition to the Boys Town Family Home Program℠ was complete.

Monsignor Hupp chats with a Family-Teaching Couple outside a newly built Family Home. A total of seventy single-family dwellings would eventually populate the Village of Boys Town as the organization transitioned to its new residential care program.

Looking back, it is easy to assume Boys Town was successful in its search for and implementation of the Teaching-Family Model, which would eventually evolve into the research-proven Boys Town Model® that is the foundation of all Boys Town programs today. In reality, this historic shift was far more difficult, created far more day-to-day uncertainty, and initially was far less clear in design and execution.

Boys Town's history had shown there is nothing more difficult to accomplish than radical organizational change. For a long time, more people opposed and resisted the changes at Boys Town than were in favor of them. The changing roles of staff members meant some employees did not have the skills or training to continue working at the Home. There was resentment and even animosity as a result of the "growing pains" Boys Town was experiencing. There were also some false starts. For example, Boys Town's support of three research centers was ended in the early 1980s because the general studies of youth development being done were not related to the new program and did not help the Home develop better ways of taking care of children.

On the job for only two years, Monsignor Hupp's leadership and organizational skills were already being severely tested.

A Community of Families

Monsignor Hupp was determined to transform Boys Town so it could meet the changing needs of children. As the Family Home Program became more established, the Village began to look like the community of care Father Flanagan had envisioned in the early days of Boys Town.

Under the new youth care system, each Family Home in the Village housed eight to ten boys. (Eventually, the Village would comprise seventy Family Homes.) The boys were of various ages, races, and ethnic and religious backgrounds, and they came to Boys Town from across the country. Each Family Home was headed by a Family-Teaching Couple, who lived with the boys seven days a week, twenty-four hours a day, meeting their daily needs, providing supervision and guidance, teaching them social skills, and providing a caring and loving home environment.

Compassion for children in need had always been a mainstay of Boys Town. Now that compassion was being combined with effective childcare technology, an approach that would give the youth their best opportunity to achieve success, both during their time at Boys Town and after they left.

A unique element of Boys Town's new residential program was its emphasis on skill teaching and relationship building. This focused care and treatment on correcting inappropriate behaviors by *teaching* youth alternative positive behaviors and social skills (following instructions, accepting "No" for an answer, respecting authority) and encouraging and reinforcing their positive behavior. The main responsibility for this teaching fell to the Family-Teachers, who had multiple opportunities every day to effect change as the boys' primary caregivers. Skills also were consistently taught and reinforced by teachers in Boys Town's schools and by coaches and instructors in other extracurricular activities. This created a consistent learning environment where youth were aware of the expectations for their behaviors. Along with their teaching, Family-Teachers and other staff were charged with developing *positive, trusting relationships* with the youth and modeling for the boys how they could develop healthy relationships with others.

PIONEERS AND ROLE MODELS

Ron and Annette Herron were the first Family-Teaching Couple hired when Boys Town adopted the original Teaching-Family Model in 1974. This milestone marked the beginning of Boys Town's modern-day residential program, where youth live with and receive care from trained married couples in a family-style home. Up to that time, large groups of youth had lived in cottages and dormitories supervised by counselors.

Ron and Annette Herron, Boys Town's first Family-Teaching Couple, outside their home with their family of boys in the early 1980s.

"Ron and Annette not only were the first but they also were the pioneers and prototypes for what Family-Teachers became at Boys Town—courageous, compassionate, technically proficient, and patient," said Dan Daly, PhD, executive vice president and director of Boys Town Youth Care. "None of the systems we depend so heavily on today—training, evaluation, supervision, and consultation—existed when they began. They had no checkbook and no self-contained kitchen. Ron and Annette helped build all of what we now take for granted."

Annette was working at the Pottawattamie Mental Health Center in Council Bluffs and Ron was teaching high school English in Underwood, Iowa, when they received a call from a Boys Town administrator they knew. Boys Town was hiring married couples to work with troubled children in a new program, he said. Would they be interested?

After extensive interviews and a few weeks of training that included traveling to the University of Kansas (where the Teaching-Family Model was developed), Ron and Annette moved in as the first Family-Teachers. On the day before Thanksgiving in 1974, they welcomed their first five boys into a cottage undergoing remodeling at 122 Maher Drive. (Ten boys would eventually live in the home.)

For several months, the Herron's Family Home was the only one on campus. Boys Town was gearing up to hire more couples, but more cottages had to be remodeled and support systems had to be developed. Meals were delivered to the Herron family from the Great Hall dining facility because their home's kitchen wasn't finished. Even with their training, Ron and Annette had to improvise at times in the teaching they did with the boys. "It wasn't easy at first," Annette said. "There were a lot of adjustments for us and the kids. Everybody was flying by the seat of their pants. We were like a little island."

As other Family Homes eventually opened, the new residential program took root and grew. Some of the new Family-Teaching Couples hired were friends of Ron and Annette. Between 1974 and 1987, Ron and Annette served as Family-Teachers for about eight years. When they weren't working in a Family Home, they filled administrative positions at Boys Town. Their last stretch as Family-Teachers was from 1983 to 1987. In all, Ron and Annette "parented" an estimated fifty boys over the years, serving as positive role models, teachers, and counselors. Years after leaving, those young men would return to visit Ron and Annette and thank them for the second chance they got at Boys Town. "That was the best job we ever had in our lives," Annette said. "Ron would say, 'It's not a job, it's a lifestyle.'"

Ron and Annette continued to work at Boys Town in administrative positions before leaving to pursue other opportunities in 1999. Ron passed away in 2011 at age sixty-one.

Day-to-day activities for youth and their caregivers in each Family Home included eating meals together, a regular study and homework hour, and time for fun and games.

A CENTURY OF SERVICE, A HISTORY OF HEALING

Two other components played a critical role in producing positive outcomes for the youth. Each Family Home had a self-government system that enabled the boys to participate in daily family meetings, where they had a voice and a vote in making decisions on how their home was run. Each youth was also placed on a motivation system where he could earn points for positive behaviors or lose points for negative behaviors. At the end of each day, each boy totaled up his points; if he had earned a required number of positive points, he could purchase privileges like watching TV, spending extra time playing outside, or doing something special with a Family-Teacher. If he didn't earn the required points, he could not purchase privileges and had to wait until the next day to start over. Eventually, a youth would move off the motivation system as he internalized positive behaviors and skills and began using them simply because he had learned it was the right thing to do. In this way, the boys learned to take responsibility for their individual behaviors, make good choices on how to behave in social situations, and build a foundation for success in school, with others, and in life after Boys Town.

Giving the youth a voice in the decisions that affected their lives was a major element of the Family Home Program. Family meetings, like the one seen here, were a daily activity that allowed the youth to discuss and vote on things like house rules, chore schedules, and family outings. This helped them learn how to contribute as part of a family and strengthened their family bonds.

STAFF DEVELOPMENT: THE KEY TO SUCCESS

In order to implement the model so it could produce the optimal positive results, Boys Town instituted major changes in how Boys Town staff members were prepared for and supported in their work with children. Four key components were the foundation for success:

- **Training.** Each Family-Teaching Couple received extensive training before they moved into a Family Home and began caring for youth. Couples lived in on-campus apartments, observed experienced couples in various childcare and home operation activities, and were required to successfully complete a rigorous three-week pre-service workshop. In the workshop, couples spent most of their instruction time role playing and practicing the skills they would use in caring for the youth and operating their home. After Family-Teachers moved into a Family Home to begin working with youth, they continued their training through specialized workshops that helped them enhance their basic skills and learn more advanced childcare techniques.

- **Consultation.** Once in a home, Family-Teachers received advice and support from an administrative staff member (consultant) who would help during crisis situations, observe the couple at work and provide feedback, and provide continuing in-service training. Once the residential program was established and growing, these consultants usually were former Family-Teachers who had received special training in consultation skills. Consultants were available twenty-four hours a day, seven days a week, by phone or in person. They also helped Family-Teachers develop a service plan for each youth, which outlined a youth's specific care needs and goals and the ways to meet them. As an important guiding member of the treatment team, consultants helped Family-Teachers develop sound professional skills and maintain their enthusiasm, concern for youth, and objectivity.

- **Evaluation.** An evaluation system was necessary to ensure accountability and the highest level of treatment success possible. On a regular basis, each youth and the people who were involved in his services (e.g., parents or guardians, teachers, principal, social worker, probation officer, judge) were asked to rate and comment on the services provided by the Family-Teachers. A steady flow of information about activities in each Family Home was provided through formal and informal reports. All of the evaluation material was used to determine whether a couple became "certified" Family-Teachers. A couple that failed to pass their first evaluation was given a second, final chance, usually within thirty days. These annual evaluations meant a Family-Teaching Couple had consistently provided a safe, caring family environment; their youth liked and respected them, and each child was learning important skills and values and was making progress toward his service plan goals.

- **Administrative.** Boys Town designed its administrative system to meet the needs of youth who were living in a family-style environment. Consistent administrative procedures eased the burden of Family-Teachers and facilitated the accomplishment of service goals for each youth. Administration provided proper supervision and support services for Family-Teachers and established policies and procedures in program areas such as admissions, staff recruitment and training, licensing, and budgets.

These components remain as the foundation of today's Boys Town's Family Home Program and provide the framework for most other Boys Town services.

Each prospective Boys Town employee was required to complete a comprehensive pre-service training program before entering a Family Home to begin caring for youth or beginning other administrative or consultation duties. Here, a class of Boys Town trainees gathers prior to their training "graduation" day.

Religious education and practice had been part of Boys Town's youth care approach since the days of Father Flanagan. In the new Family Home Program, a boy's spiritual development played a major role in treatment and was the responsibility of the Family Home as well as church and school. Family-Teachers were asked to respect and enhance the religious traditions of Boys Town youth without proselytizing or "forcing" religious practices on them. Family-Teachers also attended church with their youth, taught proper church behavior, and modeled and taught religious home habits such as prayer, reflection, and study.

Boys Town's transition to a residential care program was slow and sometimes painful. Ultimately, though, it invigorated the organization and brought hope and healing to youth. For many of the boys admitted to Boys Town, it was their first experience with a family that didn't yell at or hit each other and had two parents who cared about them, had rules, and, most importantly, never gave up on them. "Even though we're not family in blood, we are a family through God, peace, and happiness," said one youth.

This Family Home Program turned out to be exactly what Boys Town needed to address the challenging needs of a new generation of children. Over time, Boys Town would continue to improve on the Teaching-Family Model and enhance its ability to provide the best care possible for troubled youth.

Regardless of their denomination, all Boys Town youth benefited from opportunities to strengthen their faith life through daily prayers and attending worship services. From the Home's beginning, spirituality was considered to be a critical element in each child's journey of healing. Here, Monsignor Hupp says Mass in Dowd Chapel.

A Child in Need Is a Child in Need

"I hadn't been at Boys Town for more than a week," Monsignor Hupp would recall, "before I got a call from Juvenile Court Judge Colleen Buckley asking me when we would start taking girls. I told her to just give me time."

Traditionally, Boys Town had provided care only for boys. That didn't mean girls didn't face the same problems as their male peers. But when Father Flanagan first opened his Home, he focused on helping boys because of what he had seen happen to destitute men he had worked with and because boys made up the vast majority of the kids living on the streets or getting in trouble with the law.

In the early 1900s, when girls lost their parents and became homeless, they were usually taken in by relatives or moved in with families for whom they could work as maids and housekeepers. This meant there were far fewer girls who were orphans or living on their own. As times changed, it became clear girls were facing many of the same problems as boys and needed, and deserved, the same high-quality care and treatment. The Boys Town Institute (National Research Hospital) had been treating girls with communication disorders since opening in 1977. But the Home's residential care program was still limited to boys.

Monsignor Hupp had experience working with girls and was aware of their problems. He served as chaplain, teacher, and athletic coach for a girls' home run by the Sisters of the Good Shepherd Convent in Omaha from 1946 to 1950. In 1978, he accepted five girls into the Boys Town residential program in what was to be a small, short-term test. These first girls lived off-campus in a downtown Omaha home Boys Town owned. Then, in 1979, a few girls began living in a Family Home on campus. More followed and by 1985, twenty-six girls were citizens of Boys Town. "I saw it as an experimental program," Monsignor Hupp said. "I also had trouble convincing the Board of Trustees that accepting girls wasn't a mistake. But when the girls arrived, it actually improved the behavior of the boys."

In 1983, (left to right) Cindy Koppenhaver, Jeanette Hoer, Joni Bachelor, Lisa Bordogna, and Diana Luce became the first five girls to graduate from Boys Town High School. Here, the group holds a photo of some of the Home's earliest residents. The number of girls living at Boys Town increased steadily through the 1980s as the Home further evolved to meet the care and treatment needs of both male and female youth.

A family of girls and their Family-Teachers gathered in their living room for a photo in 1981.

The relatively small number of girls living on campus caused little stir at Boys Town. But there was a great commotion among alumni and the general public. The media began bombarding Monsignor Hupp with questions: Was he going to change Boys Town's name? What did he think of "People Town?" Monsignor Hupp called a meeting with the girls who were living on campus and asked what they thought. Their unanimous answer: "We want to live at **Boys** Town."

Again, Boys Town weathered the storm of controversy that came with another major change in its approach to helping children. The "experiment" was a success, and in the coming years, more and more girls would call Boys Town home and experience the life-changing benefits of effective, compassionate, family-style care.

"... when the girls arrived, it actually improved the behavior of the boys."

A Bold New Venture to Help Children with Communication Disorders

In 1974, two years after the board's approval, ground was broken and construction began on the new Boys Town Institute for Communication Disorders in Children near downtown Omaha. A year later, a Boys Town Institute clinic opened in a rental space at the then-St. Joseph Hospital.

On September 9, 1977, the institute formally opened with ceremonies including a blessing of the new building by Archbishop Daniel E. Sheehan. The $13 million facility, adjacent to St. Joseph Hospital, featured a five-floor diagnostic and rehabilitation center and an adjoining language and learning center. The complex was designed to bring together the disciplines of medicine, communication science, research, and education for the benefit of children with communication disorders. Under the leadership of Director Patrick Brookhouser, MD, the institute enabled Boys Town to take giant strides toward helping even more children and families through research into the causes of communication disorders and the evaluation and treatment of children.

The official opening ceremony (left) of the Boys Town Institute for Communication Disorders in Children included a blessing from Archbishop Daniel Sheehan of the Archdiocese of Omaha and the unveiling of a Two Brothers statue outside the facility. During a tour of the institute (below), Eunice Shriver (left) and Phil Donahue (right) listened intently as a staff member described the state-of-the-art medical equipment.

Researchers had found childhood communication disorders were an important element in educational, social, and emotional problems. Through diagnosis, treatment, and study of speech, hearing, language, and learning problems, the Boys Town Institute would improve the future of children who are deaf, hard of hearing, or have related communication disorders.

In 1978, the institute's Center for Childhood Deafness, Language and Learning was established, and in 1982, the institute earned its first one-year accreditation from the Joint Commission on Accreditation of Hospitals (JCAH). Two years later, a new clinic opened on the home campus and several new programs were developed to address issues such as the abuse of children with disabilities.

Sharing the Boys Town Approach

As the number of youth seeking long-term residential care at Boys Town continued to grow, it was obvious the Home could not keep up with the demand. In 1975, Monsignor Hupp decided to begin offering Boys Town's system of youth care to other organizations.

By this time, the residential program developed at Boys Town and the care it provided had four characteristics that made it effective and attractive to others. It was *safe*; children were healthy and truly free from the fear of abandonment and abuse. It was *effective*; kids actually made progress and got better. It was *family centered*, and the children were *happy* to be at Boys Town. The question now was whether the program was *replicable* and could be adopted in other locations.

Boys Town developed the Community-Based Systems Program (later called the Boys Town National Group Home Program) to provide training and technical assistance to group homes owned by other agencies. Within about ten years, more than ninety affiliated Family Homes in thirteen states were using Boys Town's childcare technology.

Monsignor Hupp also had received many requests from communities around the country to start other Boys Towns. In addition, he had become increasingly concerned about other childcare agencies that were affiliating themselves with the National Group Home Program and using Boys Town's name, but not fully adopting the Boys Town program. So in 1983, he announced the development of a new program called "Boys Town USA®," which would establish childcare sites around the country, with residential homes that would be wholly owned and operated by Boys Town. Later that year, the first Boys Town Family Home outside of Nebraska was opened in Tallahassee, Florida. This single-dwelling residence, with a family of six boys and a Family-Teaching Couple, was the first step in gauging whether Boys Town could deliver the same high-quality care to children away from the home campus.

Once again, Boys Town was poised to make a huge but necessary leap into unchartered territory.

Father Flanagan Award for Service to Youth

In 1975, Boys Town Executive Director Monsignor Robert Hupp wanted to promote the Home's new residential program and other initiatives that had modernized its youth care programs while also raising Boys Town's national profile. As a result, the Father Flanagan Award for Service to Youth was created to recognize individuals whose efforts to help children followed the principles of the Boys Town's founder. In announcing the award, Monsignor Hupp said, ". . . it will be given whenever the Home's directors feel a person's accomplishments merit it."

The national executive director and the Boys Town National Board of Trustees select candidates for and recipients of the award, Boys Town's highest honor. They consider how a person has furthered the principles of Father Flanagan by improving the lives of children and families. On the award are the words, ". . . for their faithfulness to the cause of service to youth, a faith and cause shared by Father Flanagan . . ."

Since its inception, only twenty-one people have received the award. They have included philanthropists, leaders in the medical field, child and family advocates, entertainers, and sports figures. The award is a nineteen-inch bronze statue of Father Edward Flanagan, created by artist Fred Hoppe, standing on a wooden base with a plate that bears the recipient's name.

The first recipient of the Father Flanagan Award for Service to Youth was Louise Tracy, widow of Spencer Tracy who won the Best Actor Academy Award for his portrayal of Father Flanagan in the 1938 movie *Boys Town*. Mrs. Tracy was honored for founding the John Tracy Clinic for hearing-impaired youth in Los Angeles; the clinic was named for the Tracys' son, who was discovered to be deaf as a child.

Louise Tracy, widow of actor Spencer Tracy, was the first recipient of the Father Flanagan Award for Service to Youth in 1975. Making the award presentation were Monsignor Hupp and Archbishop Daniel Sheehan.

Other Father Flanagan Award Recipients:

Blessed Mother Teresa met with the youth during her historic visit to Boys Town.

Entertainer Bob Hope brought laughter to countless servicemen and servicewomen.

Dr. Mildred Jefferson was recognized for her leadership in the right-to-life movement.

1976 – Blessed Mother Teresa of Calcutta, founder of the Missionaries of Charity, recognized for her zeal in enlisting nuns and brothers to serve needy children in sixty-seven countries. Mother Teresa visited Boys Town and toured the Family Homes and other facilities.

1977 – Bob Hope, entertainer and humanitarian, in recognition of three decades of entertainment tours for America's young men and women in the service.

1978 – Dr. Mildred Jefferson, recognized for her work as the three-time president of the National Right to Life Committee and a pro-life activist.

1979 – Dr. Jonas Salk, recognized for developing the first effective vaccine against paralytic polio.

1980 – Bob and Dorothy DeBolt, a Piedmont, California, couple honored for the love, understanding, and care they gave to their special family of twenty children, fourteen of whom were adopted with diverse racial backgrounds and physical handicaps.

1981 – Danny Thomas, entertainer, recognized as the founder of St. Jude Children's Hospital in Memphis, Tennessee, which treats children with catastrophic illnesses.

1984 – Julius Erving, star basketball player with the Philadelphia 76ers, recognized for his outstanding public example for the youth of America, especially his role in encouraging youngsters to stay in school and stay off drugs.

1985 – Donald R. Keough, Coca-Cola president and chief operating officer, recognized for his commitment to Special Olympics programs for the handicapped and athletic programs for girls.

1986 – Former First Lady Nancy Reagan, in recognition of her leadership in the battle against drug and alcohol abuse and for heightening awareness of drug abuse problems in the nation's schools.

1987 – Dr. Denton Cooley, founder of the Texas Heart Institute in Houston, recognized for pioneering methods to correct congenital heart defects in infants and children. Dr. Cooley also implanted the first totally artificial heart in a human.

Dr. Jonas Salk developed the vaccine for polio, saving generations of children from the dreaded disease.

Nebraska football coach Tom Osborne and his wife, Nancy, were honored for their Husker Teammates program.

Former First Lady Nancy Reagan received a big "Boys Town" welcome in 1986.

PGA golfer Tom Lehman works with numerous charities that help kids.

1990 – Michael Jordan, NBA superstar, recognized for his work in encouraging youth to stay in school and stay off drugs.

1993 – Lou Holtz, University of Notre Dame football coach, in recognition of his work to inspire youth and adults to always do their very best.

1995 – University of Nebraska football coach Tom Osborne and his wife, Nancy, recognized for helping young people find success through the couple's Husker Teammates program, which paired junior high school students with Nebraska football player mentors.

1996 – Montrose Wolf, American psychologist, in recognition of his work on developing child learning tools like time-out.

2000 – Arnold Schwarzenegger, professional body builder and actor, for his work to inform young people of the importance of physical fitness. He also was honored for his involvement with the Special Olympics and the Inner-City Games.

2006 – Former First Lady Laura Bush, in recognition of her leadership of the "Helping America's Youth Initiative." In accepting the award from Boys Town youth, she said: "When I look at you students, I see immense promise and possibility in each of you. There's no doubt about it. Father Flanagan knew what he was doing when he created this model of success nearly 90 years ago."

2007 – John Gillin, a former division vice president and senior vice president of Coca Cola, for his commitment to Boys Town's mission as the first lay chairperson of the national board of trustees. Gillin was instrumental in modernizing the board's organization and protocols and in establishing a Boys Town site in Atlanta.

2013 – Tom Lehman, PGA golfer, honored for his work with numerous charities, most which focus on helping kids. He serves on the board of Elevate Phoenix, a civic program providing long-term, life-changing relationships with urban youth, and he is also involved with Big Oak Ranch, a residential care facility for youth.

Father Flanagan High School

Boys Town had always recognized the critical needs of young people who ended up on the streets after dropping out or being expelled from school. When Dominican High School, Omaha's primary alternative school for these students, faced demolition to make way for a freeway in 1979, the Boys Town Board of Trustees authorized the construction of a new school building to take Dominican's place.

Father Flanagan High School opened in 1983 with a capacity of about two hundred students, most of whom were high dropout risks with family histories of poverty, drug addiction, alcoholism, or teenage pregnancy. Under the leadership of Father James Gilg, Flanagan High tailored its educational and social service programs to help these students complete school and improve their chances for employment and self-sufficiency. The school's program was accredited by the State of Nebraska and the North Central Association of Colleges and Schools. It offered students a complete academic curriculum, including religious education, career preparation, self-discipline skills, and parenting classes. In 1984, the school was honored by the U.S. Department of Education as an Exemplary Private School.

In 1997, Flanagan High School closed as the Omaha Public School District opened new alternative schools to accommodate the needs of the city's at-risk students.

Father Flanagan High School Principal Father James Gilg talks with one of his students in the school's main atrium. The high school was an extension into the community of Boys Town's efforts to help Omaha's at-risk youth continue their education and reach their academic goals.

Historic Recognition

In February 1985, Boys Town was named a National Historic Landmark. Every year, thousands of visitors would drive through the shady, tree-lined streets of the Village, making a stop at Dowd Chapel to visit Father Flanagan's tomb and experience the spirit of giving that makes the community unique and inspiring. Today, Boys Town is the only National Historic Landmark District in Nebraska.

Retirement and Rejuvenation

A year after Boys Town ventured out to open its first Family Home in another state, Monsignor Hupp turned seventy and retired, becoming the Home's executive director emeritus. In his thirteen years of leadership, Monsignor Hupp had compiled a long list of impressive accomplishments: the introduction of a family-style residential program that provided leading-edge care methods to better meet the needs of the youth; the acceptance of girls as Boys Town citizens; the beginning of expansion—both in a physical presence and in training—of Boys Town's treatment approach outside the village; and development of an inner-city high school in Omaha.

To carry on Boys Town's dynamic mission, the board of trustees called on Father Valentine J. Peter. Father Peter had served as Boys Town's deputy executive director in the year before Monsignor Hupp's retirement. In June 1985, he assumed the top post as the organization's fourth national executive director.

"Monsignor Hupp was a great builder," Father Peter said. "He came at a time when child care in the United States was in disarray—terrible disarray. And his greatest achievement was putting into place a brand new child care technology. He manned his pioneering effort with the best and the brightest people available. I only hope I do as good a job."

Monsignor Hupp and Father Valentine Peter share a laugh in front of the Boys Town Two Brothers statue. Father Peter spent a year working in the Village before becoming Boys Town's fourth national executive director upon Monsignor Hupp's retirement in 1985.

DAILY LIFE FOR THE BOYS AND GIRLS

The growing pains of Boys Town's transition to family-style residential care had a major impact on staff members, as well as the boys and girls who came to the Home during Monsignor Hupp's tenure as national executive director. But while the approach was new and improved, the underlying tenets of helping children turn their lives around and become productive citizens remained as constant as they had always been.

For most of these youth, the problems and challenges that brought them to the Home required more intensive treatment and care than what Boys Town had provided to its earlier citizens. Abuse, neglect, drug and alcohol use, divorced parents, family dysfunction, violence, gangs, and other troubles had put these young people behind in school, in their social development, and in finding a purpose in their lives. For many, Boys Town was the lifesaving alternative that helped them avoid going to juvenile detention or becoming a victim of violence or suicide.

In its new program, Boys Town believed providing a family environment, where caring adults taught necessary life skills and showed kids how to build healthy relationships with others, was the key to youth success. Getting boys and girls to "buy into" this approach was essential to their progress, so a lot of time was spent helping new youth adjust to their new environment and establish a daily routine that enabled them to reap the full benefits of the Boys Town Family Home Program.

For the most part, Boys Town tried to make daily life for its youth as close as possible to what kids would normally experience. Six to eight boys or girls lived in each Family Home with their Family-Teachers. In the morning, they got ready for school, ate breakfast together as a family, and headed off to classes at either Boys Town High School or Wegner Middle School.

Boys and girls follow a teacher's lesson in their Boys Town High School classroom.

Students learned job skills and helped keep Boys Town beautiful while working on campus during the summer. These girls were tending a Boys Town flower garden.

The schools' academic curriculum ensured students received a well-rounded education. Because so many students were behind—as far as two or three grade levels—there was extra emphasis on basics like reading and math. As in any high school or middle school, students ate lunch together in the cafeteria before heading to afternoon classes. The school day also included instruction for many students in one of the various trade courses offered by the Boys Town Career Vocational Center. This followed Father Flanagan's principle of ensuring youth were prepared to enter life after Boys Town with marketable employment skills.

After school, there was practice for students in sports, band, choir, Fire Cadets, and other activities. Students were encouraged to participate in extracurricular activities as a way for them to grow their self-confidence and work toward goals, either individually or as part of team. These activities also let them "just be kids" while having fun and being with their friends.

RIGHT: Opportunities for girls to participate in sports and other extracurricular activities blossomed as more female residents were admitted to the Home. Here, a Boys Town runner sprints for the finish line.

BELOW: In the Boys Town Fire Cadet program, youth received training in firefighting skills and learned how to accomplish goals as part of a team. The cadets often took part in competitions against other programs and displayed their teamwork in demonstrations on holidays and other special occasions.

Once back at their Family Homes, youth helped prepare the evening meal and enjoyed dinner together with their Family-Teachers. Afterwards, they cleaned up and then retired to a study table to do their homework. Each youth also was responsible for doing household chores. With their remaining free time, they could watch television, play board games, play outside, take a bike ride, or just hang out with their friends or the Family-Teachers.

Family-Teachers also planned family outings, like going out to dinner, going grocery shopping, or attending a movie or sports event. Each Family Home had a van so Family-Teachers could provide their youth with transportation for these activities or to get them to doctor, dentist, or therapy appointments.

To all of these "normal" activities was added a layer of continual teaching from Family-Teachers, schoolteachers, coaches, and other staff members. This teaching and the reinforcement of the use of social skills by the youth were consistent and effective because all of the staff members had been trained in the same strategies and techniques. This way youth always knew what behaviors were expected of them and the positive and negative consequences they would earn for appropriate and inappropriate behavior, respectively.

To keep track of those consequences, students carried point cards where adult staff members could record a student's use of a skill or appropriate behavior, as well as negative behaviors. At the end of the day, Family-Teachers totaled up the points assigned to those behaviors. If students earned enough positive points, they could purchase extra privileges. Not getting enough points meant no privileges until the next day when the points started over.

LEFT: High school graduates sing at their commencement exercises as they prepare to leave Boys Town and head out into the world.

BELOW: Working on the Boys Town farm, tending the gardens, and raising livestock for 4-H competitions remained popular outdoor activities for youth. These boys and girls enjoyed a hayrack ride while celebrating the fall harvest.

Whenever possible and in a youth's best interest, he or she could phone home to talk to parents and family members. Families also could schedule visits with their youth at Boys Town or arrange for home visits if a youth was doing well.

Spirituality also played an important role in the lives of all Boys Town youth as an important element of their treatment, development, and growth. The boys and girls were encouraged to continue to practice the religion or faith they grew up with or to choose a spiritual path to follow. Religious instruction was part of the school curriculum, and Boys Town families said prayers at meals and attended weekly worship services together. Family-Teachers took Protestant and Jewish youth to off-campus churches or synagogues, respectively. However, religion and spirituality were never forced on the boys and girls, following Father Flanagan's principle that every child should learn to pray, but how a child prays should be up to him or her.

In the summer, each Family Home loaded up its van and traveled to Boys Town's camp at Lake Okoboji in Iowa for a fun summer vacation. Youth—many of whom had never experienced a family vacation—enjoyed swimming, boating, water skiing, and cookouts during their time there. While summer vacation was a time to relax and have fun, Family-Teachers still continued their teaching and guidance.

Throughout the Family Home Program's formative years, thousands of youth found the help they needed at Boys Town while experiencing a happy, healthy childhood as part of a caring family. By the mid-1980s, Boys Town was well established as a model of quality, replicable residential care that could effectively serve large numbers of boys and girls.

ABOVE: Floating on an inflatable raft under sunny skies was just one of the many fun experiences Boys Town youth enjoyed each summer during their family vacation to Lake Okoboji. Boys Town families travel to the camp in their van and spend several days boating, water skiing, singing around a campfire, and playing volleyball.

LEFT: Boys Town's female residents celebrated the dedication and opening of five newly constructed Family Homes for girls in April 1988. The addition of new Family Homes became a necessity on campus as the number of girls admitted to Boys Town continued to grow through the 1980s and 1990s.

A CENTURY OF SERVICE, A HISTORY OF HEALING

FULFILLING THE VISION

For a decade, Boys Town had focused most of its energy and attention on establishing and developing its new residential program. Now that the program was in place and showing consistent success, there was an opportunity for the Home to again explore new possibilities in child and family care.

CHAPTER FOUR
National Expansion and Leadership
Father Valentine J. Peter
1985–2005

While new National Executive Director Father Valentine Peter had many new and sound ideas for Boys Town's future, he also reflected on how the contributions of his predecessors had laid the foundation and started the building process:

Father Flanagan inspired people to give their lives to something greater than themselves—namely the care of troubled children. A charismatic leader, he built Boys Town by of the power of his personality and the attractiveness of his vision. After his death, no one could replace his charisma. So Boys Town needed someone with organizational skills to put all of that fire and vision into an orderly and disciplined move forward. Monsignor Wegner's achievement was to give organizational flesh and blood to Father Flanagan's dream. Right before he died, the troubles of America's children became radically different as the scourges of drugs, alcohol, suicide, and sexual, emotional, and physical abuse infected many families. New methods, new treatments were required. Monsignor Hupp's contribution to Boys Town, the development of a new model of youth care, was also uniquely important. There is nothing harder to do than vast organizational change.

With those legacies as his guideposts, Father Peter put Boys Town on a path of far-reaching change and expansion.

OPPOSITE: Father Valentine Peter, Boys Town's fourth national executive director.

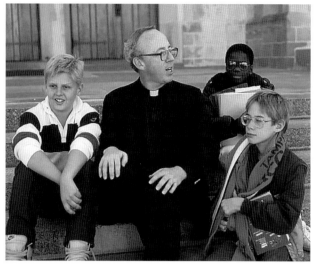

From the start of his tenure, Father Peter believed that getting to know each youth at Boys Town was an essential part of his job. As he carried out his responsibilities as national executive director, he always found time to take a group of kids to McDonald's for hamburgers or to just talk to a group about how their day was going.

Looking to the Future

Father Peter wanted to ensure the continued effectiveness of Boys Town's residential program. He also knew the Home had to be prepared for what childcare would look like ten, twenty, or thirty years down the road. He believed Boys Town had to further develop a "continuum of care" using proven childcare technologies so no matter what troubles children experienced, Boys Town would be prepared and able to provide healing and hope in the best way possible.

Father Peter also set a national goal for Boys Town of "changing the way America takes care of its children" before the year 2000. Achieving that goal involved extending and accelerating the work begun under Monsignor Hupp's leadership. First, Boys Town would need to evolve from being a local or regional organization into a national organization with a physical presence in more states. Second, Boys Town's childcare technology needed to expand and improve, moving beyond long-term residential care to a whole spectrum of child and family care.

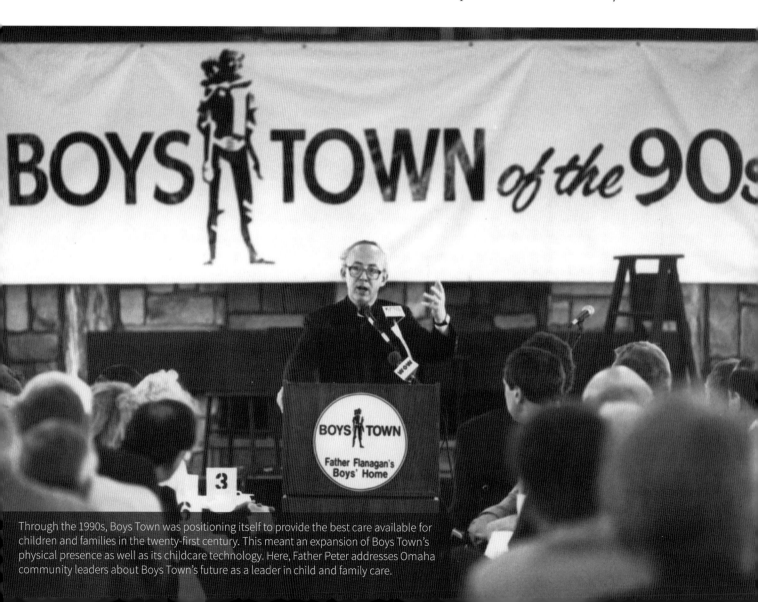

Through the 1990s, Boys Town was positioning itself to provide the best care available for children and families in the twenty-first century. This meant an expansion of Boys Town's physical presence as well as its childcare technology. Here, Father Peter addresses Omaha community leaders about Boys Town's future as a leader in child and family care.

AN EARLY CALLING

Valentine Peter was born in Omaha in 1934 and attended Holy Cross Grade School and Creighton Preparatory High School. It was as a student at Creighton Prep that he decided to become a priest. "One day, I forgot to bring my lunch," Father Peter recalled. "I was working in the school lunchroom and one of the Jesuits [the order of clergy who taught at the school] asked me: 'Aren't you going to eat your lunch?' I told him: 'I forgot it today, and I don't have any money.' The priest told me to follow him to the Jesuit dining room. I waited at the door. He came back outside and gave me a sandwich. I thought that was fabulous. So I ate the sandwich and I went to the chapel and I asked God to make me a priest like that."

After graduating from Prep, the aspiring priest spent two years at Immaculate Conception Seminary in Conception, Missouri. He studied the next several years at Gregorian University in Rome, was ordained in 1959, and attended the Second Vatican Council. After earning doctoral degrees in theology and canon law, Father Peter returned to Nebraska and taught at St. John Seminary in Elkhorn, the College of St. Mary in Omaha, and finally at Omaha's Creighton University. He served on Creighton's faculty for thirteen years before being selected as Boys Town's fourth national executive director in June 1985.

Father Peter's service to children as a youth advocate, educator, and friend spanned more than four decades. He has served on the boards or committees of more than twenty national and local organizations and also has published numerous books and articles.

After his retirement in 2005, Father Peter continued to serve Boys Town and its youth as executive director emeritus.

Father Flanagan's mission . . . is a gift to all of us . . . To carry out this mission requires an enormous effort, but the blessings are even greater.

—Father Peter

An Omaha native, Father Valentine Peter was ordained in 1959 and spent several years studying in Rome. He served on the faculty of Creighton University before being named Boys Town's fourth national executive director.

New Locations Opening

In 1988, Father Peter spearheaded an effort to transfer Boys Town's experience and technology to four new services—Parent Training, Home-Based Services (in-home crisis intervention), Treatment Foster Care, and Shelter Care. Grouped under an umbrella called Family-Based Programs, these services would ultimately become the core of Boys Town's new continuum of care.

The basic question about whether Boys Town's youth care model was replicable had already begun to be answered at the first Boys Town USA site in Tallahassee, Florida. Encouraged by that success and motivated by the clamor for similar services for youth in many other cities, Father Peter planned for a major and rapid expansion. "We're taking our healing out from the Heartland to the whole nation," he said, announcing Boys Town's goal to establish programs in seventeen major metropolitan areas.

Throughout the 1990s, Boys Town overcame myriad obstacles, including dealing with a dysfunctional child welfare system, local opposition to the establishment of much-needed Family Homes and shelters for at-risk children, bureaucracy, and the sometimes endless search for the right piece of property to gradually branch out and gain a foothold in communities across the country. Cities where new Boys Town USA affiliate (or national) sites would spring up included Orlando and West Palm Beach in Florida; San Antonio, Texas; New Orleans, Louisiana; Las Vegas, Nevada; Brooklyn, New York; Newark, New Jersey; Portsmouth, Rhode Island; Orange County, California; Washington, D.C.; Atlanta, Georgia; Philadelphia, Pennsylvania; and Chicago, Illinois.

"We're taking our healing out from the Heartland to the whole nation."

Opening Boys Town affiliate sites in states like California (opposite), New York (above), and Texas (top) were major steps toward expanding Boys Town's national impact and fulfilling Father Flanagan's vision of providing quality child and family care across America.

In its expansion, Boys Town was not just thinking outside the box; it was creating a new box by offering more effective ways to help troubled children and families on a larger scale. Since 1917, Boys Town had specialized in providing residential care—first in dormitories, then in Family Homes—to kids who could no longer live with their families. But it was clear not all youngsters with problems needed to be removed and treated away from their families and homes for long periods of time. Indeed, in many situations, it was more beneficial to provide family-based services to both parents and children, providing effective guidance while keeping families together. These kinds of services were used only when it was clear children could safely stay at home and receive adequate care.

In those early years of national growth, the long-term residential program and the Family-Based Programs operated at Boys Town USA sites in a "hub-and-spokes" arrangement. Many sites had a mini-campus with three to five Family Homes as their "hub." One or more of the four "spoke" programs also were developed and put in place. Based on the service needs of each community, some Boys Town USA sites did not begin with residential homes but rather with one or several of the "spoke" programs. Initially, the Village of Boys Town served as the pilot hub for the plan, with the spoke programs located in other nearby communities. In Nebraska, Parent Training programs were at Offutt Air Force Base in Bellevue, Treatment Foster Care was in Lincoln, and Shelter Care was in Grand Island; Home-Based Services were in Glenwood, Iowa.

An Evolving Youth Population: More Girls

Until 1985, the twenty-six girls residing at Boys Town had been a small presence amid the population of more than four hundred boys. Early in his tenure, Father Peter decided to add as many girls as possible in order to "create a normal village with normal life." In 1986 and 1987, ten new Family Homes were built and four former dormitories were remodeled into twenty-two additional homes for girls. By 1990, 210 girls were living at Boys Town out of a total population of 538. Hundreds more girls were being served by other Boys Town programs and Boys Town USA site homes.

The increased number of female students in the Village produced many systemic and cultural changes. Parts of the treatment model had to be adapted to meet the specific needs and problems of girls. Girls' athletic teams were formed, and girls were integrated into traditionally all-male activities like choir, band, and cheerleading. Policies were developed to address issues of appropriate friendships between boys and girls, and dating skills became part of every citizen's education. Boys Town even changed its program name to "Girls and Boys Town" for several years to increase public awareness that the Home served girls as well as boys.

A Family-Teacher guides two girls through meal preparation in a Family Home. What began as an experiment in the late 1970s as the first girls became residents of Boys Town had become a way of life at the Home by the 1990s as hundreds of female residents found a new direction through residential care and other services.

These were traumatic changes for Boys Town, and while they were necessary, they were not universally welcomed. Some labeled them as "scandalous," predicting that "when girls are turned loose, so to speak, they seem to 'go wild' to experience all their sexual desires."

Father Peter met the critics head on. He pointed out "girls get pregnant no matter where they live. Actually, the girls who live here are much more protected and watched over. We have very, very strict rules, and (the boys and girls) abide by them." He reminded other critics that many girls who came to Boys Town had suffered sexual abuse. "Most of our kids are victims of crimes," he told them. "The girls tell us they feel safe here at Boys Town, safe from sexual exploitation and demands that they have experienced elsewhere. To this extent, they are free to be little girls again, free to grow up healthy, and free to heal their past wounds."

Free to enjoy the happy childhood every child deserves.

"... they are free to be little girls again, free to grow up healthy, and free to heal their past wounds."

A Growing Community

At the same time Boys Town was expanding across the nation, the home campus was undergoing major changes and milestones:

- The former grade school dining hall was remodeled into the Hall of History, a museum showcasing Boys Town's remarkable history and current work for the nearly 100,000 visitors who tour the Village every year. Monsignor Hupp had commissioned the project in 1984 to gather and categorize photographs, artifacts, and documents chronicling Boys Town's history. The Hall of History opened in March 1986, in time to celebrate the one-hundredth anniversary of Father Flanagan's birth. Among the many displays and historical features in the museum are the Academy Award won by Spencer Tracy for his portrayal of Father Flanagan in the 1938 movie *Boys Town* and an entire wing devoted to memorabilia representing Boys Town alumni.

- In 1986, the U.S. Department of the Interior designated Boys Town as a National Historic Landmark. Also marking Father Flanagan's birth was the issuance of a stamp in his honor by the U.S. Postal Service. The first-day-of-issue ceremony for the four-cent stamp in the "Great Americans" series was held on campus.

The Boys Town Hall of History takes visitors on an inspiring, introspective journey through the Home's past. Hundreds of photographs, exhibits, and interactive displays tell the story of Boys Town's founding and development into one of the nation's largest child and family care organizations.

The Father Flanagan House served as Father Flanagan's residence from 1927 to 1941. Today, visitors can see the house as it was furnished in 1929 and view many of the priest's personal possessions.

- The Father Flanagan House, the residence of Boys Town's founder and a visitor attraction, underwent a major renovation. The rooms of the Father Flanagan House are presented as they appeared in 1929, two years after it was built. It features many of the personal belongings of Father Flanagan, who died in 1948. A life-size statue of the priest, donated by the Boys Town Alumni Association®, stands in front of the house. The Hall of History, the Father Flanagan House, and other attractions make Boys Town a popular stop for tourists year round, increasing awareness and gaining new supporters for the Home's mission.

With its grand Gothic architecture and twin spires, Chambers Chapel is a unique place of worship for the Home's Protestant youth and community members. The chapel was dedicated in 1991.

Members of Boys Town's JROTC often serve as the honor guard at special events, both at Boys Town and in the community. Here, the honor guard takes part in the opening ceremonies at a College World Series baseball game in Omaha.

- The Herbert B. Chambers Jr. Protestant Chapel for the Nativity of Our Lord was completed and dedicated in 1991. Funded by New Jersey businessman and philanthropist Raymond Chambers in memory of his father, the cross-shaped, Gothic-style chapel replaced the Protestant Nativity Chapel located in the field house. Built in 1953, the older chapel had become too small and cramped for the expanding population of the Home, which was approximately 60 percent Protestant.

- Boys Town started its own Junior Reserve Officer Training Corps (JROTC), a federal program sponsored by the United States Armed Forces in high schools across the United States and U.S. military bases across the world. This was another valuable activity for the youth on campus, further reinforcing the concepts of self-discipline, responsibility, and teamwork they were learning through the Family Home Program. JROTC was especially important for those youth who were planning to enter military service after graduation or to make serving in the military their career.

- Boys Town introduced an Environmental Education Plan in 1987. Youth actively participated in the plan through an agricultural education and training program. Two major achievements stemming from the plan were the Garden of the Bible, a green space between the Home's two churches that features 150 species of plants mentioned in the Scriptures (olive and fig trees, the "burning bush"), and the planting of thousands of trees across the home campus. In 1986, Boys Town was first designated a Tree City USA by the National Arbor Day Foundation, an honor it has received in many years since.

Boys Town's Garden of the Bible offers a quiet green space for solitude and reflection, both for Boys Town youth and visitors. Located an equal distance between the two on-campus churches—Chambers Chapel and Dowd Chapel—the garden features numerous plants mentioned in Scripture.

Training Others in the Boys Town Approach

In 1989, the National Group Home Program established in 1975 was expanded and renamed the Boys Town National Training Center. Prior to this, Boys Town had provided technical assistance and training to other residential care facilities for youth so they could fully replicate Boys Town's childcare technologies. Now Father Peter wanted to influence more and more childcare providers, including those who only wanted to use some of Boys Town's technology and those who worked with youth in schools and psychiatric care programs rather than residential settings. With the well-researched, outcomes-oriented technologies Boys Town had developed—technologies that actually changed the behavior of troubled children—it was the ideal time to start sharing this new knowledge and experience with caregivers who were helping children in different settings.

Over the next decade or so, the National Training Center would present Boys Town's expertise through workshops, on-site training and consultation, and specialized materials. In 1991, for example, the center conducted workshops for childcare professionals from more than three-hundred organizations in ten major cities and trained educators in seventy-four school districts. Also during this time, the Boys Town Press® was founded as the publishing arm of the organization and began producing and selling publications, videos, and other materials for professionals, teachers, and parents who wanted to tap into Boys Town's positive approach to childcare.

Opened in 1989, the Boys Town National Hotline provided a new source of assistance for children, parents, and families across the country with trained counselors available twenty-four/seven, year round. Over its history, the hotline has prevented thousands of potential suicides by counseling callers who were threatening to harm themselves or sending help to their home.

Help at the End of the Line

Reaching out across the country enabled Boys Town to bring hope and healing to many more children, either through direct-care programs or helpful resources and training. Still, there were millions of children and families who desperately needed help but were beyond Boys Town's immediate reach.

In May 1989, Boys Town established a lifeline for those troubled children and their parents. The Boys Town National Hotline® was a toll-free crisis number (800-448-3000) that was available twenty-four/seven to callers across the country. Trained professional counselors handled calls on any problem, from drug abuse, sexual abuse, and suicide to depression and parent-child conflicts. After listening to a caller's problem, the counselors offered initial advice and then, using a sophisticated computer database, referred the caller to agencies or services right in his or her own community for further assistance. In crisis situations, such as when a caller was threatening self-harm or suicide, counselors often were able to contact local police in the caller's community, send them to the caller's location, and stop the harmful action.

The hotline further expanded Boys Town's national scope and reinforced its standing as a leader in the child and family care field. By 2014, the hotline had received more than nine million calls and other contacts.

A Leader in the Research and Treatment of Communication Disorders

By 1989, when the Boys Town Institute's name was changed to Boys Town National Research Hospital, the hospital had gained international recognition as a leader in applied medical research and clinical care for children with communication disorders. Under the leadership of Dr. Patrick Brookhouser, the hospital had provided care for nearly 70,000 patients from 2,500 cities in all fifty states and more than a dozen foreign countries. No child was turned away because his or her family was unable to pay for care.

ABOVE: In 1995, Heather Whitestone McCallum (center), the first deaf Miss America, visited Boys Town National Research Hospital.

RIGHT: Boys Town National Research Hospital near downtown Omaha provides health care services to thousands of patients every year.

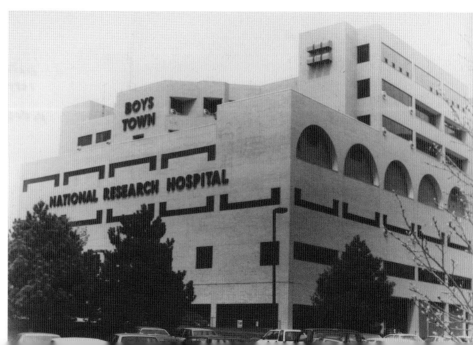

In response to the special needs of these children, the hospital developed new models of care that would become standard practices across the country. For example, the hospital's pioneering work included the development of software that is vital to universal newborn hearing screening. This technology detects hearing loss within hours of birth. Such early detection, combined with early intervention, can significantly reduce communication delays that commonly accompany hearing loss.

In the early 1980s, Boys Town National Research Hospital began offering a summer program for gifted youth who are deaf and hard-of-hearing from around the country. The program was designed to stimulate the learning potential and improve the self-esteem of teenagers. This group is studying the formation of clouds.

The hospital's research program was integral to its work from the beginning, but increased rapidly between 1979 and 1985 with grant support from the National Institutes of Health (NIH). Another increase occurred in the 1990s with the development at NIH of the National Institute on Deafness and Other Communication Disorders. The new institute's charter called for significantly more translational research and outreach activities, and the hospital was the leading recipient of funds during the institute's first ten years. (In 2016, thirty-four PhD scientists were conducting research in twenty-six laboratories.) In 1995, the hospital opened its first medically directed Residential Treatment Center (RTC) for severely troubled youth, ages five to eighteen, who require twenty-four-hour direct supervision and intervention.

With the dedication of a second Boys Town National Research Hospital on the Boys Town campus in 2006, medical and surgical services were extended to even more children and families. Other hospital highlights included:

- In 2002, the hospital celebrated its twenty-fifth anniversary and the Boys Town Board of Trustees recognized Dr. Brookhouser and his staff for its achievements in helping special needs children and caring for needy families.

- Construction began on the $9.3 million Lied Learning and Technology Center for Childhood Deafness and Vision Disorders in 2002. The center opened in 2004 and offers services for families and children that include family-centered early intervention, a model preschool program, distance mentoring and education, and cochlear implant services.

- In 2002, the Center for the Study and Treatment of Usher Syndrome was dedicated at the hospital. Usher syndrome is the leading cause of combined hearing and vision loss. The center's geneticists identified five of the eleven known Usher syndrome genes.

The Lied Learning and Technology Center for Childhood Deafness and Vision Disorders is equipped with state-of-the-art research laboratories, educational facilities, and rehabilitative services for children with hearing loss, visual impairment, and other communication disorders. Opened in 2004, the center utilizes the most advanced technology and distance conferencing solutions to offer comprehensive programs and services for patients, families, educators, and clinicians.

About 1,300 runners participated in Boys Town's first annual Memorial Day Run in 1985 on campus. The run, which now draws thousands of participants, is held each year to raise money for Boys Town National Research Hospital's Lied Learning and Technology Center for Childhood Deafness and Vision Disorders.

- In the early 2000s, the hospital launched two new websites designed to provide support and helpful information to parents and health care professionals. My Baby's Hearing (www.babyhearing.org) helps parents of infants who have recently been diagnosed with hearing loss to navigate available resources and gain the knowledge they need to help their child succeed. The website www.BoysTownPediatrics.org offers health-care topics, videos, and information on pediatricians that parents can use to help keep their children healthy.

- Since its founding, the hospital has received more than $200 million in externally funded grant support for research.

The Increasing Importance of Youth Care Research

The effectiveness of the Teaching-Family Model, its components (training, consultation, evaluation, and administration), and its replication in Boys Town's residential program had been the focus of ongoing research since 1973. It was this research that directly led to identifying the scope and specifics of the problems children and families were facing and discovering the best ways to resolve them by improving Boys Town's other child and family services.

With Monsignor Hupp's "re-making" of Boys Town in the early 1970s came an emphasis on applied research, meaning, in this case, research findings are implemented in practice so they have an actual and measureable benefit to the children who receive services. Monsignor Hupp brought in a group of applied researchers from the University of Kansas to form the Teaching Family Research Module in the Boys Town Research Center. Because this module was the only area related directly to children, it was the only area of research to continue when the board of trustees closed the Boys Town Research Center in the 1990s.

To ensure the continuance of research and evaluation of all Boys Town programs, the Program Planning, Research, and Evaluation Department was organized in 1989 to conduct research on the effectiveness of residential, educational, and family-based programs. Included in the department was the Boys Town Reading Center, which conducted research on literacy programs for the at-risk students in Boys Town's middle school and high school. Many of these students came to Boys Town with reading skills three to four years below their grade level. In the 1990s, the center developed the Reading Is Fame® program, an intensive instructional approach that helped youth improve their reading by two grade levels for every year of instruction.

The overall goals of the Program Planning, Research, and Evaluation Department researchers were to improve the care and education of Boys Town youth and disseminate knowledge about effective programs and innovations to other professional and childcare audiences. It was this department that expanded Boys Town's continuum of services and the new technology that fueled the national expansion of the 1990s. Again, Boys Town was leading the way in advancing child and family care.

In 2000, Boys Town took another significant step forward by establishing the Boys Town National Research Institute for Child and Family Studies℠ (NRI) to conduct further applied research that focuses on understanding the nature of problems children and families face and identifying the most effective ways to help them. The NRI employs experienced and knowledgeable research scientists and analysts and is dedicated to collaborating with experts in the social science fields. The institute developed several research partnerships with universities—most notably the University of Nebraska-Lincoln—and has published hundreds of articles that support the effectiveness of the Boys Town Model®, particularly as it is applied in the Boys Town Family Home Program.

The Voices of Boys Town raise the roof during a performance at a dinner kicking off Boys Town's seventy-fifth anniversary celebration in 1992. Borsheim's Jewelers hosted the event and presented a commemorative Faberge Brotherhood Egg to Boys Town.

The NRI/University of Nebraska-Lincoln collaboration is unique in that no other child and family service organization has such a productive research partnership with a leading university. Research has not only expanded knowledge of and practices for child and family care, but also has attracted more than $14 million in grant funding, further widening Boys Town's research footprint.

Ongoing research shows Boys Town gives many at-risk children their best chance to build bright, productive futures. Years after receiving care, Boys Town youth—even those with the most severe problems—achieve success as adults. This research shows these kids grow into adults who are nearly identical to the general population in key success factors such as positive mental health, life satisfaction, employment, and family relationships.

Today, applied research is still at the epicenter of Boys Town's evolution and expansion. Boys Town is one of the few leading child and family service organizations that devotes an entire department to developing and disseminating applied research.

Charting an Ambitious Future

With its ambitious geographic and programmatic expansion, by its seventy-fifth anniversary in 1992 Boys Town was serving 16,000 boys and girls annually through direct youth care services at Boys Town sites around the country and health care services provided by Boys Town National Research Hospital. There also had been explosive growth in Boys Town's indirect services, especially in training and the production of materials that could assist others in helping troubled children and families, and in a national hotline that was accessible to millions more. In Father Peter's first seven years as national executive director, Boys Town had grown into one of the largest child and family service organizations in the United States, with an annual operating budget of $84 million. "At Boys Town, we feel there is a moral imperative urging us to help even more children," Father Peter said at the time. "Our children are on the edge of an abyss, a huge void created by economics and apathy. Unless we heal these boys and girls, we will soon be a nation not of just troubled children, but of lost children."

Child and Family Care for the Twenty-first Century

Throughout the 1990s, Father Peter focused on developing "child and family care for the 21st century," positioning Boys Town to enter the new millennium as an innovator and a model organization others would want to emulate and learn from.

When Father Flanagan first founded his Home for Boys, he was keenly aware of the important role environment played in shaping children and their behaviors. He knew that by providing abandoned, wayward children with a positive environment, training, and good role models, he could change their lives for the better.

This thinking had always been at the core of Boys Town's work and mission. Now, Boys Town was beginning to place more emphasis on the "environmental" element of treatment in its programs. This enabled caregivers to identify and assess the many important factors—both positive and negative—in a child's or a family's environment when preparing a service plan. Treatment then could focus on reinforcing positive factors that could help at-risk youth and families get better and effectively address negative factors that may be contributing to problems.

Simply stated, this environmental approach helped Boys Town determine how children got where they were and how they could get where they wanted to be. Caregivers didn't work just with the youth; they worked with a whole network of people, places, and things that daily influenced how a youth lived and functioned. This included the youth, his or her family, peers, schools, teachers, the neighborhood, and the community.

"Unless we heal these boys and girls, we will soon be a nation not of just troubled children, but of lost children."

Boys Town believed this approach would improve the quality of care it provided and enhance the already-positive outcomes youth and families were experiencing.

Meanwhile, Boys Town's national expansion efforts enabled the organization to become a champion and a voice for the cause of at-risk children and families, providing new and unique services to address serious problems that threatened their stability, safety, and well being. Throughout the late 1990s and early 2000s, most sites made their mark as "go-to" agencies in their respective communities, forming productive partnerships with other providers and community organizations. As the demand for certain kinds of care ebbed and flowed, some sites (Atlanta, Philadelphia, Newark, and Chicago) were closed, often due to a lack of state and local support. This enabled Boys Town to refocus its resources to areas where they were most needed.

By 2005, Boys Town was being recognized as one of the largest and most effective child and family care organizations in the United States. And with new advances in programs and services, Boys Town was successfully implementing what Father Peter had described as the "head" and the "heart" approach. The "head" was the research-based childcare technology that focused on helping children with their problems through education, training, and self-empowerment. The "heart" meant nurturing children through love and compassion and making them feel valued and wanted. Both elements had to be used to effectively help kids.

"The heart without the head is pure sentimentality," Father Peter said. "And the head without the heart is pure manipulation."

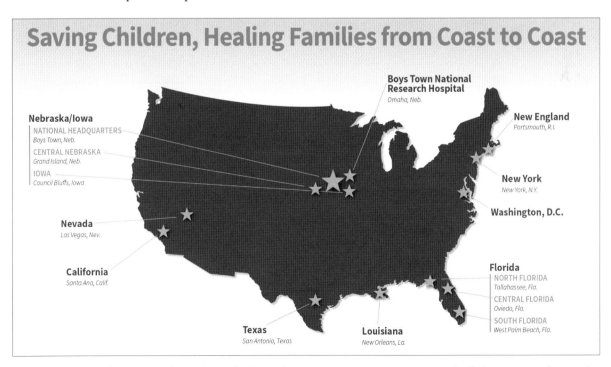

Boys Town's national expansion ultimately resulted in twelve primary sites across America, each offering a variety of research-proven child and family services. These include residential care through the Family Home Program (at several sites), in-home services, foster care, parenting classes, and behavioral health clinics. Boys Town and its affiliate sites directly serve more than 30,000 children and families every year, and Boys Town National Research Hospital serves more than 40,000 children annually.

Setting Boys Town's Sites on Widespread Care

Each of the Boys Town national sites developed during Father Peter's tenure offers its own set of continuum services and programs, including shelter or short-term residential care, foster care, in-home care, community support services, and behavioral health services. All of these services are based on the research-proven Boys Town Model of care, so they have the same expectations for positive results and outcomes.

Several Boys Town sites provide residential care to youth through the Family Home Program. At those sites, boys and girls live in Family Homes with Family-Teaching Couples, just as they do in the Village of Boys Town, Nebraska. Daily life—including learning social skills, doing household chores, enjoying activities together as a family, and going on outings—is much the same as it is for youth in the Village. However, youth at Boys Town national sites attend schools in the community and often receive specialized services (therapy and counseling for behavioral or mental health disorders and medical care) through local resources and providers. All national Boys Town sites partner with area schools, agencies, foundations, and businesses to garner local support and constantly enhance the quality and variety of care they provide in the community.

The first of Boys Town's national sites, **Boys Town North Florida**, has been serving children and families since 1983. Every year, its continuum services touch the lives of more than 5,000 people in the Tallahassee area.

Boys Town Central Florida began serving children and families in 1986. The largest Boys Town campus area outside the Village of Boys Town, its continuum services touch the lives of more than 7,600 people in the Orlando area annually.

Boys Town Texas has been serving children and families of the Lone Star State through a variety of programs since opening its doors in 1989. Every year, its Integrated Continuum of Care® services touch the lives of 81,000 people in Texas.

Since opening in 1989, **Boys Town Louisiana** has served the needs of tens of thousands of children and families in the region. Every year, its continuum services touch the lives of more than 7,600 people in Louisiana.

Opened in 1990, **Boys Town New York** serves a culturally diverse population of adolescents from all five boroughs of New York City. Its Integrated Continuum of Care services touch the lives of 63,000 children and families every year.

Since opening in 1991, **Boys Town New England** has brought life-changing care to thousands of children and families in Rhode Island and nearby states. Its continuum services touch the lives of more than 8,000 people in Rhode Island and Massachusetts every year.

Boys Town Nevada opened its doors in 1991, bringing a unique, innovative approach to child and family care to those in need in the Las Vegas area. Annually, the site's continuum services directly serve more than 1,500 children and nearly 600 families in Nevada.

Boys Town South Florida opened in 1991 with a variety of family-focused services to assess children's needs and keep struggling families together. Every year, its continuum services touch the lives of 17,000 people in south Florida.

Since opening its doors in 1991, **Boys Town California** has continued to expand its services to meet the needs of troubled children and families. Its continuum services touch the lives of more than 48,000 people in California every year.

Boys Town Washington DC has provided life-changing services for children and families in the nation's capitol and surrounding areas since opening in 1993. Its continuum programs touch the lives of more than 6,200 people in the District and surrounding areas every year.

Four main components comprise the **Boys Town Nebraska** and **Boys Town Iowa** sites. Each serves a specific purpose but all are united by the common goal of providing effective, life-changing care for children and families.

The Village of Boys Town, Nebraska – The Village serves as the organization's national headquarters and is the site of its largest residential program (Family Home Program). It is also the center of research and program development. Boys Town offices in south Omaha and north Omaha provide parenting classes, in-home services, and other assistance to residents of surrounding neighborhoods.

Council Bluffs, Iowa, Office – Boys Town's in-home services have been helping Iowa families stay together or reunite since 1989. Similar services are provided through Boys Town offices in several other Iowa cities and towns across the state.

Grand Island, Nebraska, Office – Boys Town's programs in Grand Island opened in 1989 to help bring effective care to children and families across central Nebraska. The site provides two important levels of service—emergency short-term residential care for girls and boys in crisis and foster care. Additional offices in Nebraska also provide services.

Boys Town National Research Hospital – The hospital has been internationally recognized as a leader in clinical and research programs focusing on childhood deafness, visual impairment, and related communication disorders. It has developed national medical programs that are now instituted in hospitals and clinics across the country. Today, the hospital, accredited by The Joint Commission, offers a broad range of surgical and clinical services, including ear, nose, and throat services at the Boys Town Ear, Nose, and Throat Institute; general pediatric care with Boys Town Pediatrics; and pediatric specialty care, including gastroenterology, allergy, asthma, pulmonology, behavioral health, audiology, and ophthalmology. It annually serves more than 44,000 children and families from across the United States.

A Friend and a Leader

From his first days at Boys Town, Father Peter made it a point to get to know each and every one of the children in his care. He had a unique ability to remember kids' names, their hometowns, and other information about their backgrounds, something that endeared him to the boys and girls and let them confide in him as a friend and advocate as well as a priest who cared about their well being. In addition to his administrative and leadership duties, Father Peter was always on the go for his kids, attending school functions, welcoming new Boys Town citizens, greeting visitors to the Home, or just taking a few minutes to offer a boy or girl a word of encouragement, kindness, or prayer.

Boys Town youth could always count on Father Peter to join them for a fun event or just a friendly chat. Building relationships with the boys and girls on campus and those being served through Boys Town services at other sites was one of Father Peter's great strengths.

Father Peter also routinely took groups of children to lunch and invited Family Homes to his living quarters in the Dowd Chapel rectory for dinner or Sunday after-church meals. He did whatever he could do to ensure Boys Town's children knew they were in a place where people truly cared about them and would do everything he could to help them overcome their challenges and find success. Few if any children ever left Boys Town without a memory of a personal conversation or a kind act initiated by Father Peter. For most, that memory would stay with them for a lifetime.

ABOVE: Sarah Williamson gives a fist pump upon learning she has been elected Boys Town's first female mayor in 1991. As an adult, she has served as the director of the Boys Town National Alumni Association and has worked for Boys Town as an Assistant Family-Teacher® and a family consultant with In-Home Family Services.

BELOW: Father Peter says good-bye to the Boys Town student body during a retirement ceremony at Palrang Field House.

Mayoral Elections Revived

After a hiatus of several years, Father Peter revived the annual election process during which the boys and girls voted for a new mayor and vice mayor of Boys Town. Father Flanagan had started the elections as a way to teach the early citizens of the Village about government and civic responsibility.

During the elections, candidates for the two offices campaign by making signs, creating slogans, and giving speeches to the student body. In 1991, the youth of Boys Town elected Sarah Williamson as the first female Boys Town mayor. Today, the mayor of Boys Town presides over special occasions, welcomes dignitaries and other visitors to the Village, and serves as an ambassador of Boys Town at community events.

From a Legacy to New Leadership

In 2005, Father Peter had reached the retirement age of seventy. To find the best person possible to step in as his successor, the Boys Town Board of Trustees launched a national search, eventually reviewing applications from nearly 150 candidates.

When the search began, Archbishop Elden Curtiss of the Archdiocese of Omaha asked a priest who was working at the St. Augustine Indian Mission in Winnebago, Nebraska, to submit an application. The priest, Father Steven Boes, was raised in Elgin, Nebraska, and had been serving children at the mission for eight years as a teacher, advocate, and counselor. He followed the archbishop's advice and pursued the position.

It was a wise decision. In the end, the board chose Father Boes, another priest with Nebraska ties and experience working with children, as Boys Town's fifth national executive director. Father Boes was an avid mountain climber and compared his passion for scaling high peaks with the lofty challenges he would face as Boys Town's new leader. "I think it's a great symbol for me. I am a risk-taker who always prepares well," Father Boes said at his inauguration. "I always study the mountain, I always do my homework. It's a pretty good analogy for what's going to happen here" at Boys Town.

Over the next dozen years, Boys Town's continued growth and evolution under Father Boes's leadership would prove to be both fortuitous and groundbreaking.

ABOVE: Father Peter gets a farewell hug from two of Boys Town's younger citizens after announcing his retirement as national executive director in 2005.

BELOW: Father Peter welcomes newly appointed Boys Town National Executive Director Father Steven Boes (left) in 2005. Father Boes is the fourth successor to Boys Town founder Father Edward Flanagan.

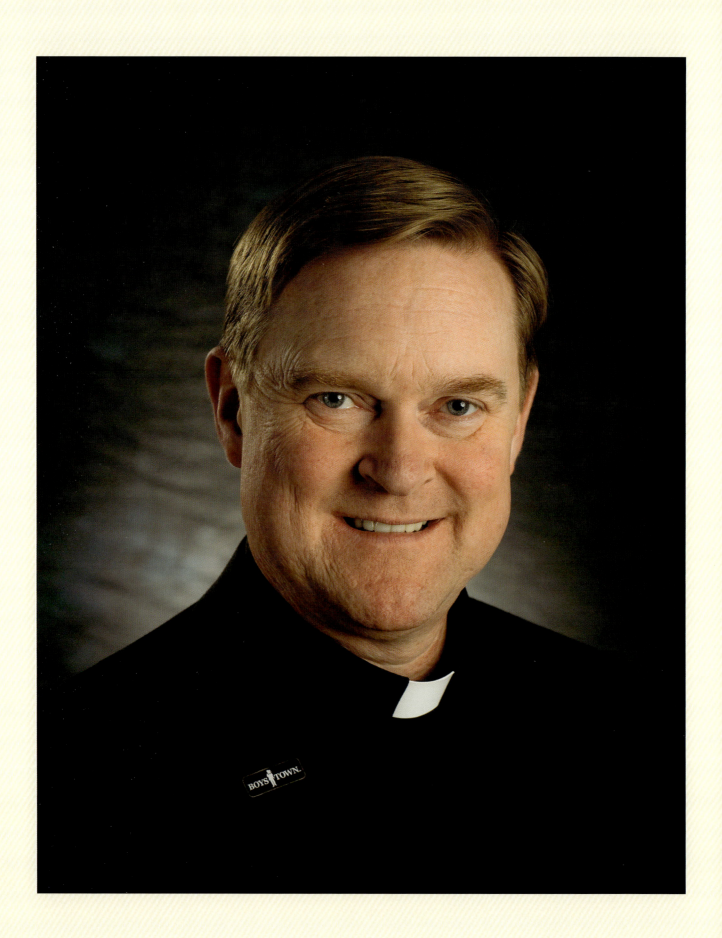

A CENTURY OF SERVICE, A HISTORY OF HEALING

CARRYING THE DREAM FORWARD

As Father Steven Boes began his tenure as Boys Town's fifth national executive director, the world continued to grow smaller due to rapid advances in electronic technology. The Internet, smartphones, texting, tweets, blogs, personalized webpages (Facebook), and other means of immediate communication enabled people to connect with friends—and strangers—with lightning speed. Teens were especially attracted to and enthralled by the newest electronic gizmos and wizardry, and parents often struggled to keep up, not always knowing whether the flood of cyber tools and toys were a blessing or a curse.

CHAPTER FIVE

From a Revolution to Evolution
Father Steven E. Boes
2005–Present

OPPOSITE: Father Steven Boes, the fifth national executive director of Boys Town.

Big changes also were happening on the child and family care landscape. Many states and communities were dealing with broken or dysfunctional child welfare and juvenile justice systems, while looking for ways to cut costs and still provide effective services. More young people seemed to be struggling in school and with problems like drug and alcohol abuse, gangs, gun violence, bullying, and respecting authority. Mental and behavioral health issues plagued many families across the country, and unemployment and foreclosures added even more friction and despair to American households. To meet these challenges, Boys Town would have to work smarter and be more proactive, more strategic, and more innovative in its efforts to change the way America cares for children, families, and communities.

SERVING CHILDREN, SERVING GOD

Steven Boes was born in Carroll, Iowa, and raised in Elgin, Nebraska. The oldest of the six children, he graduated from Elgin High School and attended the University of Nebraska-Lincoln for two years before deciding to become a priest.

Father Boes was ordained a priest for the Archdiocese of Omaha in 1985. He holds a bachelor's degree in sociology from St. John Vianney College Seminary at the University of St. Thomas in Minnesota, master's degrees in theology and divinity from St. Paul Seminary College at the University of St. Thomas, and a master's degree in counseling from Creighton University in Omaha. Father Boes is a nationally certified counselor and has received Creighton's Distinguished Alumni and Outstanding Priest awards. He also has been a member of the Equestrian Order of the Holy Sepulchre of Jerusalem since 2005.

For twelve years, he worked as a parish priest, primarily as a youth minister and a Catholic school teacher. In the eight years before he came to Boys Town, Father Boes was the director of the St. Augustine Indian Mission in Winnebago, Nebraska.

In the two decades before coming to Boys Town, Father Boes worked as a youth minister and a Catholic school teacher and served as director of the St. Augustine Indian Mission in Winnebago, Nebraska.

An organization like Boys Town was a natural fit for Father Boes. Upon starting as national executive director, he compared helping children, especially those who are at-risk or troubled, with the beadwork band a Winnebago artist made for his trademark cowboy hat, which Father Boes wears daily as he carries out his responsibilities at Boys Town. The artist intentionally put a bead out of place, Father Boes said, "because God places a flaw in us, an imperfection, and that doesn't make us less beautiful . . . With hurting kids, it's a great message for them."

Father Boes loves to be active and can often be found running or skiing around the Boys Town lake, bicycling around campus, or lifting weights at his home gym. Every year, he heads to Wyoming to fly fish, hike, and climb mountains. An avid climber, Father Boes has scaled most of the 12,000-foot mountain peaks in Wyoming and a few others in neighboring states.

In order to help young people overcome their problems and become productive citizens, they need a healthy and safe family environment where they can learn and grow.

—Father Boes

Father Boes has sometimes compared his mountain-climbing experiences with the constantly challenging battle Boys Town faces in changing how America cares for children and families.

A group of excited Boys Town children leads Father Boes to his formal inauguration ceremony in June 2005. Father Boes spent the previous night in the Father Flanagan House, sleeping in Father Flanagan's bedroom.

It took a combined effort of the Boys Town Board of Trustees and leaders of Boys Town youth care and health care programs to create a five-year strategic plan to chart Boys Town's future work. Here, employees receive an annual update on the plan from Father Boes (left); Daniel Daly, PhD, executive vice president and director of Youth Care; and John Arch, executive vice president and director of Boys Town National Research Hospital.

Developing a strategic plan was a major goal for Boys Town in the first few years Father Boes was on the job. Boys Town wanted to double the number of children and families it served by providing a wider spectrum of connected, consistent services and resources. Other priorities were increasing public awareness of its mission and engaging more people as donors and supporters by educating them about the Home's relevance and effectiveness in the child and family care field. To accomplish these goals, Father Boes enlisted the assistance and input of Boys Town leadership and the Boys Town Board of Trustees, as well as outside consultants who brought modern marketing expertise and experience into the mix. Father Boes summed up the forward thinking and progress Boys Town was making this way:

Father Flanagan was a true visionary. When he founded Boys Town as a humble home for wayward youngsters nearly a century ago, his bigger dream was to someday reach out to help children and families all across America. Through sound leadership and ground-breaking innovations, that vision was realized as Boys Town grew into a national leader in child and family care. What began as an immigrant priest's revolutionary idea to change how America cared for children is now one of the country's largest nonprofit child and family organizations.

Boys Town has always enthusiastically accepted its leadership role in reshaping and reforming child and family care. We have an obligation to help fix what is broken, to improve what works well, and to share our expertise, experience, and knowledge so that more children and families can benefit.

That's why Boys Town continues to evolve and grow, both in our life-changing programs and the number of people we serve. As the needs of children and families have become more complex, we have responded by developing new ways to make a positive difference in their lives.

"We have an obligation to help fix what is broken, to improve what works well, and to share our expertise, experience, and knowledge..."

The First Strategic Plan (2008–2012): Dramatic Results

In 2008, Father Boes launched Boys Town's first five-year strategic plan, which introduced a refined version of what was now called the Integrated Continuum of Care and established a road map for implementing the continuum's multiple services and programs at Boys Town sites nationwide. The continuum, a tightly connected spectrum of service levels based on the research-proven Boys Town Model of care, would serve as the centerpiece as Boys Town moved forward and outward.

At the same time, Boys Town National Research Hospital, under the direction of Dr. Patrick Brookhouser, was expanding its services through its new hospital in the Village of Boys Town and its new pediatric care clinics across the city of Omaha. This partnership, which combined life-changing youth care and health care services, would further differentiate Boys Town from other providers and ensure that children and families received the right care, at the right time, in the right way.

Most of the major achievements at Boys Town from 2008 to 2012 occurred as a result of this plan, whose success relied on the expertise and experience that helped create it, as well as the willingness and commitment of Boys Town staff members to implement and follow it. "Boys Town employees have excelled at 'living' the plan instead of just putting it on the shelf," Father Boes would later say.

Boys Town Integrated Continuum of Care®

> Residential Treatment Center

> Intervention and Assessment Services

> Family Home Program

> Foster Family Services

> In-Home Family Services

> Community Support Services

SM

An enhanced version of Boys Town's unique Integrated Continuum of Care enabled the organization to provide life-changing services and programs for even more children and families across the country.

DR. PATRICK BROOKHOUSER: A CHAMPION FOR CHILDREN, A VISIONARY FOR HEALTH CARE

Dr. Patrick Brookhouser pioneered Boys Town's health care efforts to treat children with communication disorders and conduct groundbreaking research for new treatment methods.

When Patrick Brookhouser, MD, founder of Boys Town National Research Hospital, passed away on September 3, 2011, at age seventy, the entire Boys Town family felt both a professional and personal loss.

Dr. Brookhouser was a gifted physician and surgeon and a steward of Father Flanagan's dream to help children. He was recognized by his medical colleagues, locally and across the United States, for his contributions to the field of otolaryngology and otology, along with the groundbreaking research he initiated in the treatment and prevention of hearing loss and other communication disorders, especially in children.

A visionary, Dr. Brookhouser was the founding director of the hospital in 1972. Since officially opening in 1976, the hospital has provided care and treatment to more than 300,000 patients from across the country and a number of foreign countries. It has developed into one of the most influential specialty hospitals and research institutes in the world.

Dr. Brookhouser was the president and CEO of the Lied Learning and Technology Center for Childhood Deafness and Vision Disorders at Boys Town National Research Hospital, and for over a quarter century he served as Father Edward J. Flanagan Professor and Chair of Otolaryngology and Human Communication at Creighton University School of Medicine.

An advocate for both medical education and research, Dr. Brookhouser's national leadership roles included chair of the Residency Review Committee for Otolaryngology; a director of the American Board of Otolaryngology; membership on the National Advisory Councils of the National Institute on Deafness and Other Communication Disorders and the National Institute for Child Health and Human Development; and president of the Triological Society and the American Society of Pediatric Otolaryngology.

An Iowa native, Dr. Brookhouser received his bachelor of science degree (summa cum laude) from Creighton University and was awarded his doctor of medicine degree by Johns Hopkins University School of Medicine. He completed residency training in otolaryngology/head and neck surgery at the Johns Hopkins Hospital. He was a Fellow of the American College of Surgeons, as well as a member of Alpha Sigma Nu (the national Jesuit Honor Society) and the medical honor society Alpha Omega Alpha. He was also honored by induction into the Johns Hopkins Society of Scholars and by the Distinguished Alumnus Award given by the Johns Hopkins University Alumni Association.

Dr. Brookhouser held the rank of Knight Commander in the Equestrian Order of the Holy Sepulchre of Jerusalem and was a member of the Omaha Archbishop's Committee for Development.

It may seem like a small thing, but I will miss Dr. Brookhouser's voice. His was always a strong voice of support for Boys Town values. I often took the pleasure of hearing Pat's voice for granted. Yet, for thousands of America's kids, Dr. Pat Brookhouser's surgical and administrative skills are the reason they can hear anyone at all, and that is no small thing. My pledge to you is that we will continue to hear his voice in the years to come and continue the work he began in the founding of Boys Town National Research Hospital.

—Father Steven Boes
President and National Executive Director, Boys Town

As much joy as Dr. Pat Brookhouser derived from treating children with communication disorders, his real passion was conducting research in this area. Thirty-eight years later, Pat's dream is a research powerhouse with 21 independent laboratories, 24 PhD scientists, and more than $175 million in grant funding since 1976. Pat gave unselfishly to his medical specialty, his patients, and his colleagues.

—Robert H. Miller, MD
Executive Director, American Board of Otolaryngology
Former Trustee and Chair, Boys Town National Healthcare Committee

Dr. Brookhouser was a man of great vision, courage, and determination. He saw the future with such clarity that it could have been written as history. He was fearless in his willingness to take risks because his vision was so clear. And, he never faltered in his perseverance to see his vision accomplished. The world and Boys Town National Research Hospital were blessed by his life.

—John K. Arch
Executive Vice President of Healthcare, Boys Town
Director, Boys Town National Research Hospital

Serving More Children and Families, Growing In-Home and Preventive Programs

In 2007, Boys Town provided direct youth care services to 13,033 boys and girls nationwide. In 2011, that number had skyrocketed to 28,065. Also, Boys Town health care programs served more than 38,000 children. What had been a five-year goal of the strategic plan—to double the number of kids being helped—was accomplished in four years. Also during this period, the number of people nationally whose lives were being touched by Boys Town youth, health, family, and community programs every year grew to 1.6 million.

Boys Town knew there would always be children who need the intensive, skills-focused intervention provided through its Family Home Program. These children have been removed from their homes and families due to serious problems and challenges and could get the most benefits from successfully completing a service plan in a Boys Town Family Home.

But Boys Town also understood the value of keeping troubled families together whenever possible and providing care and assistance to the whole family in their home. That is why, starting in 2008, Boys Town initiated a major internal culture shift, redirecting its focus to serving more children while they remained with their own families. Not only was this a more cost-efficient approach than depending heavily or solely on out-of-home placements, but it also could produce many of the same positive outcomes as residential services because all services were based on the same model of care.

One focus of Boys Town's strategic plan was to provide services to more struggling families in their own homes so children and their parents could stay together (whenever possible) while overcoming their problems. During these home visits, a trained family consultant (pictured at right) helps parents develop new child-rearing skills and connects them to community resources so they can solve problems on their own after services end.

By 2011, of the nearly 29,000 children Boys Town served across the nation, 75 percent of them safely and effectively received care while living with their own families. This was significantly higher than the 30 percent of children who received services through Boys Town in-home programs in 2007. In 2013, of the 35,500 children and families directly served by Boys Town, 92 percent received services while children lived in their homes. And this focus on preventive in-home care would continue into the future.

This culture shift enabled more families to stay together and kept large numbers of boys and girls from entering an already overburdened child welfare system. When children could stay with their families and parents could learn how to solve problems before they become crises, everyone benefited, including the communities in which they lived.

Besides keeping families together, Boys Town In-Home Family Services also was helping reunite children with their parents when out-of-home placement had become necessary. Even in situations where abuse, neglect, or drug and alcohol use led to the removal of children from their homes, Boys Town often was able to help families resolve their dysfunction and learn skills that enabled them to reunite, healthier and happier.

Improving and Maintaining the Quality of Care

Boys Town has always had a stellar reputation for providing high-quality care for children and families. To build on that reputation, Boys Town completed a major overhaul of its In-Home Family Services and Foster Family Services® so they could better meet the future needs of children and families. Research also continued on the long-term effectiveness of these and other programs, and Boys Town pursued evidence-based status for a number of services. Attaining evidence basing is important because it attracts more contracts for services, which eventually allows Boys Town to become the preferred provider for certain types of care across the country. This, in turn, helps more kids and families get the help they need.

Expanding the Scope of the Integrated Continuum of Care across the Country

From 2008 to 2012, many Boys Town national sites steadily added new Integrated Continuum services. In many cases, this included In-Home Family Services and Common Sense Parenting® (CSP) programs to further reinforce Boys Town's family-based approach to care. Boys Town Outpatient Behavioral Health℠ Services clinics also began providing therapy and counseling for children with behavioral, emotional, and mental health issues and their families at affiliate sites serving Nevada, Texas, and Nebraska/Iowa. In subsequent years, similar clinics would open at several other Boys Town sites, including those in Florida and Washington, D.C.

Linking Youth Care and Health Care to Help More Kids

Because Boys Town was one of the few child and family organizations in the country that offered both youth and health care services, there was a great potential to strengthen the connection between the behavioral change Boys Town Youth Care programs promoted and the medically based care Boys Town Health Care programs provided. This included having behavioral therapists working alongside pediatricians at Boys Town clinics, further studies on reducing psychotropic medications for children by implementing behavior-change strategies, and assessing the biological effects those strategies have on children through neurobehavioral research.

BOYS TOWN INTEGRATED CONTINUUM OF CARE

The Integrated Continuum of Care is unique to Boys Town and provides a tightly linked spectrum of research-proven services, all based on the Boys Town Model of care. Children and families can begin services at any point and move to other levels, depending on their progress or needs. This unique approach enables Boys Town to help more children and families in more ways, with the same expectations for positive results. For children, this means being successful in school, at home, and on the job while growing into productive citizens. For families, it means having a safe home, being able to solve problems, and staying together. For communities, it means stronger, empowered families and citizens who contribute to the good of society.

The **Boys Town Residential Treatment Center** serves children ages five to eighteen who have severe behavioral and mental health problems. The goal is to help boys and girls gain the self-assurance and academic and social skills needed to succeed in life. The proven treatment program is specifically designed to offer medically directed care for youth who require supervision, safety, and therapy but do not require inpatient psychiatric care. The program offers round-the-clock supervision and numerous other safety and program features.

Boys Town's Intervention and Assessment Services® provide emergency, short-term, twenty-four-hour care in a residential setting for boys and girls ages ten to eighteen. Many of these youth have been abused and/or neglected, are runaways, or have come through the juvenile justice system. When youth enter these services, professionally trained staff members begin assessing their safety, health, and service needs in order to plan for the best permanent care arrangement.

In the **Boys Town Family Home Program**, youth with serious behavioral or emotional problems live in a family-style home and receive teaching and care from professionally trained married couples called Family-Teachers. Six to eight boys or girls, usually ages ten to eighteen, live in each home. The couple and a full-time Assistant Family-Teacher are responsible for providing structured supervision for youth in their daily living and care activities. This includes meeting the educational, medical, psychological, emotional, and behavioral needs of the youth in care. A major focus of this program is teaching youth social, independent living, and educational skills and helping them build healthy relationships with others. With a focus on reunification, the Family-Teaching staff works with families to achieve permanency, safety, and child well being.

Boys Town Foster Family Services is a community-based program where professionally trained foster parents provide care and support to children of all ages, infancy through adolescence, and help meet their behavioral, emotional, and educational needs. With a focus on reunification, Foster Family Services utilize a strength-based, team approach to work with families to achieve safety, permanency, and well being. Foster parents receive twenty-four/seven support from Boys Town.

The main goal of **Boys Town In-Home Family Services** is to prevent children from being placed outside of the home and/or to reunify them with their family if outside placement is necessary. These services provide a family-centered, skill-based intervention for families that are in or near a crisis situation. Boys Town family consultants are available twenty-four/seven and work with families in their homes to help parents and other caregivers build on their strengths, improve their parenting skills, and identify community resources and supports. Services focus on the entire family. Consultants also help families learn how to solve problems that may threaten their stability or the children's safety after the intervention ends.

Boys Town Community Support Services® enable children and parents to tap into a wide variety of resources to learn how to help themselves through advice from our experts or receive direct care through specialized services. The main goal of this service level is to help people help themselves by providing tools, training, and other techniques based on Boys Town's research-proven approach to the care and education of children and families. Most resources focus on prevention rather than intervention.

- **The Boys Town National Hotline (800.448.3000)** is a free resource and counseling service that assists youth and parents twenty-four/seven, year round, nationwide. The hotline receives about 150,000 calls a year.

- **Boystown.org/parenting** is a free online resource that provides practical, skill-based materials and information for parents and caregivers of children of all ages.

- **Common Sense Parenting** provides parents and other caregivers with proven techniques that can help them build good family relationships, prevent and correct misbehavior, and improve positive behavior. These informative classes are usually presented in the community and at schools.

- **The Boys Town Press** produces books, audio products, DVDs, display materials, and other resources to assist children, parents, caregivers, educators, and other professionals.

- **YourLifeYourVoice.org** is a special website that enables and encourages teens to share their problems and concerns in positive ways and provides access to immediate help from a Boys Town hotline counselor in a crisis.

- **Boys Town Outpatient Behavioral Health** therapists work with children of all ages and their families to identify and treat difficult youth issues. Children benefit from individual service plans that focus on teaching skills and achieving lasting positive results.

- **Boys Town School-Based Programs℠** provide a variety of training and instructional resources for teachers, administrators, and other school staff. Training is based on the Boys Town Education Model®, which focuses on skill teaching, relationship building, and effective discipline procedures.

- **Boys Town Schools®** include school programs operated by Boys Town that help students with learning or behavioral problems to be successful in the classroom. This includes students who are being served by Boys Town programs or have struggled or failed in mainstream schools. Specially trained Boys Town teachers and administrators provide instruction to help meet children's unique learning needs.

To support the mission, Boys Town National Research Hospital developed a pediatric health care network to provide an array of services to treat physical and mental illnesses. Boys Town Youth Care and Health Care services joined forces by imbedding Youth Care's behavioral health psychologists in pediatric clinics. This has become the model for expanding Boys Town's behavioral health services nationally.

Besides offering surgical and clinical services at two Omaha locations, the hospital also provides a broad range of clinical services, including ear, nose, and throat services; general pediatric care with Boys Town Pediatrics®; and other pediatric specialty care, including orthopaedic, gastroenterology, allergy, asthma, pulmonology, behavioral health, audiology, and ophthalmology. Accredited by The Joint Commission, the hospital annually serves more than 44,000 children and families from across the United States.

Besides offering care and treatment through its five Omaha-area pediatric clinics (opposite), Boys Town National Research Hospital provides educational programs, as well as fun and informative activities, for children and families. The hospital operates a preschool for students who are deaf and hard-of-hearing (above), sponsors the Beeping Easter Egg Hunt for youngsters who are visually impaired (left), and welcomes kids and their parents to an annual Healthy Kids' Carnival that features games, prizes, and health-related parenting advice and information (below).

BOYS TOWN HOSPITAL OPENS UP NEW WORLD OF SOUND FOR TODDLER

As a toddler, Chloe Brauer of Beatrice, Nebraska, received a very special birthday gift—the gift of hearing.

Just five days after turning one, Chloe had her second cochlear implant programmed at Boys Town National Research Hospital, allowing her to hear. This life-changing event for Chloe and her family also marked the five-hundredth cochlear implant milestone for the hospital.

Chloe was born with bilateral hearing loss. "The dream that you have for your child is broken," said Natalie Brauer, Chloe's mother, recalling how she and husband Brian felt upon hearing the news. "She's never going to hear my voice."

Chloe was referred to Boys Town National Research Hospital for further hearing testing and a cochlear implant candidacy evaluation. A cochlear implant is a high-tech device surgically implanted behind the ear and attached to the cochlea. The implant is connected to a processor that sends sound signals to the inside of the ear, allowing children and adults to hear.

The hospital's Cochlear Implant Center has been helping children and adults with severe or profound hearing loss for more than two decades. The center offers a team of ear, nose, and throat physicians; audiologists; speech-language pathologists; clinicians; and counselors who work together to determine if a cochlear implant would provide the best outcome for the patient and tailor the best medical care and rehabilitation services for each patient.

Chloe received her first implant on July 24, 2012, followed by her second implant on August 21. Eight days later, hospital staff happily celebrated the milestone with Chloe, her parents, and other loved ones as the second implant was activated, allowing the little girl to hear with both ears.

As a service to patient families, the hospital's Cochlear Implant Team was the first to offer live audio and visual webcasting of a cochlear implant programming session so family, friends, and loved ones anywhere in the world can witness the first time a patient hears sound. This meant family members and friends back home in Beatrice were able to watch as Chloe responded to the first sounds she could hear.

Chloe and her family will make the four-hour round trip to Omaha many more times for follow- up visits with the multi-disciplinary team of physicians, audiologists, speech pathologists, researchers, and early intervention educators at the Cochlear Implant Center. So far, Chloe's progress has been excellent.

As Chloe gets older, she will learn to put the sound of her voice and other sounds together, eventually forming words, sentences, and spoken language. For now, Chloe's parents are thankful their little girl can now hear their voices. "My dream has come true," said Natalie.

A whole new world of communication opened up for Chloe (left) and her big sister Sydney when Chloe became the recipient of the hospital's milestone five-hundredth cochlear implant.

Improving National Outreach through Technology

By 2011, more people than ever were benefiting from Boys Town's expertise and resources because of innovative services developed through the strategic plan. The **Boys Town National Hotline** (pictured below) was approaching the nine million-call mark while continuing to help children and parents across the country. In 2011, teens made 600,000 visits to a new Boys Town National Hotline website—**YourLifeYourVoice.org**—to share challenges they faced and to get answers to difficult questions. The website offered a safe environment for teens, many of whom were more comfortable reaching out for advice or assistance online rather than through a phone call. Helpful articles, videos, blogs, and tips on effective parenting were just a mouse click away for parents at a free online website, **BoysTown.org/parenting**. This gave parents across the country immediate access to parenting tips and strategies based on Boys Town's positive approach to child rearing. The **Boys Town Press**, Boys Town's publishing department, continued to provide quality resources in the form of books, audio products, DVDs, and other products to help children, parents, caregivers, educators, and other professionals. In health care, the My Baby's Hearing website (**babyhearing.org,** available in English and Spanish) continued to help parents of infants who had recently been diagnosed with hearing loss find the resources and information they need.

1-800
448-3000

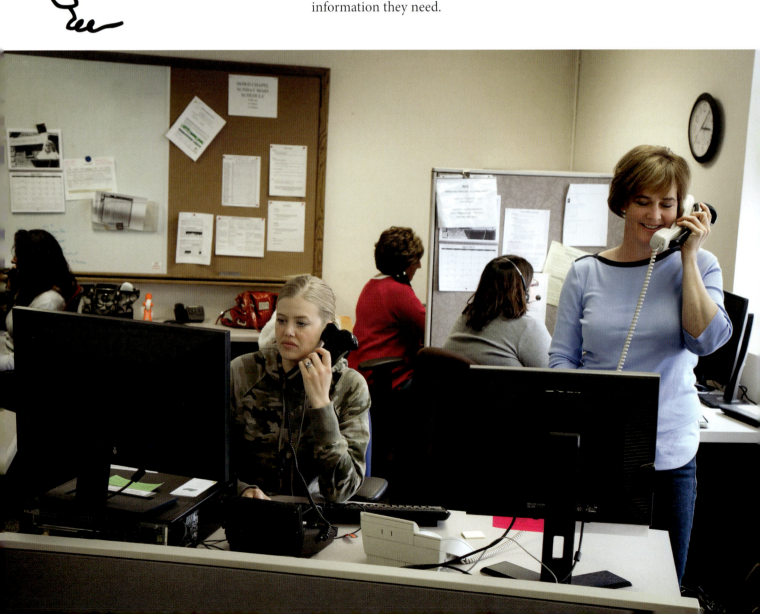

The Boys Town National Hotline also facilitates another technology-based resource, the Nebraska Family Helpline. A service of the Nebraska Department of Health and Human Services, the helpline fields calls from families in need of assistance and connects them with the appropriate state agencies. The helpline is a perfect example of how states can partner with a private organization like Boys Town to effectively address child and family problems and improve the care and treatment they provide.

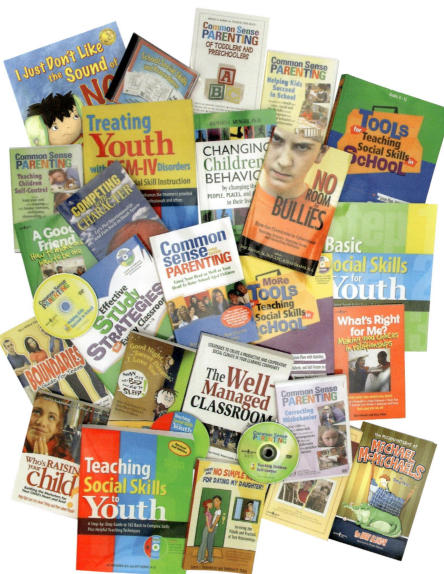

Technology has enabled Boys Town experts to share their knowledge and guidance with parents, children, teachers, and professional caregivers through a variety of channels. These self-help resources enable Boys Town programs to touch the lives of more than two million people nationwide every year.

Extending Boys Town's Leadership Role in Reforming Child and Family Care

As Boys Town ramped up its efforts to provide valuable child and family services, it also became more involved in efforts to reform child welfare systems. Unfortunately, through the eyes of children and families in need of help, the disjointed and inconsistent ways these services are delivered often make victims out of the very people they are supposed to be helping.

In response, Boys Town launched a more concerted campaign to increase awareness about the benefits of Integrated Continuum of Care services and other resources among decision makers, including state and federal legislators, government and community agencies, and judges and others in the juvenile justice system.

For example, Boys Town has taken a national leadership role in advocating for quality residential care, like that which is offered through the Boys Town Family Home Program. This effort champions quality residential care as a necessary treatment option for troubled youth whose problems require more intensive care and attention. Boys Town agrees that whenever possible, at-risk youth should receive

help while they remain with their own family. But it also contends there will always be youth with severe emotional or behavioral problems whose treatment needs cannot be met through services like foster care and family-based programs.

By 2015, Boys Town was making significant progress in increasing awareness and building support on this front in states where it has affiliate sites. This included discussions with state lawmakers, providing testimony at legislative hearings, presentations at conferences and forums, and the dissemination of research-supported information on the benefits of quality residential care.

Taking a leadership role in efforts to reform the child welfare and juvenile justice systems, Boys Town has made important inroads with decision makers at the local, state, and federal levels. Father Boes has served as guest chaplain and delivered the opening prayer to the U.S. Senate and to Congress. He also has met with members of Congress like former U.S. Representative Lee Terry of Nebraska (pictured at right). Boys Town leaders, staff members, and former youth have testified at numerous legislative and committee hearings about the need for quality care and treatment for children and families. Boys Town has its own administrator who networks with government officials, providing information and testimony and working to pass legislation that will benefit children and families.

Understanding the Role of Psychotropic Medications

Through its practice and research, Boys Town has achieved national prominence in understanding the appropriate role psychotropic medications play in the treatment of youth with behavioral and mental health disorders. Consequently, Boys Town has become an advisor to elected officials and other decision makers, as well as national institutions, in this area and on similar topics. Youth Care researchers have published more than four hundred articles in journals, with several focusing on the prevalence rates of psychotropic medications.

Centers of Excellence Promise Expanded Services

In Boys Town's first capital construction project in decades, construction began in 2011 on two new mental and behavioral health treatment centers in the Village of Boys Town, Nebraska. These two centers of excellence added a new element to the life-changing services Boys Town already provided and met a critical need for expert mental health care in the region.

With a welcoming, family-friendly atmosphere, the new Boys Town Center for Behavioral Health® opened in the spring of 2013, providing outpatient services for girls and boys of all ages who have serious behavioral and emotional problems. Children and their parents could now meet with therapists in therapy rooms designed for confidentiality, comfort, and safety.

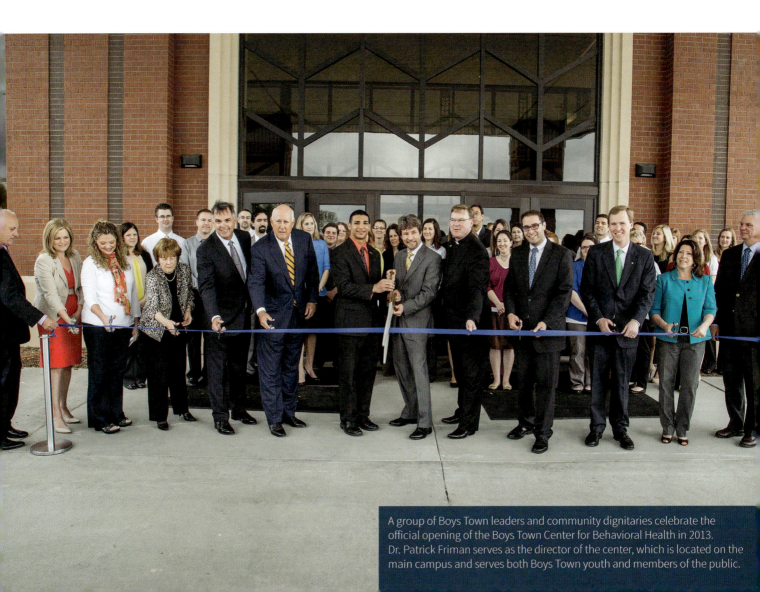

A group of Boys Town leaders and community dignitaries celebrate the official opening of the Boys Town Center for Behavioral Health in 2013. Dr. Patrick Friman serves as the director of the center, which is located on the main campus and serves both Boys Town youth and members of the public.

The Residential Treatment Center at Boys Town National Research Hospital-West provides specialized treatment for children with serious behavioral and mental health disorders.

Additional space also was available for individual meetings with families and staff training. The center expanded Boys Town's existing mental health services, significantly increasing the number of children who received much-needed services.

Also opening in the fall of 2013 was the new Boys Town Residential Treatment Center at Boys Town National Research Hospital-West in the Village of Boys Town. The center, with thirty-four beds, offered help for girls and boys who have severe mental health problems and who may pose a danger to themselves or others. Some of these girls and boys also had a long history of failed placements in foster homes and other youth care programs.

A special feature of the Center for Behavioral Health is a play area for children who are waiting for their appointments. This helps children feel more at ease and reduces their anxiety.

Village of Boys Town Earns '100 Best' Honor Multiple Times

In the 2000s, the America's Promise Alliance named the Village of Boys Town one of the "100 Best Communities for Young People" several years in a row. This distinction honored the hard work and dedication of the Boys Town community in helping troubled youth prepare for a brighter future.

Established in 1997, America's Promise Alliance (the Alliance) is the nation's largest partnership organization dedicated to improving the lives of youth. The Alliance's main priority was to ensure young people have the resources they need for high school graduation and beyond. The "100 Best" award is one element of its campaign to end the school dropout crisis.

The Village of Boys Town proudly displays its "100 Best Communities for Young People" signs. The Boys Town Music Hall is in the background.

Cause for Canonization of Father Flanagan

In March 2012, the Archdiocese of Omaha began the process of determining whether Boys Town founder Father Edward Flanagan should be declared a saint. At the request of the lay-led Father Flanagan League Society of Devotion (FFLSD), Archbishop George Lucas opened the cause for canonization by declaring Father Flanagan a "Servant of God."

The FFLSD was formed in 1999 with the purpose of "opening" Father Flanagan's sainthood cause and educating people about the priest's life and mission as a mentor and protector of youth. For years, the group organized pilgrimages to Boys Town and Father Flanagan's tomb in Dowd Chapel so followers could honor the priest's life and work and pray to God through the intercession of Father Flanagan for their needs. League members also collected testimonials, with particular attention to miracles believed to have resulted from Father Flanagan's intercession.

"I'm happy that Father Flanagan's work is being recognized," Father Boes said as the cause for sainthood was opened. "Miracles occurred every day in his work to heal children in mind, body, and spirit. These miracles still take place today at Boys Town, where we continue his mission to save children and heal families."

Father Flanagan represents the eternal values of selflessness, service to others, sacrifice, and love for the defenseless and downtrodden. He would be a saint for modern times because of his tireless work to reform how America cares for its children, and his life can serve as a model of holiness for young people, now and for generations to come.

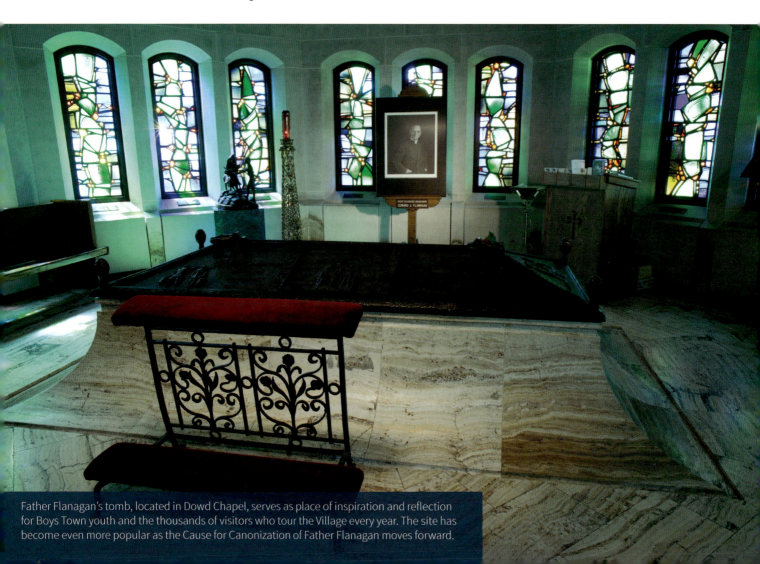

Father Flanagan's tomb, located in Dowd Chapel, serves as place of inspiration and reflection for Boys Town youth and the thousands of visitors who tour the Village every year. The site has become even more popular as the Cause for Canonization of Father Flanagan moves forward.

"Miracles occurred every day in his work to heal children in mind, body, and spirit. These miracles still take place today at Boys Town, where we continue his mission to save children and heal families."

The canonization process has four steps: Servant of God, Venerable, Blessed, Saint. The first step of the process took place in Omaha with the Omaha archbishop appointing a tribunal to investigate the life and virtues of Father Flanagan. Medical teams investigate potential miracles associated with the priest. The archbishop reviews the tribunal findings and decides whether to advance the cause to the next steps. (In June 2015, the archbishop, in a formal ceremony, advanced the cause to the Vatican in Rome for further investigation.)

The second, third, and fourth steps take place at the Vatican. A tribunal appointed by the Holy Father further investigates the life and virtues of Father Flanagan and potential miracles associated with him. After the tribunal makes recommendations to the Holy Father, he decides whether to declare the priest a saint of the church.

The canonization process takes many years and requires an extensive investigation of Father Flanagan's life. To be canonized a saint, there must be proof that at least two miracles attributed to him occurred after his death.

During a special Mass in June 2015, Omaha Archbishop George J. Lucas blesses and officially seals boxes of documents being sent to the Vatican as part of the Cause for Canonization of Father Flanagan. The event marked the end of the diocesan phase of the cause. A special tribunal in Rome will review the thousands of pages of documentation on Father Flanagan's life and work and make its recommendations to the Pope.

Preparing for the Next Phase

In 2012, after his first five years as national executive director, Father Boes was asked about the challenges Boys Town would face over the next half-decade.

One of the biggest challenges we will face is changing the way America thinks about families. Just as Father Flanagan said there are no bad boys, we need to convince America that there are no bad families. In every family, there is always someone who is willing and able to care for a child, whether that's a parent, grandparent, aunt, uncle, or another relative. That's how children can remain in a family, which we believe is the best place for any child to be. America's mindset must be changed in order to make effective changes in the system. As we continue to serve America's children and families, we must be open to new ideas to help mold and shape our organization.

As always, Boys Town prepared to take this and other challenges head on. The principles and philosophy about the care of children Father Flanagan created ninety-five years earlier were as true and relevant as when Boys Town was founded, and the modern-day Boys Town again made a plan to achieve more effective and more relevant care for more kids and families.

Strategic Plan Two (2012–2017): Reaching Out to Strengthen Communities

When Boys Town rolled out its second five-year strategic plan in 2012, much progress had been made in establishing the Integrated Continuum of Care as a model of comprehensive services and extending Boys Town's national reach through direct care programs and technology-based resources. But more work needed to be done to ensure children and families in greatest need could access services and resources and find new and better ways to help children lead happier, healthier lives.

Under Father Boes's leadership, the new five-year strategic plan called for Boys Town to work with local leaders and agencies to identify areas in their communities with the greatest need for child and family services and then locate offices, programs, agencies, and resources where those services could be readily available. From the onset, Boys Town made it clear that local leaders and advocates would guide and direct these community initiatives, and a collaborative partnership was the only way to achieve success. These community initiatives and collaborations were to be developed across the country, beginning in communities where Boys Town already had a physical presence.

On a second front, Boys Town sought to enhance and expand its research capabilities by creating the Boys Town Center for Neurobehavioral Research at the National Research Hospital in the Village of Boys Town. The center would use leading-edge imaging technology to improve the understanding of how biology and behavior work together to influence child development and why children behave in certain ways. Research outcomes are expected to lead to groundbreaking treatment strategies and techniques for changing children's behaviors.

"One of the biggest challenges we will face is changing the way America thinks about families."

Every Boys Town national site has launched community initiative projects as part of Boys Town's current five-year strategic plan. In each initiative, Boys Town staff members work with local leaders and agencies to connect with children and families in greatest need and provide life-changing services, hope, and healing.

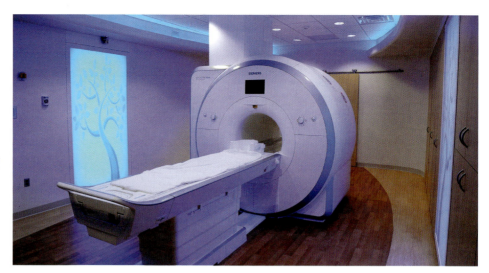

The state-of-the-art Boys Town Center for Neurobehavioral Research features the latest in fMRI technology, which is expected to produce major breakthroughs in the treatment of children with serious behavioral and mental health disorders.

A capital campaign to fund this effort started in 2013, and in 2015 Boys Town added advanced functional magnetic resonance imaging (fMRI) technology that can produce real-time images of how a child's brain responds to behavioral treatment interventions. Funding also was sought for endowed chairs, staff, and additional equipment necessary to launch this major research endeavor. Most importantly, the research findings would be shared with other childcare organizations and advocates and would actually be applied to enhance existing strategies and develop new, more effective ones.

In both community initiatives and research, Boys Town continued to make huge investments of time, resources, expertise, and collaboration for the benefit of children, families, and communities.

Community Initiatives: A Blueprint for the Future

In 2013, Boys Town launched a number of community-focused projects at its national sites. These projects and related efforts to promote awareness and engagement helped strengthen communities by enhancing children's school performance, providing guidance to families in crisis, offering therapy for children affected by trauma or other negative factors, and giving families ways to obtain and hold jobs and manage their finances. Besides expanding programs and services, Boys Town also opened new offices in many areas, making it easier for families to access valuable resources and assistance and establishing Boys Town's physical presence in specific neighborhoods. Self-help resources, like parenting classes and public presentations on important topics, also were made available.

As part of Boys Town's community initiatives, many national sites also began collaborating with schools so more students and families could have access to and benefit from Boys Town services. In most programs, school staff, including teachers and counselors, were able to refer those in need to the appropriate Boys Town program. At some sites, Boys Town consultants have offices in the schools so they can work directly with students and school administrators. At many of its affiliate sites, Boys Town formed partnerships with local businesses and organizations to address specific community needs.

The Boys Town Center for Neurobehavioral Research in Children

Many of the children who come to Boys Town have suffered or been exposed to significant trauma, violence, abuse, and neglect. These early life experiences often cause serious mental health problems such as mood disorders, problems with impulse control, self-harm, and aggression.

Medical research has given mental health and behavioral experts a better understanding of how these early life experiences affect and alter brain development and function in children. In response to these new research findings, Boys Town launched its Center for Neurobehavioral Research in Children in 2012. The center, a collaborative effort between Boys Town National Research Hospital and Boys Town Youth Care services, studies and improves methods for intervening early in the lives of children with behavioral and mental health problems.

Research is the key to deepening knowledge about the factors contributing to behavioral and mental health problems. This knowledge has profound implications for prevention and treatment, giving caregivers opportunities to change the course of a child's life by intervening early and effectively.

Boys Town's long history of providing effective treatment for children with a wide range of disorders and Boys Town National Research Hospital's successful history of research over the past forty years positions the Center for Neurobehavioral Research at the forefront to offer evidence-based solutions for treatment to the larger mental health community.

An important tool in the center's research is functional magnetic resonance imaging technology. This safe, noninvasive way to study brain activity uses a magnetic field to detect oxygen levels and blood flow, enabling researchers to compare the brain activity of children and to watch the brain react to different kinds of therapy.

Boys Town's research studies combine the latest brain imaging technology with behavioral measures that are well established as part of the organization's model of care. Boys Town is uniquely positioned to do this critical research in more realistic environments, to produce results that are more useful in the everyday care of children, and to rapidly apply research findings in its own work. The center also partners with outside researchers, both locally and nationally, to develop the best practices to treat behavioral and mental health problems in children.

The Boys Town Center for Neurobehavioral Research provides a unique opportunity to explore the biological bases of behavioral problems in children and enhances Boys Town's intervention methods. This neuroscience approach is providing immediate benefits to children and is leading to a better understanding of the causes of behavioral and mental health problems in children—giving them their best first chance at a happier, healthier life in a place historically known for giving children second chances.

Boys Town's Career Readiness Center has been preparing youth for real-world jobs for decades.

Career Readiness Center Expansion

Throughout the Home's history, the Boys Town Career Readiness Center has served a vital role in preparing youth to enter the workforce as adults. Students learned the fundamentals of a trade or a skilled labor job so they could continue their education at a trade school, or, in some cases, immediately begin working once they graduated high school.

Students work with an instructor in a health services course at the Boys Town Career Readiness Center. Changes in workplace needs spurred Boys Town to expand the center and its offerings in order to better prepare graduates for jobs in the trade and skilled-labor fields.

As technology advanced in the 1990s, many of the center's trade courses were replaced with offerings that focused on helping students develop computer skills. Also at that time, a large number of Boys Town youth were entering military service or going to college after graduation, so there wasn't as great a need for training in trade-oriented occupations.

Twenty years later, however, Boys Town's observation of workplace trends indicated an increasing demand for workers who had received at least some training in a trade or skilled-labor field. Also, not every Boys Town student wanted to or was ready to attend college, and the U.S. military—a mainstay for as many as one-third of the students in a Boys Town High School graduation class in the past—was no longer a viable option for life after Boys Town. With combat operations ending after two major wars in Iraq and Afghanistan and higher standards being set for potential enlistees, the armed forces were not recruiting as aggressively as they once were and all branches were moving toward downsizing.

As a result, Boys Town started an extensive remodeling and expansion project in the Career Readiness Center on the home campus in 2014. In collaboration with local businessmen, the project added a number of courses designed to give students the foundational skills and direction they need to enter a career field. These courses include welding, small-engine repair, horticulture, the culinary arts, auto mechanics and auto body repair, sports medicine, and landscape design. Plans also included expanding current Career Readiness Center offerings in health occupations, construction-related careers (plumbing, electrical, framing, and roofing), and communication and media sciences (journalism, video production and broadcasting, media design, audio production, and photography).

In addition to equipment, tools, and other materials, each of these courses required hiring highly trained, certified instructors who can engage students, train and teach them, and help them plan their career path. Ideally, these instructors would have ties to local companies and businesses who would consider hiring Boys Town graduates.

Boys Town invested in and asked for the public's support of this campaign because it provides students their best opportunity for success after high school. Boys Town believes the better prepared youth are to continue their education or enter the workforce after they leave Boys Town, the more likely they will be to achieve their goals and grow as productive, contributing members of society.

BOYS TOWN EFFORTS FIND ALLY IN TV STAR JOSH TEMPLE

As the host of several popular home improvement reality shows on the HGTV and DIY networks, Josh Temple is a familiar sight on television these days. Recently, he's been a familiar sight in the Village of Boys Town, Nebraska, too. In fact, Temple's connection with Boys Town goes back to 2013, when he flew in to do a meet-and-greet with the kids and staff. While he was here, he fell in love with the Village and its history and mission.

Upon his return to Los Angeles, Temple kept in touch with Boys Town. Later he returned to film a public service announcement and to talk more with kids, staff, and donors about his desire to help create new opportunities for trade education for at-risk youth.

Recently, Temple has chaired a round table discussion at Boys Town with Omaha-area business and construction company owners to discuss what they are looking for in potential employees and how Boys Town can help young people acquire trade and skilled-labor job skills. These types of informational gatherings contributed to Boys Town's decision to move forward on expanding the Career Readiness Center.

TV reality star Josh Temple shares a laugh during dinner with female residents of a Boys Town Family Home. Temple has visited the Village of Boys Town several times to help promote Boys Town's mission and its efforts to improve job skills for graduates.

Several Boys Town students congratulate Laura Bush as she receives the Father Flanagan Award for Service to Youth in 2006.

Other Milestones and Achievements

- Former First Lady Laura Bush and professional golfer Tom Lehman visited Boys Town to receive the Father Flanagan Award for Service to Youth. Mrs. Bush received the award in 2006 and Lehman was a recipient in 2013.

- Boys Town High School sports teams achieved excellence with the basketball team winning the Nebraska Class C-1 state championship in 2006 and 2012 and the boys' track team winning three consecutive Class C-1 state championships in 2009, 2010, and 2011.

RIGHT: Father Boes and his Boys Town kids cheered on the boys' basketball team to Nebraska state championships in 2006 and 2012.

BELOW: Members of Boys Town's 2009 Nebraska state championship track team proudly display their hardware.

- In 2014, the Boys Town National Hotline celebrated its twenty-fifth anniversary and reached the milestone of receiving nine million calls and other contacts.

- By 2015, Boys Town youth care and health care services were providing direct care to more than 74,000 children and families nationwide, and Boys Town programs were touching the lives of more than two million people across the country every year.

- Boys Town unveiled its totally renovated website, www.boystown.org. The new site provides valuable and useful information to visitors who want to learn more about Boys Town and its mission and how they can support the organization's work through engagement and donations. The site also helps children and families find Boys Town services and programs that may benefit them.

- Boys Town joined Nebraska Families Collaborative (NFC), a partnership of local organizations that contracts with the State of Nebraska to provide child and family care services.

- The state's Nebraska Family Helpline began providing services, using the Boys Town National Hotline's facilities. This service helps families access and move through the Nebraska child and family care system more efficiently to get the assistance they need.

- Boys Town Day Schools, both in the Village of Boys Town and in other communities, began providing an education alternative for students who have been suspended or expelled from their regular school due to serious behavioral problems. The goal is to keep students in the classroom and learning so they don't fall behind or drop out of school.

While the remaining chapters of Boys Town's work under Father Boes's leadership remain to be written, one thing is certain: Boys Town is well positioned to have an even greater impact in the years to come, both as an effective treatment and research organization and as a leader in improving care systems for children, families, and communities. Boys Town's experience and expertise is second to none, and as it continues to share those assets through community initiative projects throughout the country, even more at-risk children and struggling families will be able to find the help they need.

As Boys Town moves into its second century, it will continue to shine as a beacon of hope for America's children, families, and communities.

DAILY LIFE FOR THE BOYS AND GIRLS

During the tenures of Father Peter and Father Boes, daily life for the children at the Village of Boys Town, Nebraska, was very similar and consistent, both in their Family Homes, in school, and in their many experiences as residents of their "home" community.

Since the 1980s, the Village has provided care to children in up to seventy family-style homes, each headed by a specially trained married couple called Family-Teachers. Each Family-Teaching Couple provides a warm, caring, and structured family environment for six to eight boys or girls. Located on more than nine hundred acres on the west edge of Omaha, the Village is home to more than four hundred boys and girls at any one time. Most are between the ages of ten and seventeen when they become citizens of Boys Town. Many are struggling with behavioral, emotional, and/or mental health problems. Some have been referred through the juvenile justice system.

The picturesque Village's tree-lined streets, neat buildings, and beautiful lake give the community a welcoming, "small town" feel, which encourages youth to develop a unique sense of belonging and identity. Over time, every boy and girl develops a deep sense of pride in where they live.

ABOVE: Boys Town residential youth take pride in where they live, whether it is on the home campus or at a national site. Outdoor activities like keeping lawns tidy and maintaining landscaping allow family members of all ages to pitch in and make a difference

LEFT: Youth develop a deep sense of belonging and community pride as residents of Boys Town. Whether they are walking to school, cheering on their sports teams, worshiping in church, or learning new skills in their Family Home, every boy and girl knows he or she is in a safe, welcoming place and is part of the greater Boys Town family.

"It's been said that it takes a village to raise a child. For children and parents looking for life-changing care and guidance, that village is Boys Town."

Boys Town offers a fresh start for youth who are in trouble and need positive guidance in their lives. In this research-proven residential program, kids learn the skills that will help them achieve their goals while living in a safe, comfortable home with other youth and responsible adults. At the same time, they attend school right on Boys Town's picturesque campus (older students go to Boys Town High School; younger students attend Wegner Middle School), making new friends and enjoying the fun experiences that should be part of childhood and adolescence. From sports and JROTC to student government and prom, every girl and boy who comes to Boys Town can find opportunities to demonstrate their talents and acquire new ones. Six times, Boys Town has been named one of the "100 Best Communities for Young People" by the America's Promise Alliance.

ABOVE: A group of boys enjoy a pick-up football game in the yard outside their Family Home.

RIGHT: Two youth sort through flowers in the Boys Town greenhouse. Flowers and plants grown in the greenhouse were planted around the Village or sometimes sold to staff members during the holidays.

On a typical day at Boys Town, the boys and girls attend school, participate in school activities, prepare and eat meals with their Family-Teachers and other youth, complete chores and homework, and go on an outing or play a game as a family. Some youth may go to work at an off-campus job. Weekends also are structured but every Family Home makes it a point to have the youth and their Family-Teachers enjoy activities together, both on and off campus. Family-Teachers monitor the behaviors of all the youth in their care and communicate with teachers and parents on school progress and behaviors. One of the primary tools Boys Town employs to help youth learn and use new skills and positive behaviors is a motivation system. Every day, youth earn positive points for their positive behaviors and negative points for their negative behaviors. When they accumulate a set amount of positive points for the day, they can exchange them for privileges like snacks, free time, and special activities.

LEFT: Boys Town students study hard at school and work hard at their chores, but there's always time for fun and recreation in every Family Home.

BELOW: Boys Town youth enjoy a hayrack ride around the Village.

Youth and their Family-Teachers also gather every day for a family meeting. At these meetings, youth discuss important issues, learn how to solve problems involving the home and family, give feedback to one another, build healthy family relationships, and develop and practice skills that help them make good decisions.

At Boys Town, dedicated professionals help youth improve in body, mind, and spirit. Academics, life skill development, social and extracurricular activities, and spiritual growth are equally important as boys and girls work on overcoming their past problems and lay the foundation for a productive future. Everything is geared toward providing effective, individualized therapeutic care that helps each child learn to make better choices and change for the better.

At the same time, they enjoy numerous opportunities to just be kids, from summertime fishing to riding a bike across campus to sledding in the winter to cheering on the Boys Town Cowboy sports teams. In all of these activities, the focus is always on teaching youth the skills that will help them achieve success and develop healthy, positive relationships. Every summer, the youth enjoy a family vacation at Boys Town's camp on Lake Okoboji in north-central Iowa, where Family-Teachers continue their teaching and make all of the fun activities part of each youth's therapeutic care.

Boys Town cheerleaders and other student-athletes gather after a home football game.

ABOVE: Cold weather, plenty of snow, and hot chocolate afterwards makes sledding one of the favorite fun winter activities for youth living at the Village of Boys Town.

LEFT: In the summer, picnics and cookouts are regular happenings for the boys and girls.

Boys Town has its own police department and fire department (pictured), and a Village board handles issues related to Boys Town's standing as a municipality.

An elected board governs Boys Town. The Village's police and fire departments ensure the safety of all residents, staff, and the community. Recreational facilities include the recently renovated Palrang Memorial Field House, which features basketball courts, a swimming pool, a one-eighth mile indoor track, a weight room, racquetball courts, a climbing wall, and a ropes course.

Besides having the organization's largest residential program, the Village of Boys Town also is the national headquarters for administration, training, research, and program development.

A Positive Approach for Positive Results

The length of stay in today's Family Home Program can vary, depending on a youth's progress and needs. Boys Town research has found children do best in the residential program when they complete a stay of twelve to eighteen months. Boys Town advocates for what is best for each youth, which may mean encouraging parents to have their child stay in the program for the optimal length of time.

Boys Town also has many resources to help meet the needs of youth with emotional, behavioral, and mental health issues and drug or alcohol problems. At the Center for Behavioral Health, a large team of therapists works very closely with each Family Home to ensure youth receive individualized, specialized care whenever necessary.

Education

Academic success is a vital component of the Boys Town residential experience. Boys Town believes children must receive a good education so they can contribute to society, go on to college, get a job, and live independently once they leave.

At the time of their admission, 53 percent of today's Boys Town youth have not been attending school regularly and 85 percent are having school difficulties (attendance, behavior, learning/academic). All Boys Town youth attend either Wegner Middle School or Boys Town High School. Both schools provide comprehensive academic and vocational classes, which include instruction in reading, writing, science, social studies, and mathematics. Students also attend classes in art, music, religion, and physical education. Academics, social skills, and employability skills are emphasized, and students can receive vocational training in more than a dozen career areas. Boys Town also has its own sports teams, band, choir, student government, student newspaper, and JROTC program.

The academic curriculum and specialized programs at both Boys Town High School and Boys Town's Wegner School (above) are designed to help students overcome past struggles in the classroom and thrive as engaged, achieving learners.

Junior high and high school students who are behind in their reading ability can be enrolled in Boys Town's Expedition Literacy (formerly Reading Is FAME) program. Research on this program, which was developed specifically for Boys Town students who have reading difficulties, shows boys and girls, on average, gain two years of reading ability for every one year of instruction. Students also receive individual assistance through Boys Town's community mentoring program.

Both Boys Town schools are fully accredited by the Nebraska Department of Education and the North Central Association Commission on Accreditation and School Improvement (NCA CASI). This accreditation includes meeting all guidelines for special education under the Individuals with Disabilities Education Act (IDEA). All teachers are trained in the Boys Town Education Model, which compliments the Boys Town Model of care used in Family Homes. This model has been implemented in numerous school systems throughout the country.

Many students who were failing in a public school setting begin to make progress in the well-structured environment of Boys Town. Students also benefit from individualized attention, which is possible because the average class size in the schools is ten to twelve students. This enables students who are struggling academically to get the help they need to catch up and move toward graduation. Nearly 90 percent of the boys and girls who successfully complete the Family Home Program graduate from high school.

Research shows Boys Town gives these children their best chance to build bright, productive futures. In fact, educational success is often the first sign a boy or girl will experience positive transformational change at Boys Town. And years after receiving care, Boys Town youth—even those with the most severe problems—achieve success as adults.

Boys Town students also get a real-life lesson in civics each spring as citizens run election campaigns for the office of Boys Town mayor and vice mayor. Candidates make signs, come up with slogans, and make campaign speeches, urging their fellow students to vote for them. In May, all Boys Town citizens go to the polls to elect their favorites and winners are announced to the student body and the public. The mayor and vice mayor serve as ambassadors of Boys Town, greeting special guests and attending events and ceremonies as representatives of the Home.

Family Involvement and Contact
Boys Town highly encourages families to be involved in their children's care, from the admission process to service planning and implementation. Family involvement is another key to youth success, especially when reunification is a service and therapeutic goal.

Parents and other family members can regularly communicate with youth through phone calls, visits to the campus, regular mail, and online visits. (The type and frequency of contact between youth and their families usually depends on a youth's needs and his or her individual progress.) Boys Town youth are not permitted to have or use their own computers and cell phones.

Visits home for youth typically occur twice a year, usually at Christmas and during a two-week summer break. Other visits home or family visits to campus are welcome as long as they do not disrupt a youth's care or progress. These visits are arranged according to each youth's service needs and his or her home situation.

Graduation is perhaps the biggest and most important family celebration day of the year. Each May, up to one hundred students who have stayed at Boys Town to complete their high school academic classes dress in gowns and mortarboards to walk across the Music Hall stage and receive their diplomas. Family members, friends, Boys Town staff members, and others who have helped the students reach this monumental achievement fill the Music Hall to cheer on the graduation class and share their happy day. For many students, graduating from high school seemed like an impossible dream when they first come to Boys Town. But through their hard work and the efforts of dedicated caregivers and teachers, they are able to reach their goal and make their families proud. After the commencement ceremony, there are plenty of hugs and tears as graduates celebrate their special day with family members.

Graduation is an exciting time at Boys Town when graduates and their families celebrate the end of one journey and the beginning of a new one. Nearly 90 percent of Boys Town students earn their high school diploma.

Medical

Besides addressing the emotional and behavioral needs of youth, Boys Town also makes sure they receive quality medical care. Youth receive a complete physical examination at admission and see Boys Town National Research Hospital physicians for regular check-ups and when they are sick or injured. Dental and eye care is usually provided by local health care providers who have experience working with Boys Town youth.

Boys Town National Research Hospital has two locations—one near downtown Omaha and one in the Village of Boys Town. The hospital also has pediatric clinics throughout the Omaha area which employ some of the top pediatricians in the area.

Family-Teachers and other Boys Town caregivers also promote a healthy lifestyle for youth, including exercise and healthy eating habits.

Faith and Religion

Boys Town Family-Teachers and their youth say prayers at mealtime, observe daily prayer time in their homes, and regularly attend worship services together every week. There is a Catholic and a Protestant church in the Village, and children who profess other faiths are taken to their place of worship in the community. Boys Town believes, just as its founder Father Edward Flanagan did, that it's important for children to find their commitment to God in their own way. In fact, Father Flanagan famously said, "Every boy must learn to pray; how he prays is up to him." That's why Boys Town honors and respects children's religious beliefs, while nurturing their spiritual growth. Also, Boys Town is and always has been supported by loyal, generous donors of many religions and beliefs.

Religion and faith are an important part of Boys Town's approach to care, and religious instruction is included in the school curriculum. Boys Town's experience indicates care is more effective when youth have a strong foundation of faith.

As part their faith life journey, older students often attend retreats off campus, like this one at the Holy Family Shrine Chapel outside Omaha. Helping youth build and strengthen a spiritual foundation has been an essential part of Boys Town's care since its founding.

Extracurricular Activities and Athletics

Boys Town students can choose from a variety of extracurricular activities that promote good health, strong discipline, work ethic, and team and personal achievements. Involvement in these types of activities teaches and reinforces students' moral and character development and improves their ability to build healthy relationships and take on responsibilities. Student life activities include:

- Drama Club, Science Club, Chess Club, and Math Club
- Band and Marching Band
- Vocal and Instrumental Music
- Cheerleading
- Flag Corps
- Varsity and Junior Varsity Sports
- Intramural Athletics
- Interscholastic Athletics
- Student Council
- School Dances (Homecoming, Prom)
- JROTC Program and Drill Teams
- Fitness and Wellness Facility
- Indoor Climbing Wall and Ropes Course

Members of the Boys Town Marching Band proudly wear the uniform as they play at sports contests and special celebrations and participate in parades and other music-related events in the community.

ABOVE: The Boys Town Cheer Squad prepares to fire up fans at a Homecoming bonfire. Friday night football games and other sports contests are great places for students to socialize, represent Boys Town and their school, and use the social skills they learn every day as residents of the Family Home Program.

LEFT: Every spring, Boys Town's JROTC cadets show off their marching and close order drills in a Pass and Review ceremony at the field house. Boys Town students, staff, community members, and military dignitaries attend the event.

Boys Town High School offers a wide range of athletic opportunities for students. "Cowboy" athletic teams compete against schools from Nebraska and neighboring states. Students also can participate in intramural sports and in Boys Town-sponsored summer sports camps.

A crucial element of the athletic program is character development for student-athletes. Boys Town's Competing with Character® is an established program all coaches use to instill teamwork, values, fairness, good sportsmanship, and ethical behavior in their players. At Boys Town, athletics is a powerful vehicle for teaching valuable life lessons to the boys and girls.

Boys' sports:
- Football
- Basketball
- Track
- Baseball
- Wrestling
- Cross Country
- Swimming
- Soccer

Girls' sports:
- Volleyball
- Basketball
- Soccer
- Track
- Cross Country
- Softball

Football and volleyball are just two of the many sports in which Boys Town youth can have fun and learn important character traits like discipline, teamwork, good sportsmanship, and self-confidence. Student-athletes at Boys Town High School compete throughout the year against teams from across the state of Nebraska. At Boys Town national sites, youth in residential programs can participate in athletics at the local high schools they attend.

Athletic/Recreational facilities:

- Palrang Memorial Field House (138,000 square feet)
- Indoor and Outdoor Track and Field Facilities
- Indoor Football Practice Facilities
- State-of-the-Art Weight Room (5,000 square feet)
- State-of-the-Art Wrestling Facility (4,000 square feet)
- Football Stadium
- Five Indoor Basketball Courts
- Two Indoor Swimming Pools
- Collegiate-Level Baseball Field
- Recreational Softball Field

RIGHT: A center of daily recreational and athletic activities, the expansive Palrang Memorial Field House hosts indoor sports contests, youth sports camps, and physical education classes for Boys Town students. The field house also is used for large gatherings and special events, like the JROTC annual Pass and Review and the New Year's Eve celebration for youth. Boys Town staff members also can exercise and work out at the facility.

BELOW: Whether youth live in the Village of Boys Town or at one of Boys Town's affiliate sites, they are part of a caring, nurturing family that works together, plays together, prays together, and helps bring hope and healing to young lives. At Boys Town, boys and girls find the courage to change the trajectory of their lives and chart a new course for success.

EPILOGUE

Father Boes has said Boys Town really began when Father Flanagan experienced a miracle in his own heart, a miracle of caring and faith that led him to take that first small step—welcoming that first group of youngsters and opening his first Home for Boys. This small step also triggered Father Flanagan's campaign to change and transform America's larger childcare system. Since then, Boys Town has become a transformational place where miracles of the heart happen every day for children and their families. And it has carried on its founder's vision for bringing needed system changes and reforms to better protect and serve young people.

A t one hundred years strong, Boys Town is proud of its legacy of service and its century-long commitment to the well being of children, families, and communities. Its roots run deep and everything it does today has been layered onto the solid foundation Boys Town has accomplished since its beginnings.

Boys Town has always been in the "business" of helping people lead better lives. For some, this means escaping the hurt and pain of abuse and neglect. For others, it means learning how to head off a crisis and bring order and stability to a dysfunctional home so a family can stay together. For still others, it means tapping into Boys Town's vast experience and expertise to ensure children are being nurtured and raised with positive values and skills that will enable them to be successful as adults and caretakers of their own families.

Boys Town's first one hundred years were only the beginning. Unfortunately, there will never be a shortage of children, families, and communities that need the unique kind of help Boys Town provides.

Boys Town has worked hard to position itself for the next leap forward in child and family care. That leap will involve providing opportunities for life-changing care for *every child, every family,* and *every community* across the country. This will happen through Boys Town's high-quality programs and services, advocacy for best practices and system reform, enhanced research, closer working relationships with schools and communities, a broader national impact, and a focus on influencing decision makers to do what is best for the greatest number of children and families. It also will involve a sharing approach that enables other organizations to adopt Boys Town's Model of care and use its research findings to improve and enhance their own child and family programs.

When he founded Boys Town as a humble home for wayward youngsters, Father Flanagan's bigger vision was to someday reach out to help children and families all across America. Today's Boys Town is that vision realized, reshaping the lives of troubled boys and girls and changing the way America cares for children, families, and communities.

As Boys Town moves into its second century, it will continue to shine as a beacon of hope for all of America, ignited by faith, dedication, and love; sustained through knowledge, research, and experience; and forever burning brightly because so many people believe every child deserves a happy, healthy, productive life.

In the hearts of those who have been helped, those yet to be helped, and those who are loyal supporters of Boys Town's mission, the dream lives on!

Children Saved, Families Healed

Boys Town is in the "people" business. The mission has always been to make the world a better place for children and families. It has succeeded because so many continue to believe every child deserves to be

valued and have the chance to reach his or her full potential.

Boys Town has mountains of research and data that confirm their positive approach to child and family care works—children and families who turn to Boys Town for help do get better.

However, the lasting measure of their success over the past one hundred years lies in the tens of thousands of individual success stories of people who have turned to Boys Town to overcome painful pasts and seemingly insurmountable challenges and find brighter futures.

From the orphaned and abandoned boys of Boys Town's early years to the present-day boys and girls whose lives are mired in drug and alcohol abuse, school failure, and emotional and behavioral challenges, Boys Town has shined as a beacon of hope, a refuge where youth can learn to lift themselves up and grow into productive citizens.

In more recent decades, Boys Town has focused heavily on helping the family, keeping parents and their children together through preventive services and programs that reunify broken families that are unable to mend on their own. In

strengthening families, the communities in which they live are also strengthened.

The hallmark of the boys and girls and families who benefit from Boys Town's help is courage—the courage to change, to learn new skills and new ways of behaving, and to chart a new course in life. This courage has been evident in every child and family that has put their trust in Boys Town so their journey of healing could begin.

Every child who comes to Boys Town is special. Each one is unique, and each has his or her own story of heartbreak and dreams for a better life. Boys Town lifts them up, heals their wounds, and saves them, one child at a time.

Father Flanagan was right when he said when a child is valued and loved, he or she can do amazing things. That's why "miracles of the heart" happen every day at Boys Town.

The photos in this section represent just a few of the countless children and families that found their second chance for a happier, healthier life at Boys Town over the past century.

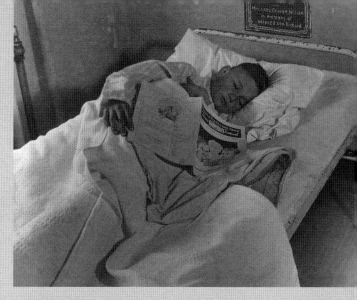

LEFT: The boys always found time for fun activities like jumping rope.

RIGHT: A Boys Town resident of the 1920s falls asleep while reading the *Father Flanagan's Boys' Home Journal* in bed.

ABOVE: Father Flanagan and his boys were grateful for a local businessman's gift of a pool table for their recreation room.

LEFT: In the early days, many boys who came to the Home didn't have enough to eat. That wasn't the case when they gathered for meals in the Boys Town dining hall.

ABOVE: On lazy summer afternoons in the 1930s the boys went fishing in the Boys Town lake.

RIGHT: A typing class hones their skills on manual machines in the 1940s.

Father Flanagan gathered with a group of boys in their Sunday best before leaving on a fact-finding trip to Asia in 1947.

A Forever Family

Ben and Patty Valdez really weren't planning to adopt children when they decided to become Boys Town Texas Foster Parents in 2013. But when three-year-old Sunny and eighteen-month-old Robert—siblings who were victims of severe neglect—arrived at the couple's home as their first foster children, there was an immediate bond. "It was almost like they had belonged in our family forever," Patty said. "Sunny walked into our house and she covered her little mouth. She was crying; she was so happy to be here. It didn't even take a few days before they began calling us Mom and Dad."

Eventually, the siblings' birth parents surrendered their parental rights and the Valdezes were able to move forward with adoption proceedings. In January 2014, six months after that emotional first meeting, Ben and Patty welcomed Sunny and Robert home for good.

Patty said she and Ben couldn't believe how quickly the adoption occurred, especially since they had originally only planned to be foster parents. Even making that commitment had required a lot of thought and prayer. But, she said, they both already had what children who were looking for a forever family needed. "We had a love for kids in our hearts."

Today, the Valdez house is a busy, active place where a brother and sister are safe and happy, and their mom is familiar with every children's cartoon character that appears on TV. Both Sunny and Robert have grown and thrived over the past few years. Ben, who owns a scrap metal recycling business, takes his daughter to school every morning. Ben and Robert are "best friends," and Robert cries when Dad has to leave for work. (Sometimes, Ben is able to take Robert to work with him.)

Patty is a stay-at-home mom and loves every minute of it. "A lot of my free time is not free anymore and it doesn't bother me one bit," Patty said. "Before, my house was really quiet. Now it's full of laughter. Boys Town opened this door to our hearts and then filled it with beautiful colors. They've been very helpful and supportive, and I wouldn't trade them for the world."

ABOVE: In 1952, one of the boys built his own car to race in the local Soap Box Derby.

BELOW: This spaghetti night in the 1950s brought out the boys' more creative eating techniques.

A Bright Future

Thomas McRae Jr. lived in twenty-two foster homes before he was old enough to drive.

Growing up, Thomas never really knew what it meant to be part of a family. His mother chose a life of drugs over him. His dad tried but was unable to care for the youngster. Entering the foster care system at age eleven brought only more confusion into Thomas's life. Every day held the possibility he would have to move again, starting all over in a new home, a new school, and a new neighborhood. Constantly living in fear and uncertainty, it was no surprise the youngster often acted out with anger and aggression.

Ironically, it was just such a confrontation between Thomas and one of his foster parents in the fall of his senior year in high school that led him to a Boys Town Family Home in his home city of Washington, D.C. Thomas's stay with Boys Town was only supposed to last a couple of days. But his attorney advocated for a longer placement. It turned out to be the turning point in the teen's life.

The Boys Town Family Home was unlike any place Thomas had ever lived. His Family-Teachers, Hubert and Chauna Geter, were responsible for his daily needs and for teaching him the skills that would help him succeed in school, with others, and in life. They made sure he did his homework, completed chores around the house, and built strong relationships with the other boys in the home.

In the eight months Thomas lived with the Geters, he found a new direction and purpose. "I had the greatest Family-Teachers in the world," Thomas said. "They were so inspiring, so motivating. They taught me what it means to have a mother and a father. They taught me patience and kindness. Had it not been for them, I would not be the man I am today."

Since graduating high school and leaving Boys Town, Thomas has experienced one success after another. He went to college, majoring in psychology with a concentration in philosophy. One summer, he worked on Capitol Hill as part of an internship with the Congressional Coalition on Adoption. He has been a featured speaker at a number of events, and his plans include obtaining a master's degree in social work and pursuing a career as a clinical psychologist for foster youth.

"What Boys Town does is invest in you," Thomas said. "You just have to be willing to take the investment and run with it. They took this lost kid and made him into something great. I can't thank them enough for helping me find Thomas."

ABOVE: A pick-up football game on the lawn outside a dormitory was a great way to have fun and get to know the other boys.

LEFT: A group of boys hit the books in their high school classroom in 1967.

LEFT: With the advent of the Family Home Program in the 1970s, Boys Town adopted a family-style care approach that brought eight to ten boys together as a family in one home under the care of married couples called Family-Teachers. The Family Home Program enabled Boys Town to help youth with more serious behavioral and emotional problems. In every home, saying grace before meals was an important part of the daily routine.

BELOW: Water basketball was just one of the fun activities the youth enjoy during their annual summer vacation to Boys Town's camp on Lake Okoboji in Iowa. The structure and teaching the youth experience at Boys Town continues during time at the camp.

The first girls began receiving care as residents of Boys Town in 1979. The transition to having girls on campus went smoothly and the number of girl residents steadily grew into the 1980s.

A New Life

Sitting in a jail cell, Brandee Steffes knew her life was spiraling out of control. She desperately longed to be with her baby boy, Pierce, and realized she could lose him for good. It was up to her to change. The problem was, she didn't know how or where to start.

Brandee reached a moment of reckoning after being arrested in July 2012 for assaulting her mother's boyfriend and kicking out the window of a police car. She was intoxicated at the time.

Soon after, Brandee and her son were referred to Boys Town Iowa's In-Home Family Services. Jaymes Sime, a Family Consultant with the program, met with the young mother at the county jail. "Brandee appeared really beaten down and defeated," Jaymes said. "She was in no shape to care for herself, let alone her one-year-old son, Pierce."

Pierce was placed in a foster home. In the meantime, Brandee pled guilty to the charges she faced, paid restitution for the property damage, and was sentenced to jail time and probation. Eventually, Jaymes helped get Brandee transferred to a residential correctional facility (RCF) that housed inmates while providing them with treatment and transition services.

Five weeks after her arrest, Brandee was allowed her first visit with Pierce. Brandee lit up when she saw her little boy. She made the decision to do whatever it took to keep him in her life. "Pierce was about 15 months old and she hadn't seen him in more than a month," Jaymes said. "She missed him badly and was unsure of how the process was going to play out. That was the moment she knew what she wanted."

With Jaymes's assistance, Brandee started working part-time through temporary employment agencies to pay her rent at the residential facility and catch up on her other bills. He also helped Brandee establish a support system so she could stay sober and access other needed services. Brandee reached a major milestone when she was able to transition out of the RCF in November 2012 and move into a home in the community. A month later, Pierce and Brandee were reunited. Jaymes continued to work with Brandee to improve her parenting skills and help her maintain a stable home life for her son.

Brandee eventually enrolled in classes at Iowa Western Community College to earn her associate's degree. While there, she was selected to lead "The Winner's Circle," a support group for formerly incarcerated women who were transitioning back into the community.

In June 2013, Brandee and Pierce completed Boys Town's services. Six months later, Jaymes got a message from Brandee that read, "I received a letter yesterday. Apparently, I made the honor roll last semester!"

Brandee has helped facilitate substance abuse treatment classes and groups and speaks at various places to share her story to help others with their recovery. Her journey of hope and healing continues as she and Pierce rebuild their lives. But thanks to Boys Town, she was empowered to pick herself up off a jailhouse floor and embrace with optimism the bright possibilities for the future.

"My experience with Boys Town will always be a memorable one," Brandee said. "They played a key role in reuniting my son and I. In the beginning, they were the rope I clung to for survival. Jaymes was a godsend. He gave me the encouragement and hope that I needed during those tough times. He helped me see things in a clearer, more positive light. He pushed me to network out and gain the support systems I needed for success. Jaymes will always be family to us."

ABOVE: As Boys Town continued to grow and evolve in its care methods and national presence in the 1990s, one thing that didn't change was the long-time tradition of older youth helping and looking out for their younger "brothers" and "sisters."

BELOW: The Boys Town horse farm provided riding sessions for special needs children in the 1990s. The sessions were just another innovative way Boys Town was changing the lives of young people.

These Boys Town girls just wanted to have fun, hanging out and sharing a laugh.

Back on Track

Growing up in a dysfunctional family with little guidance or support, Aeryn Vaneck made one bad choice after another. She got caught up with the wrong crowd, abused drugs, and was chronically truant at school.

When Aeryn did attend school, she barely managed to maintain a "D" average. Her attendance was so erratic she eventually just dropped out. With no structure at home and no one supporting her, Aeryn's life spiraled out of control.

Frequent arguments with her family led Aeryn to run away for long periods of time. But life as a runaway proved disastrous. She got in trouble with the law and was arrested several times. Aeryn was already on probation when she was picked up for stealing. Standing before a juvenile court judge, she was charged with grand larceny. The judge, who was familiar with Boys Town Nevada, believed the site's residential program offered the best, and perhaps the last, opportunity for Aeryn to get her life back on track.

Aeryn was immediately placed in one of the site's Family Homes, a jarring change for a young lady who was accustomed to living by her own rules. But the highly structured, family-style environment turned out to be both a rude awakening and a welcome rescue. The new surroundings brought limits and responsibilities and required an immediate attitude adjustment for Aeryn. That wasn't easy, but the teen slowly warmed up to her Family-Teachers, who listened and provided unconditional support. Their calm, reassuring presence enabled Aeryn to think more clearly about her choices and the direction of her life.

With patience, structure, and teaching from her Family-Teachers, Aeryn began to take responsibility for her actions and her emotions. She learned self-control strategies as well as decision-making and life skills that empowered her to think through her feelings instead of impulsively lashing out or running away.

Aeryn also recommitted herself to her education. She returned to high school with a more positive attitude, determined to make up for lost time. In the classroom, she successfully put into practice many of the skills she learned at Boys Town. She worked diligently on her studies, even taking additional coursework so she could get back to her grade level. Her determination and perseverance paid off as she upped her grades to a "B" average and graduated with her class, something she never dreamed was possible.

Most recently, Aeryn was balancing college and a job and had reconciled with her family.

"Boys Town was like a savior," Aeryn said.

Learning for Life

From the earliest days of instruction in reading, writing, and arithmetic by Father Flanagan himself to today's modern school system and sophisticated classroom management model, Boys Town has promoted education as the cornerstone of success for the youth in its care.

Many of the boys and girls who have called Boys Town their home or whose families received their services were far behind in their academic studies. They'd lost interest in school, were suspended or expelled because of behavior problems, or just dropped out. Most were years behind their grade level in classwork.

Boys Town's positive approach to youth care meshes education with spirituality, social skills, physical and emotional well being, and preparation for independent living in order to treat the whole child and strengthen body, mind, and spirit. A unique feature of Boys Town is its schools have always been part of the overall youth care program. Boys Town citizens are expected to attend classes, complete homework, study for tests, and graduate from high school. They also are encouraged to continue their education in college or a trade school if they so choose.

For decades, Boys Town has operated two schools for its home campus residents. Boys Town High School serves youth in grades nine through twelve, and Wegner School serves youth in grades five through eight and lower grades as the need arises. Boys Town youth attend school year round, including half-days during the summer months. Students also benefit from the Boys Town Reading Center, which provides a specialized curriculum designed to improve reading skills for at-risk adolescents. A mentoring program in which Boys Town staff members and residents from the local community volunteer to provide one-on-one assistance for Boys Town youth is beneficial also.

Education is equally important for youth served at Boys Town sites around the country. Those youth attend local schools, a number of which have adopted the Boys Town classroom management system. Boys Town's family-based and community-based services also help parents learn strategies that promote school success for their children.

At Boys Town, education does not begin and end in the classroom because youth continually learn life skills that enable them to care for themselves after they leave Boys Town. On the home campus, they also can learn the basics of vocational and trade occupations through courses at the Career Readiness Center, which is part of Boys Town High School.

Like all Boys Town programs, the education system has evolved over the years to meet the changing needs of youth and society. From the early residents of Father Flanagan's first home to the boys and girls who are struggling through life today, young people have learned how to become learners again and achieve their academic and long-term life goals.

This section highlights Boys Town's long-time focus on schools and education and the critical roles they have played in one hundred years of effective care.

ABOVE: Learning a trade or a craft was an essential part of each boy's education in the early days of Boys Town. This woodworking class of the 1930s applied their skills to building an ornate birdhouse.

LEFT: The members of Boys Town's first high school graduation class in 1937 were ready to use what they had learned at the Home to make their mark in the world.

BELOW: By 1947, Boys Town's graduation classes were significantly larger. Here, soon-to-be graduates gather with Father Flanagan in front of Dowd Chapel. Of this group, only six boys were from Nebraska.

RIGHT: Just as in any high school, Prom and Homecoming dances were special events at Boys Town. Boys Town residents asked girls from Omaha-area high schools to be their dates for these celebrations.

BELOW: Graduates in gowns and mortarboards process to their commencement exercises in the late 1940s.

RIGHT: Learning at Boys Town involved strengthening the mind, spirit, and body. Rope climbing was a favorite activity for physical education classes.

ABOVE: A student checks his calculations during a chemistry class in the 1950s. A well-rounded education enabled many Boys Town grads to go to college, become business owners, or enter the workforce with trade skills.

RIGHT: Auto mechanics was a popular class, allowing students to learn repair skills while having fun working on cars.

ABOVE: All-school assemblies, like this one in the Boys Town Music Hall, brought younger and older students together for educational or entertainment presentations.

LEFT: Besides academic and trade classes, Boys Town students had opportunities to participate in art, music, and drama. This quartet showed off their singing and instrumental skills to entertain their fellow residents.

BELOW: Students congregate outside the high school, waiting for the morning bell to ring.

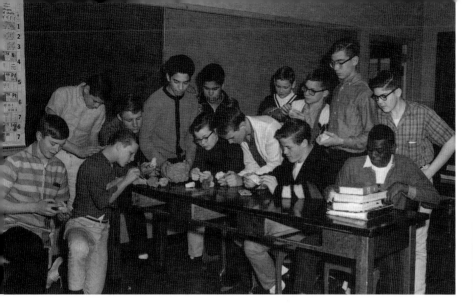

LEFT: A 1960s science class closely examines rocks as part of a geology lesson.

BELOW: Boys Town often invited special dignitaries to be part of its commencement ceremonies. In 1967, Vice President Hubert Humphrey presented diplomas to graduates.

ABOVE: Students put the finishing touches on a wedding cake in a baking and culinary arts class. The Boys Town Career Center offered a variety of specialty trade courses to prepare Boys Town youth for employment after they left the Home.

BELOW: An instructor guides a student through a lesson on a linotype machine in a print shop class.

ABOVE: The king and queen of a Boys Town Junior-Senior Prom enjoy their moment in the spotlight. Boys Town believes all students need fun social activities as well as quality academic opportunities in order to grow into well-rounded adults.

ABOVE: Students at Wegner Middle School who had earned Reading Club awards gathered for a photo with then-Executive Director Father Val Peter. Father Peter affectionately called these kids "the shrimps."

BELOW: The entire Boys Town student body posed for a photo at the football stadium in the early 1970s.

ABOVE: The class of 1988 celebrates the end of their Boys Town journey and the start of a new adventure as young adults.

LEFT: Learning the importance of community service is a big part of every youth's experience at Boys Town. This group of girls braved the cold to ring bells for the Salvation Army during the Christmas holiday.

Just like their predecessors, today's Boys Town students receive a comprehensive education that prepares them for the challenges of independent living and a successful, productive adult life.

LEFT: Boys Town's outdoors ropes course is a way for students to have fun while learning trust, self-confidence, and teamwork. Boys and girls also enjoy the exhilaration of a climbing wall inside the Palrang Field House.

BELOW: Hundreds Boys Town staff members and community members help youth sharpen math, reading, social studies, or science skills through the Boys Town mentoring program. Mentoring has long been an important element of the Home's educational system, and these volunteers log thousands of hours annually to provide extra instruction and practice for students in areas where they are behind.

This artfully designed Boys Town High School yearbook will be a cherished keepsake for students of the Class of 2014. A yearbook has been published every year at Boys Town since 1952.

Mission Accomplishers

Even before he opened his Home for Boys, Father Flanagan had become acquainted with groups of like-minded individuals who wanted to be part of his mission to help the homeless children of Omaha. These

supporters would later become the first fundraisers and board members of the fledgling haven Father Flanagan was trying to develop and grow.

In the Home's early days, many volunteers aided Father Flanagan in his daily efforts to care for the boys. These included nuns, brothers, local residents, and members of the priest's own family. For example, Father Flanagan's mother, Honora, organized a group of women, later known as the Mothers' Guild, to sew and mend clothing for the youngsters.

As the Home's financial situation improved, Father Flanagan was able to hire full-time staff members such as cooks, teachers, doctors, nurses, and caregivers for the boys. These men and women dedicated long hours, often for little pay, to keep Boys Town going. During the Great Depression, staff members sometimes weren't paid for months, but the majority stayed on to help Father Flanagan take care of the youth.

In later decades, with young people coming to Boys Town with more complex problems and a greater focus on helping families, Boys Town hired staff members for specialized positions, both in direct care and administrative and support areas. Today, Boys Town has more than 2,500 employees at its sites across the country.

Over the past century, men and women across America have become strong advocates of Boys Town and

the revolutionary concepts Father Flanagan proposed for changing the way children were cared for and treated. These advocates ranged from ordinary citizens to presidents, and their support was largely responsible for Boys Town gaining a foothold and then growing into one of the largest child and family care organizations in the United States.

As a result of this groundswell of support and Boys Town's professional and effective fundraising and marketing efforts, tens of thousands of people around the world have proudly called themselves Boys Town donors. Today, the generosity of individuals, organizations, foundations, and corporations helps account for a large portion of Boys Town's annual budget of more than $400 million.

Hundreds of volunteers also help support Boys Town's work, serving in many diverse roles, from mentors for students and tour guides in the Village of Boys Town to sponsors for fundraising events or special activities for children at Boys Town's national sites.

The sampling of photos and stories in this section are offered in gratitude to the countless staff members, advocates, volunteers, and supporters whose dedication and commitment have kept Father Flanagan's dream and mission alive for one hundred years and counting.

ABOVE: In the early days of the Home, local residents and social groups often volunteered to help Father Flanagan care for the boys. These ladies visited Boys Town in 1922 to help with a summer picnic.

LEFT: Office staff of the 1930s worked in a plain but functional space as they kept files on the boys up to date and typed letters to supporters and donors.

Father Flanagan with male staff members in 1935. Among them is Pat Norton (front row, in light suit), Father Flanagan's nephew, who served as Boys Town's business manager for many years.

ABOVE: These lunch ladies in the 1940s made sure the boys had delicious, nutritious meals during the school day.

RIGHT: Henry Monsky (left), a businessman, attorney, and Jewish leader, helped Father Flanagan launch his dream by loaning him $90 for the first month's rent on the first Home for Boys in downtown Omaha. Monsky and Father Flanagan were long-time friends and shared similar views on the state of childcare and the juvenile justice system in America. This close friendship was very unique for its time, but Father Flanagan commonly forged many bonds with like-minded individuals of different races and religions. Monsky, who served as an advisor and legal counsel to the priest, died in 1947.

BELOW: In the 1940s, Father Flanagan brought a number of Japanese American families from internment camps in California to Boys Town. Father Flanagan disagreed with the government's order to confine these families after Japan attacked Pearl Harbor, and he tried to help as many families as possible. These men were former internees who were rescued from the camps; some were later hired as employees of Boys Town.

LEFT: Boys Town school faculty celebrated a special event with cake and ice cream in the 1950s. Teachers and other school staff members form the backbone of the Home's educational system, often providing the first real opportunity students have to learn and flourish in the classroom.

BELOW: The Alexian brothers served as teachers and caretakers at Boys Town under the direction of Monsignor Nicholas Wegner.

A teacher's aide works one on one with a student on a school assignment in the early 1970s.

Manual typewriters and dictation machines were state-of-the-art equipment for Boys Town office staff of the 1960s.

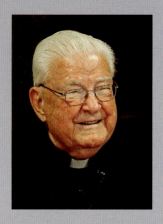

LEFT: Monsignor Peter Dunne's first assignment as a priest was at Boys Town in 1948, where he worked alongside Boys Town founder Father Edward Flanagan. Monsignor Dunne left Boys Town in 1958 to serve as a pastor in Nebraska parishes for more than thirty years, but returned to the Home upon his retirement in 1989. He served the youth and others at Boys Town in a variety of roles until his death in 2015 at age ninety-six.

ABOVE: Family-Teachers have been the mainstays of Boys Town's residential care program since the Home moved to a family-style model in the mid-1970s. This Family-Teaching Couple was overseeing the girls in their care as they prepared for a cookout.

LEFT: For more than fifty years, Pierre Bossant prepared delicious meals for Boys Town youth, staff, and visitors. Bossant was born in Paris and moved to Omaha in 1960, starting at Boys Town soon after. He also served as the personal rectory chef for the Home's executive director and other priests.

BELOW: Retirees and others from the community regularly volunteer at Boys Town to help with day-to-day tasks and projects. This group is sorting historical photos at the Boys Town Hall of History.

ABOVE: Throughout Boys Town's history, its boards of trustees have been instrumental in promoting growth, maintaining financial security, and adhering to the principles established for youth and family care by Father Flanagan. This is the 1982 board of trustees, including Executive Director Monsignor Robert Hupp (seated, second from left).

RIGHT: For decades, the Boys Town Police Department has worked to ensure the safety of youth and staff members in the Village. Officers receive special training in the proper handling of youth issues.

RIGHT: Over the decades, Boys Town sought out people who could bring diversity to the Home's leadership and serve as role models for its young residents. Jesse Owens was one of those people. Owens gained worldwide fame by winning several gold medals at the 1936 Berlin Olympics, overshadowing Adolf Hitler's efforts to portray the Aryan race as superior. Following those successes, Owens became an advocate for civil rights, promoting programs to assist youth in need. From 1974 to 1977, Owens (pictured here with Monsignor Robert Hupp) served as a member of the Boys Town Board of Directors. During his tenure, he helped guide the Home into its current Family Home Program and often met with the students to discuss his life and how he overcame the challenges he faced.

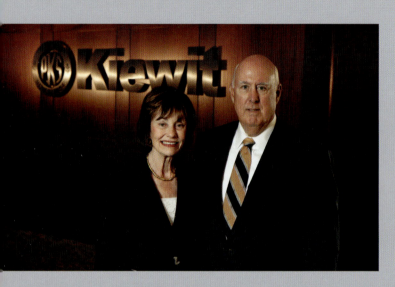

ABOVE: Ken Stinson, board chair for Peter Kiewit Sons' Inc. in Omaha, has shared his time and talents as a Boys Town donor, leader, fundraiser, and friend for more than a decade. He was a member of the Boys Town National Board of Trustees for six years, serving as board chair for the last three. As a Boys Town fundraiser, even after leaving the board, Stinson has helped garner millions of dollars in financial support for programs that benefit children and families, both locally and nationally. Stinson and his wife, Ann, have personally seen how Boys Town can bring life-changing care to people's lives. "Families who are struggling and who have youth problems . . . have come to me because they know I have an affiliation with Boys Town and asked, 'What do I do? Where do I go?' And I typically refer them to some of the very good people at Boys Town, and they inevitably come back and say, 'Thank goodness, Boys Town saved our family.' I don't know of a better place I could have referred them to."

BELOW: Geoffrey and Pam Farmer have been Boys Town Texas Foster Parents since 2009 for one simple reason: so they can love and guide children who can no longer live at home and place them on the right path for life's journey. "The most important thing is the impact you have on a child's life," said Pam, who with her husband now care for several youth at a time in a Foster Family Home at the site's campus in San Antonio. "If you impact one person to be a better person in society, you've done the best thing you can do." As foster parents, the Farmers have helped change the lives of dozens of young people. But the work they do has been a two-way street. "Pam and I came into this thinking we would make a difference in kids' lives," Geoffrey said. "It's been just the opposite. Foster Parents are the ones who reap the rewards. We benefit much more than the kids."

LEFT: As a self-contained community, the Village of Boys Town depends on an army of support staff to keep the Family Homes, schools, administrative offices, and the rest of the physical plan running in a safe, efficient manner. From plumbers and painters to electricians and carpenters, Boys Town's maintenance workers ensure the Village's smooth operation.

RIGHT: Like the coaches who came before them, long-time Boys Town head football coach Kevin Kush and his staff have guided many talented student-athletes and teams to success on the gridiron. But besides instilling his players with a competitive drive, Kush has taught an even greater lesson—to win with grace, to lose with dignity, and to always compete with character, representing Boys Town's highest ideals.

LEFT: Since 2004, Godfather's Pizza Inc. (GPI) has been a proud national sponsor of Boys Town, featuring the Boys Town National Hotline number on millions of pizza boxes each year. Over the past ten years, Godfather's Pizza has donated more than $2 million to support Boys Town and youth and families it serves. Godfather's Pizza employees also contribute their time, talents, and financial gifts every year to ensure every youth who stays at the Village of Boys Town over the holidays has a happy Christmas. The company regularly invites Boys Town boys and girls to its corporate headquarters in Omaha to have fun making pizza and learning about the food service industry. The dedication and commitment of Godfather's Pizza and its employees to Boys Town's mission is a wonderful example of corporate and community support.

RIGHT: Boys Town donors are fiercely loyal to the Home's mission of helping children, especially those with severe emotional and behavioral disorders. Thanks to a gift from long-time donor Harriet Karol, children who are receiving care at the Boys Town Residential Treatment Center have a special playground where they can have fun and be carefree. "The play area was very important to me," Karol said. "It's a place where children can forget their past problems and believe they can have a much better and more wonderful life . . . the life they truly deserve to have."

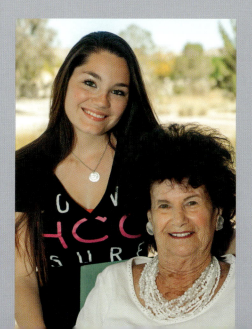

LEFT: Janet Mann was twelve when she sent her first donation to Boys Town, a quarter from the money she had earned babysitting. The feeling that first simple gift gave her was enough to make Mann a lifelong donor and supporter of Boys Town. Little did she know that decades later, the very organization she had supported so faithfully through the years would save her teenaged granddaughter, Becca, who found the help she needed while a resident of a Family Home at Boys Town Nevada.

More Than Just Winning

Since its founding, sports and other activities that provide boys and girls opportunities to have fun and just be kids have been essential elements of Boys Town's healing environment.

In the early years, the boys played marbles and baseball and learned how to box. Later, organized sports were introduced as part of the school system. Coach Maurice "Skip" Palrang helped build Boys Town's football, baseball, and basketball teams into powerhouse programs that took home state championships in Nebraska and found success against challengers from across the country.

In the late 1960s, the Boys Town Booster Club began fundraising efforts to bolster the athletic programs and ensure that any Boys Town youth who wanted to play organized sports could do so. The boosters' annual banquet, featuring a well-known sports figure as the keynote speaker, has raised millions of dollars to buy uniforms and equipment, improve athletic facilities, and support coaches and staff who dedicated themselves to helping their student-athletes learn how to compete through fair play and teamwork. Also, former Boys Town student-athletes are inducted into the Alumni Sports Hall of Fame every year during the booster banquet.

When girls were admitted to Boys Town in 1979, the Home's athletic programs expanded so new female citizens could compete in sports like basketball, track, volleyball, cross country, and others.

Today, Boys Town High School offers a wide range of athletic opportunities for students as they carry on the Home's rich legacy of sports success. As a member of the Nebraska School Activities Association and the Centennial Conference, Boys Town Cowboy athletic teams compete against schools from Nebraska and neighboring states. Students also can participate in intramural sports and in Boys Town-sponsored summer sports camps. (At Boys Town's national sites, youth participate in sports programs at the local schools they attend.)

At Boys Town, athletics is a powerful vehicle for teaching valuable life lessons and developing good character in the boys and girls. Boys Town's Competing with Character is an established program all coaches use to instill the values of fairness, good sportsmanship, and ethical behavior in their players. The coaches also share this program with coaches, parents, and players from other schools and athletic clubs.

Besides sports, Boys Town students also enjoy a variety of social and extracurricular activities that promote good health, strong discipline, work ethic, and team and personal achievements.

Even more than victories, learning life lessons has created a foundation of success for generations of Boys Town youth.

This section salutes the role sports and competition has played in shaping the lives of Boys Town youth over the past century.

LEFT: A young pugilist-in-training raises his arms in triumph beneath a pile of boxing gloves. Father Flanagan loved boxing and saw it as a proper way to teach the boys how to defend themselves. Professional fighters like heavyweight champion Joe Louis were some of the boys' favorite Boys Town visitors.

BELOW: The Boys Town Field House was constructed in 1947 and was later named for Boys Town's legendary multi-sport coach, Maurice "Skip" Palrang. The field house was and continues to be the headquarters for Boys Town athletic programs, boasting a large arena, an indoor track, a weight room, and an Olympic-size swimming pool.

Father Flanagan joins the Boys Town boxing team as they proudly display their trophies after winning their own invitational match in the 1940s.

ABOVE: Baseball was the national pastime in the 1940s, and its popularity at Boys Town was unmatched. In 1949, this Boys Town American Legion team boards a plane with Coach Ike Mahoney to play in a national tournament at the old Polo Grounds in New York City.

LEFT: Boys Town swim teams won numerous state championships in the 1950s and 1960s. Here, Boys Town swimmers are poised for the starting gun.

While the high school boys were enjoying success on the gridiron, the younger kids at Boys Town were developing their own winning ways as they learned the finer points of the game. This team celebrated an intramural junior division championship in 1956.

ABOVE: Boys Town football teams dominated their opponents, locally and nationally, from the 1940s through the 1960s. These seven lettermen formed the nucleus of Coach Skip Palrang's 1956 squad.

RIGHT: Women's sports began to share the spotlight after Boys Town began admitting girls to its residential program in 1979. A Lady Cowboy shows good form as she goes up for a jump shot over an opponent.

BELOW: Wrestling has been a standout sport at Boys Town for decades, and Cowboy wrestlers symbolize the tough competitive spirit all Boys Town student-athletes bring to their contests.

ABOVE: Volleyball gave girls another opportunity to represent Boys Town in competitive sports. This match was being played in the Palrang Field House.

BELOW: Track and field competitions give Boys Town athletes an opportunity to excel as part of a team and as individuals. In the past, indoor meets often were held in Palrang Field House.

LEFT: In 1997, only four young ladies comprised the entire Boys Town women's track team. Through determination and talent, the team ran away with the Nebraska State Class B championship.

RIGHT: Modern-day Boys Town football teams have made their mark on the high school scene, earning state rankings and striving toward championship games. On fall Friday nights, home football games in the Village bring together the entire community—youth and staff—to cheer on the Cowboys.

ABOVE: Basketball traditionally has been a sport of excellence at Boys Town, with Cowboy teams winning seven state championships since 1953. Former Boys Town coach George Pfeifer, whose teams won back-to-back state championships in 1965 and 1966, once summed up why sports play such an important role in the lives of Boys Town kids. "You know, they come with a hole in their heart," he said. "Nobody cares about them, nobody encourages them—they just think there's no way they can make it. We set up goals and objectives. We praise them when they succeed. When a kid comes up to you and says, 'God, I wish you were my dad' . . . then you know you made a difference."

No matter the season, Boys Town sports teams can be found competing with good sportsmanship, respect for their opponents and officials, and a deep pride in representing their school and their Home.

Sports bring the pure joy of playing a game and competing to every Boys Town youth who wants to participate. Boys Town student-athletes consistently earn praise from their opponents for their exemplary behavior on the field, court, or track—another indication of how Boys Town continues to use sports to help at-risk youth grow, overcome their troubled past, and prepare for a successful adult life.

Celebrations and Lasting Memories

When Father Flanagan began working with homeless and abandoned children, he quickly discovered many of them had never celebrated the holidays or other important life events. Some of his early boys didn't even know what it was like to have a birthday party. Father Flanagan made it part of the Home's mission to ensure that the children in his care enjoyed these childhood experiences.

Since Father Flanagan opened his Home for Boys just a couple of weeks before Christmas, that holiday has held a special significance at Boys Town. In the early years, Father Flanagan and his boys would decorate a tree and he would seek donations from the public so each boy received a gift. Christmas celebrations got bigger and better as the Home grew into the Village of Boys Town and more boys became citizens. In the 1950s, a new tradition called Twelfth Night became the centerpiece of the holiday season, with the boys enjoying a different activity every night for twelve straight nights after Christmas. Even today, Twelfth Night remains a cherished memory for older Boys Town alums.

Father Flanagan and his successors also saw to it the children celebrated Easter (usually with a big Sunday dinner after church), the Fourth of July, Halloween, Thanksgiving, New Year's, and other national holidays. Besides being fun and making memories, these practices also taught the boys and girls the importance of family traditions, traditions they could start and carry on with their own children and families someday.

Summer picnics also became a fun event the kids looked forward to, starting as far back as the 1920s. The first picnics were sponsored by donors and often included a day at the local amusement park in Omaha. As Boys Town's population grew, the picnics became day-long events with games, food, and fellowship. The picnic tradition continues today.

Another favorite summer event is each Family Home's vacation at Boys Town's camp at Lake Okoboji in Iowa. Boys Town families load up their vans and head to the lake to enjoy several days of water skiing, boating, volleyball, swimming, and campfire singalongs. For many boys and girls, it is the first family vacation they've ever taken.

Boys Town has always believed every child deserves the joy of just being a child. Much of this joy comes from the holiday celebrations and fun events that create the lifelong memories of a healthy, happy childhood. It is this joy and these memories that often help boys and girls overcome the pain of their past and look forward to the future with hope and confidence.

This section highlights some of the holiday and milestone celebrations that create lifelong memories for Boys Town kids.

LEFT: Many children arrive at Boys Town never having celebrated a special life event as part of a family. That is as true today as it was in the early days of the Home. Jimmy Graham (standing) was one of those kids in 1949. Before coming to Boys Town, Jimmy had never had a birthday party. That all changed when he turned eleven, thanks to the kindness of Coach Skip Palrang. Palrang provided a cake, soda pop, and invited guests so Jimmy's first birthday party would be one he would always remember. Boys Town not only provides boys and girls with second chances but also many "firsts."

BELOW: One of the most important events in the life of a Boys Town youth is being sworn in as an official Boys Town citizen. The swearing-in ceremony takes places shortly after a youth's arrival and usually is held on Fridays during the lunch hour at the Boys Town Visitors Center. Many visitors and staff members are on hand each week as a group of new youth takes the oath, promising to work hard and do their best during their time at the Home. The public welcome celebrates the start of a youth's journey of healing and hope.

The arrival of the Easter Bunny made this recent Easter celebration even more special for a Boys Town family of youth. All holidays—religious and secular—are woven into the fabric of daily life at Boys Town so youth can understand their significance and learn about traditions they can someday share with their own families and children.

A traditional egg hunt in the front yard was a highlight of Easter Sunday for these Boys Town youth. The holiday celebration also included dressing up, attending church services, and a special family dinner.

ABOVE: American flags, patriotic signs, and festive costumes made for an eye-catching group as Boys Town youngsters marched in a May Day parade in 1920. Father Flanagan, at left, celebrated with the boys as the parade wound through neighborhood streets near downtown Omaha.

LEFT: For many years, Boys Town supporters treated the youth to a Fourth of July cookout complete with hot dogs and soda pop.

BELOW: Father Peter is surrounded by a cast of spooky, funny, and cleverly costumed characters at Halloween in 1989. Dressing up for trick or treating is another of those fun moments when Boys Town youth can just be kids and create a lifetime memory.

RIGHT: Flag-waving youth commemorate Veterans Day with an informal parade across the Boys Town campus.

BELOW: Under Father Flanagan's watchful eye, a small army of boys dressed as Pilgrims process in a 1920 Ak-Sar-Ben Parade honoring the tercentenary of the *Mayflower*'s landing at Plymouth.

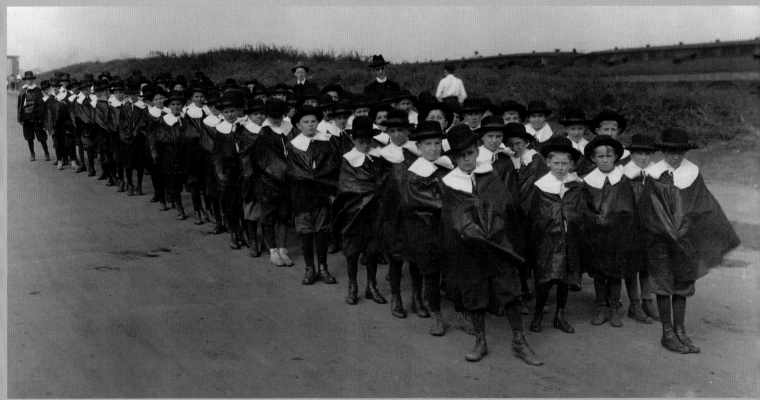

A staff member in a Pilgrim garb carves the Thanksgiving turkey for a table of boys in the Great Hall in 1974. This would be one of the last times all the boys would gather together for this holiday feast. In the years that followed, as the family-style residential program was implemented campus wide, the boys and their Family-Teachers in each Family Home began having their own Thanksgiving Day dinner, with the youth helping to prepare and serve the food.

ABOVE: Christmas pageants have been a tradition at Boys Town since the early years of the Home. These younger boys, dressed as angels and Wise Men, acted out the Christmas story on the altar of Dowd Chapel (left). Today, Wegner School students put on *The Greatest Story Ever Told* at Christmastime (right), using their musical and acting skills to share the holiday spirit with staff members and visitors.

BELOW: When the boys lived in dormitories, the Christmas season included competitions to see which dorm could create the best holiday display. These boys outdid themselves with a large, tinsel-covered tree surrounded by a snow-covered village with its own railroad system.

LEFT: On Christmas Day, the boys eagerly tore into their presents, many of which were donated by Boys Town supporters. Caregivers made sure every boy knew the joy of opening a gift purchased just for him.

BELOW: Christmas may have looked different once youth began living in Family Homes, but the thrill of opening presents on Christmas morning was still as special as ever. For many boys and girls, the first real holiday celebration of their lives was the first Christmas they spent at Boys Town.

LEFT: The boys and girls had a ball on New Year's Eve as they prepared to usher in 1990.

BELOW: In recent years, a new tradition in the form of a Hanukkah parade has been a highlight of the holiday season at Boys Town. Jewish members of the Omaha community drive to the Village, where Boys Town youth, administrators, and staff members greet them. A youth lights the candles of a Menorah and the group celebrates with music and dancing.

Hitting All the Right Notes

Bands and orchestras. Traveling road shows. Choirs. Live radio and television performances. Record albums. Concerts and performances at sports events. All of these musical and entertainment opportunities have

struck a harmonious chord throughout Boys Town's history, serving both as creative outlets for the youth and ways to show how young lives were being changed thanks to the public's support of Boys Town's mission.

In the early days, Father Flanagan believed learning to play a musical instrument was a fine way for his boys to master a skill through practice and self-discipline. Once a number of the boys were able to play with proficiency, Father Flanagan hired band directors to organize and lead the group of young musicians. One of the first directors was Dan Desdunes, an African American musician whose hiring was a groundbreaking event that illustrated Boys Town's commitment to diversity, both in its staff and the youth it served.

The boys also used their musical and stage talents to drum up financial support for Boys Town. Billed as the "World's Greatest Juvenile Entertainers," troupes of boys traveled to Nebraska towns in horse-drawn wagons (and later by train) to put on shows and ask for donations.

In the 1950s, the Boys Town Acapella Choir, under the direction of Father Francis Schmitt, gained national acclaim on annual tours that took them to cities

across the United States and Japan, Canada, and Cuba. Carnegie Hall, President Truman, Ed Sullivan, and Disney World all hosted the famous group over several decades. The choir also performed on television and radio programs and was featured as part of live television broadcasts of Christmas Midnight Mass from Boys Town's Dowd Chapel. Later, the choir recorded record albums with the Everly Brothers and Gordon MacRae.

Today, the Voices of Boys Town, a choral group of girls and boys, regularly performs at Boys Town ceremonies and often sings the National Anthem before college and professional sporting events. The Boys Town Marching Band plays at sporting events and marches in parades. Even Boys Town alumni have a chance to relive their glory days, practicing as a choir and singing at Mass during Boys Town Alumni Association's reunion conventions.

In this section, a curtain call is offered for the role music and entertainment have played in helping Boys Town youth lead well-rounded lives.

Dan Desdunes (far right, in overcoat) was a well-known African American musician and civil rights advocate from New Orleans who led the Boys Town Band in the early days of the Home. Hiring Desdunes for such a high profile position, where he served as an instructor and a role model for the boys, was further proof of Father Flanagan's efforts to bring diversity to the Home's work, both in the youth who received care and the staff who provided it.

In the 1920s, the Father Flanagan's Boys' Show traveled in horse-drawn wagons (and later by train) to small communities across the Midwest, singing, dancing, playing the favorite songs of the day, and performing skits for crowds in order to raise funds and increase the public's awareness about Boys Town. Local families welcomed the youngsters, often providing meals and posing for photos.

ABOVE: In 1925, the Boys Town Band marched in a parade in Omaha that celebrated the seventh annual American Legion Convention. Father Flanagan rode on a float with a sign that proudly proclaimed, "Father Flanagan Takes Homeless Boys." This photo was taken in front of the *Omaha Daily News* offices.

RIGHT: Concerts in famous venues like New York's Carnegie Hall and live national radio broadcasts had made the Boys Town Acapella Choir world famous by the late 1930s. Sometimes called America's answer to Austria's Vienna Boys' Choir, the Boys Town group was comprised of youngsters of all ages, many of whom started their vocal training once they moved to the Home.

Another specialized area of entertainment the boys enjoyed was baton twirling, which was an essential skill for drum majors in the marching band. These grade school boys were learning the finer points of baton positioning in this 1940s class.

Boys Town had both a high school band and a grade school band in the 1950s. The boys learned to read music, play instruments, and perform as a finely tuned unit. Being part of a musical group at Boys Town was a proud achievement and allowed the residents to represent their Home during performances at special events and shows for visiting dignitaries.

Boys Town's music programs of the 1960s did not ignore classical music, with a string ensemble that served as yet another outlet for the boys' talents.

RIGHT: During a tour in 1979, the Boys Town Choir appeared with the Osmond Brothers on a television program called *Superkids*. The choir provided back-up vocals as Jimmy Osmond (foreground) sang the Boys Town anthem, "He Ain't Heavy . . . He's My Brother."

BELOW: A procession of giant balloon characters followed the Boys Town Marching Band during a parade in downtown Omaha in the 1990s. The band was a well-received representative of the Home that helped keep Boys Town in the public's eye and showed how young people were able to overcome their troubled pasts and achieve their goals.

The Voices of Boys Town open a 1991 College World Series baseball game in Omaha with a rousing version of the National Anthem. The Voices of Boys Town eventually became the main vocal musical group after the Home began accepting girls in 1979. They regularly perform at sporting events and other public ceremonies, locally and regionally. Above, a recent edition of the group performs at Omaha's Holland Performing Arts Center as part of a Christmas concert.

Once a citizen of Boys Town, always a citizen of Boys Town. The Boys Town Alumni Choir brings together former youth from many different eras during Boys Town Alumni Association Biennial Conventions at the Home. After a practice session in Dowd Chapel, the singers provide music for Sunday Mass on the last day of the reunion event.

Stage plays like this production of *Rumplestiltskin* at the Boys Town Music Hall give the boys and girls an opportunity to hone their acting skills and entertain audiences.

The Boys Town Marching Band takes the field during halftime of a football game in 2015. Just as in the early days of the Home, music is an essential component of learning, discipline, and teamwork for the youth and an enjoyable outlet for self-expression.

Be Our Guests!

Both the Village of Boys Town and Boys Town's national sites have welcomed a multitude of famous guests and other visitors over the years. From Babe Ruth to Jackie Joyner-Kersee, from Harry Truman to Laura Bush, from Bob Hope to Kathy Ireland, athletes, politicians, entertainers, and other celebrities have visited to learn about the mission and sometimes lend their star power to promote Boys Town's work.

Father Flanagan actively solicited these visits, inviting the popular movie stars and athletes of the 1920s and 1930s to tour the Village and meet the boy citizens. The parade of celebrities continued during the tenures of his successors, bringing much-needed publicity to the Home and providing a special moment and memory for the children. In the 1960s, the recently completed Boys Town Music Hall played host to international theatre troupes and traveling symphonies. In 1968, Senator Robert Kennedy made a stop at Boys Town while campaigning for president.

Since 1968, Boys Town youth have had the opportunity to meet many famous athletes who served as guest speakers at the annual Boys Town Booster Banquet fundraiser. Boys Town also has welcomed a number of well-known recipients of the Father Flanagan Service to Youth Award. Other notable visitors include former Secretary of State Colin Powell and the Prince of Monaco. At Boys Town's national sites, famous guests have included Dana White, president of the Ultimate Fighting Championship (UFC), and Josh Temple, host of several popular home improvement reality shows on the HGTV and DIY networks.

While famous people have played a role in Boys Town's history and development over the years, the Village also has become a must-see stop for tourists and travelers who want to experience the spirit of caring that lives there. Every year, tens of thousands of people drive through the Village and tour its many attractions.

This section is dedicated to all Boys Town visitors, especially those who have made a stop at Boys Town part of their celebrity itinerary.

Humorist Will Rogers gets a firm handshake from one of the boys as Father Flanagan looks on during Rogers's visit to the Home in 1928.

During a 1945 appearance at Boys Town, actor/singer Bing Crosby crooned his way into the hearts of his admiring audience. Crosby would later donate radios to the Home so the boys could listen to music in their dormitories.

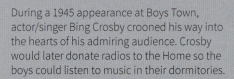

LEFT: President Truman, a great admirer of Father Flanagan, was welcomed by the Boys Town Choir and Father Edmond Walsh during a 1948 stop. The visit came several months after Father Flanagan's death

BELOW: Television personalities often found their way to Boys Town in the 1950s. One of the most popular was James Garner, best known as the star of TV's *Maverick* western series. Garner, accompanied by Boys Town Executive Director Monsignor Nicholas Wegner, drew a large crowd of young fans.

Boys Town was, and remains, a popular stop for vacationing families from all over the country. This family took a break from traveling in their Ford station wagon to tour the Home in 1963.

ABOVE: A student presents Lady Bird Johnson with an honorary Boys Town High School diploma at a welcoming ceremony in the 1960s.

BELOW: This group of visitors found a shady spot under a tree for a picnic while touring the Village in 1975. Boys Town welcomes thousands of tourists throughout the year, and Boys Town youth often lead large bus tour groups, providing historical information about the Home and sharing their unique perspective as residents.

In May 1968, presidential candidate Robert Kennedy made a swing through Nebraska while on the campaign trail and stopped at Boys Town. During his visit, Kennedy briefly spoke to the boys and then began a tour of the Village in the back of a convertible. As Kennedy's car pulled away, a group of boys ran behind it. When one of the boys—nine-year-old Joe Marsh—fell to the pavement and cut his lip, Kennedy told his driver to stop and asked one of his assistants to bring Marsh to the car. Kennedy checked to see if the youngster was all right, wiped his bloody lip with a handkerchief, and gave him a hug. Three weeks later, Kennedy was assassinated in Los Angeles after winning the California primary.

ABOVE: This Boy Scout troop from Japan visited Boys Town in the summer of 1976, posing in front of a statue that symbolizes Father Flanagan's great commitment to helping wayward children.

RIGHT: Blessed Mother Teresa of Calcutta journeyed to Boys Town in 1976 to receive the Father Flanagan Award for Service to Youth. Presenting the award are Monsignor Robert Hupp (right), Boys Town's executive director, and Archbishop Daniel Sheehan of the Archdiocese of Omaha.

AIDS/HIV spokesperson Ryan White (right) visited a Boys Town High School classroom in 1988 to talk about his experiences after being diagnosed with AIDS at age thirteen. A hemophiliac, White became infected from a contaminated blood treatment. He and his mother fought for his right to attend school, gaining international attention as a voice of reason about the disease. White died in 1990 at age eighteen, just months before Congress passed the AIDS bill that bears his name—the Ryan White CARE (Comprehensive AIDS Resources Emergency) Act.

ABOVE: A Boys Town staff member explains a Hall of History exhibit to Wanda Johnson, 1989's Miss Indian America.

RIGHT: In 1938, child actor Bobs Watson captured America's hearts as the lovable Pee Wee in the movie *Boys Town*. Fifty-three years later, Watson returned to Boys Town as a Methodist minister to share a special sermon during the dedication of the newly built Chambers Chapel. Here, Watson talks about the filming of the movie with a Boys Town resident.

ABOVE: Michael Jordan received a warm greeting from a young Boys Town resident when the NBA superstar came to the Home in 1990 to receive the Father Flanagan Award for Service to Youth.

RIGHT: General Colin Powell "ordered" Boys Town students to get a good education when he and his wife, Alma, paid a visit to Boys Town in 1992. The couple chatted with Boys Town residents and Powell gave a brief speech in Palrang Memorial Field House. Mrs. Powell has been the chair of the America's Promise Alliance, which has named Boys Town one of America's "100 Best Communities for Young People" several times.

RIGHT: In 1999, Indianapolis Colts quarterback Peyton Manning worked out his throwing arm for the youth prior to giving the keynote address at that year's Boys Town Booster Banquet. Manning had just finished his rookie season with the Indianapolis Colts and joined the ranks of other notable sports figures who have visited Boys Town as booster banquet speakers.

BELOW: Mickey Rooney, another star of the *Boys Town* movie, made several visits to Boys Town over the years. In 2003, on the film's sixty-fifth anniversary, he was named Boys Town Mayor for Life.

ABOVE: First Lady Laura Bush talked with a family of girls at their Family Home during a 2006 visit to Boys Town. Mrs. Bush came to the Village to receive the Father Flanagan Award for Service to Youth.

LEFT: Albert II, the Prince of Monaco, toured the Hall of History with National Executive Director Father Steven Boes when he visited Boys Town in 2007.

Proudly Answering the Call

As sailors, they braved the perils of the open sea; as airmen, they took the fight to the enemy high above the earth; as soldiers, they battled their way through steamy jungles, over scorching desert sands, across

muddy farm fields, and up and down frigid mountain ranges. They served in different branches of the service and fought in different times and places. But they all called Boys Town home.

Since Boys Town's founding in 1917, thousands of its former citizens have proudly served in the country's armed forces, both in wartime and in peace. Nearly seventy are known to have died in combat, and scores more were wounded. From Pearl Harbor, where three of Father Flanagan's "boys" were killed in the attack that drew the United States into World War II, to the most recent conflicts to defeat America's enemies in the Middle East, former citizens of Boys Town have answered the nation's call, representing themselves honorably and bravely on the battlefield.

In peacetime, Boys Town alumni have distinguished themselves as leaders and loyal watchmen of freedom, at home and abroad. For many, military service continued the structure and discipline they learned at Boys Town and provided a springboard for their success in future careers.

Boys Town is proud of all of its former citizens—men and women—who have served in uniform and made the sacrifices such service requires. They hold a special place of honor at Boys Town and at all of its sites, where children have found healing and hope for one hundred years.

This section salutes those former Boys Town youth who have served and honors those who made the ultimate sacrifice.

Boys Town alum Joe Ortega, class of 1947, proudly named his F-51 Mustang *Spirit of Boys Town* during the Korean War, where he flew dozens of combat missions. Ortega also would see combat in the Vietnam War and serve as a training instructor during a long U.S. Air Force career.

The surprise Japanese attack on the American naval base at Pearl Harbor on December 7, 1941, drew the United States into World War II. Three former Boys Town boys serving on warships that day lost their lives in the raid. George Thompson (left) and William Debbs (center right) were on the USS *Oklahoma* when it was sunk by Japanese torpedo bombers. Donald Monroe (right) was helping to prepare breakfast for the crew of the USS *Arizona* shortly before a bomb hit its forward ammunition magazine and destroyed the ship. A fourth Boys Town boy, Walter Clark, survived the attack while stationed aboard the USS *West Virginia*. Clark would later see action in the Pacific Theater as the United States drove toward total victory.

Vernon Baker arrived at Boys Town at age ten and spent three years at the Village in the late 1930s. With the support and encouragement of Father Flanagan, Baker went on to graduate with honors from high school in Clarinda, Iowa. He joined the U.S. Army in 1941 and fought alongside fellow African Americans in the Ninety-second Infantry Division. From his service in Italy during World War II, Baker earned a Purple Heart, a Bronze Star, and the Distinguished Service Cross. In 1997, he was awarded the Medal of Honor by President Bill Clinton. The ceremony at the White House came fifty years after Baker's service due to racial disparity in the way Medal of Honor recipients were selected during World War II. His official Medal of Honor citation reads: "When his company was stopped by the concentration of fire from several machine gun emplacements, he crawled to one position and destroyed it, killing three Germans. Continuing forward, he attacked an enemy observation post and killed two occupants. With the aid of one of his men, Lieutenant Baker attacked two more machine gun nests, killing or wounding the four enemy soldiers occupying these positions. He then covered the evacuation of the wounded personnel of his company by occupying an exposed position and drawing the enemy's fire."

Serving as a corporal in the U.S. Marine Corps during the Korean War, Bob Mitchell was wounded in action twice. He later served two tours of duty in Vietnam, where he was wounded three times and earned a Silver Star for bravery. After twenty years in the U.S. Marines, Mitchell returned to Boys Town to work for his brother Charlie (also a Boys Town grad) at the Boys Town Print Shop.

Boys Town alum Lloyd Bucher was the commander of the USS *Pueblo* when it was attacked and captured by North Korean forces in January 1968. One crewman was killed and several others, including Bucher, were wounded. Bucher and his remaining eighty-two-man crew spent 336 days in captivity, suffering torture and malnutrition, before being released in late December 1968. Bucher retired from the U.S. Navy in 1973 after a nearly twenty-eight-year career. In 1990, Bucher and his crewmembers received long-overdue Prisoner of War (POW) medals.

Former Boys Town Citizens Known to Have Died While in Military Service
(with graduation date and service branch)

WWII• MORRIS L. ASHMEAD 1933 USN • JACK C. BAILEY 1941 USA • GERALD F. BLOCK 1935 USA • CHARLES W. BRAZDA 1936 USA • DUANE E. BROWN 1941 USA • JAMES G. BURNS 1938 USA • WILLIAM H. CAPPS 1932 USA • EDWARD J. CARR 1941 USN • JAMES A. CONROY 1941 USN • VERNON A. CROWLEY 1941 USN • EDWIN C. DE ROSIER 1935 USA • WILLIAM DEBBS 1937 USN • FRANKLIN R. DENNICK 1936 USAAF • ANTON P. DRUSKIS 1935 USA • GEORGE F. FRITZ 1940 USA • THOMAS A. GAPA 1936 USMC • ROBERT E. GOUGH 1936 USAAF • DALE W. GRAFE 1939 USA • ROBERT F. GRANT 1929 USN • RICHARD HAIDUSEK 1941 USN • MARVIN D. HARDING 1932 USA • CHARLES W. HOLMAN 1922 USAAF • JAMES P. KEANE 1939 USA • JOHN C. LECOUNT 1934 USA •

ON · KENNETH L HEARN · JOHN M
N E LAMBERT · ELTON LE BOUEF Jr ·
RN D McCOMB · JOHNNIE LEE McD
S P MOLESE · MICHAEL E PETERSON
OW · FORREST M STAFFORD ·
M · GREGORY J VANDEWALLE · JOHN
· JULIAN ALONZO · JOE ARREGUIN ·
· ALLAN R CHAFFIN ·
BERT G FULLER · ROGER L GARRETT ·
· NORMAN R HOCKER ·

ABOVE: John Mollison, who graduated from Boys Town in 1964, retired as a colonel from the U.S. Air Force after a distinguished twenty-three-year military career. Mollison flew 171 combat missions as a F-4 Phantom navigator during the Vietnam War, earning three Distinguished Flying Crosses and eight air medals. After retiring from the air force, he returned to Boys Town to serve as an administrator and later as the director of the Boys Town Alumni Association.

LEFT: U.S. Army veteran Ron Dennis (center, holding hat) safely returned to Boys Town in 1991 after serving in Iraq during Operation Desert Storm. Dennis joined Father Peter and several current youth in prayers for former Boys Town residents who also were in the armed forces and still fighting overseas.

CHARLES C. MAGNUSSON 1943 USN · JOSEPH J. MARINO 1939 USN · ROBERT E. MCCARTHY 1939 USMC · PATRICK K. MCKENNA 1941 USN · DONALD MONROE 1936 USN · DAVID H. NEWBERRY 1941 USN · KATSU OKIDA 1943 USA · WILLIAM PARNELL 1943 USMC · MARTIN F. PELUCH 1939 USN · ARTHUR C. PFEIFER 1942 USA · MAYNARD R. REINER 1937 USA · LOUIS A. REWITZER 1932 USMM · GERALD R. SALLENG 1930 USA · CECIL H. SMITH 1934 USA · PAUL C. SOLT 1935 USA · EARL S. THARP 1936 USAAF · GEORGE A. THOMPSON 1934 USN · CLARENCE J. VAINREB 1936 USA · RAYMOND A. VORCE 1931 USA · GEORGE M. WICKENHISER 1920 USMM · ROBERT I. WISKOCHIL 1938 USMC · CHARLES E. WOOD 1926 USA · **KOREAN ERA**· GENE P. BLAKE 1952 USA ·

ABOVE: Boys Town is extremely proud of its war veterans and all of its former residents—men and women—who have served their country in uniform. They hold a special place of honor at the Home and are part of a tradition of service to country that began nearly a century ago and continues today. In 1991, Boys Town dedicated a memorial to its former residents who served in the United States Armed Forces. Inscribed on the memorial are these words from President John F. Kennedy's inaugural address: "Ask not what your country can do for you, ask what you can do for your country." Those words embody the ideal of service and sacrifice of so many who call Boys Town their home.

RIGHT: Sergeant Huey Fassbender was killed in Iraq on January 6, 2005, along with six fellow soldiers when an improvised explosive devise (IED) hit the Bradley Fighting Vehicle in which they were riding. Fassbender, twenty-four, was the first Boys Town alum to die in combat since the Vietnam War. He was serving in a National Guard unit out of his home state of Louisiana and received the Purple Heart and a Bronze Star.

THOMAS J. BLATARIC 1945 USA • MYRON L. CUTLER 1945 USA • GORDON F. ENOS 1947 USA • ARNOLD LEDERER 1942 USA • JOHN T. LEWIS 1952 USA • JAMES R. SHEPARD 1944 USMC **VIETNAM ERA•** TERRANCE R. ANDERSON 1961 USA • RICHARD B. BENNETT 1962 USMC • GERALD J. BERGER 1958 USMC • LARRY J. BOSTED 1963 USMC • DAVID M. CARR 1964 USN • ROBERT J. CORDOVA 1965 USN • DOUGLAS L. FREDERICK 1966 USMC • LOUIS M. GARCIA 1967 USA • GIUSEPPE J. GIANNELLI 1964 USA • GEORGE A. HAIN 1967 USA • RAYMOND C. HANIK 1967 USA • KEVIN W. HARRIS 1970 USMC • THOMAS A. HAUSERMAN 1967 USN • RUBEN M. HERNANDEZ 1951 USA • WILLIAM F. HEWITT 1963 USMC •

LEFT: In her ten years in the U.S. Marine Corps, from 1993 to 2003, Boys Town graduate Michelle Rock Fredricks became an expert in intelligence analysis and served in a number of posts overseas and in the Washington, D.C., area. From 1996 to 1999 she was a liaison between senior U.S. Marine Corps officials and the chairman of the Joint Chiefs of Staff. She later worked as a contractor for the Defense Threat Reduction Agency and supported combatant commanders during Operation Iraqi Freedom and Operation Enduring Freedom. Rock Fredricks reunited with Father Val Peter in Washington, D.C., during a Boys Town Alumni Association event several years ago.

ABOVE: Firefighting became Greg Hoyt's specialty during his service in the U.S. Air Force. Hoyt, a 2006 Boys Town graduate, was stationed at McConnell Air Force Base in Wichita, Kansas, and later was deployed to Udeid Air Base in Qatar in the Middle East.

LEFT: When former President Gerald Ford passed away in December 2006, Boys Town graduate Stephanie Gaudreau was hand selected as the only woman for the Navy Ceremonial Guard of Honor that stood watch over Ford's casket. The Guard of Honor was present during a prayer service for Ford in Palm Desert, California, and during a later ceremony in Grand Rapids, Michigan. Gaudreau joined the U.S. Navy in early 2006 shortly after graduating early from Boys Town.

THOMAS G. HUDSON 1957 USA • LEONARD A. HULTQUIST 1954 USMC • JOSEPH F. KEENEY 1967 USA • RICHARD J. KREDELL 1957 USN • WILLIAM C. LEBBS 1951 USAF • ROBERT E. LUTZ 1955 USN • HOWARD J. MOORE 1966 USA • NATHANIEL H. MURPHY 1967 USA • STEPHEN M. NOGGLE 1964 USA • JAMES W. SAMPERS 1956 USN • JOHN K. SCHMITT 1966 USA • ROBERT J. SIMONS 1944 USN • FORREST M. STAFFORD 1953 USN • ZBIGNIEW J. TOMASZEWSKI 1963 USN • JOHN E. WALKER 1958 USN • THOMAS R. WEIL (GANUNG) 1954 USAF • DAVID J. WILLETTE 1956 USN • **COLD WAR ERA** • JAMES T. ACKLIN 1968 USAF • **IRAQ/AFGHANISTAN** • HUEY P. L. FASSBENDER 1997 USA

A Cornerstone of Healing

When Father Flanagan founded Boys Town in 1917, he did so with a deep and abiding faith in God and a passionate concern for America's hurting, troubled children. Those rock-solid underpinnings of

spirituality and humanity have been inseparably linked throughout Boys Town's history and continue to serve as the foundation of the life-changing care boys and girls receive and the spiritual environment in which they learn and grow.

While promoting and encouraging a faith life for the children in its care, Boys Town has always remained nondenominational and nonsectarian. Boys Town accepts children of all religions and makes sure they are able to attend worship services and practice their religious traditions. Caregivers help children grow or start their faith lives without proselytizing and with an utmost respect for the beliefs of each child.

The presence of two churches in the Village of Boys Town reflects the importance of spirituality in Boys Town's mission. Dowd Chapel is where Catholic youth worship, and Chambers Chapel is the place of worship for Protestant youth. Worship services are also open to the public. Children who profess other faiths are taken to their places of worship in the community.

Boys Town strives to instill in children the central position God must hold in their lives if they are to recover from their emotional wounds and find peace.

When boys and girls take that message to heart, they grow in their faith during their time at Boys Town and maintain a strong spiritual life long after they leave.

Father Flanagan's dream of helping lost children of all faiths was uniquely ecumenical in 1917 and is a testimony to his love for God and for his fellow human beings. That spirit flourished under the leadership of his first three successors— Monsignor Wegner, Monsignor Hupp, and Father Peter—who carried on Boys Town's work to lift children out of the darkness and into the light.

Today, National Executive Director Father Steven Boes echoes the powerful spiritual messages of his predecessors to the children: "Faith is the foundation that gives us hope. It replenishes the spirit and gives rise to new beginnings. With the help of God's love, you can find a new direction in your life. Listen carefully to God in prayer and to those around who love you. Leave behind the false self— who you are not—and find your real self."

This section highlights some of the spiritual icons, symbols, and events that have spiritually lifted up and empowered Boys Town youth.

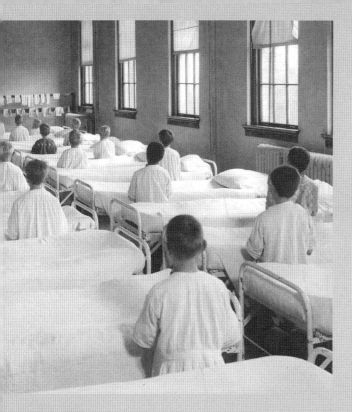

LEFT: Starting the day with morning prayers became an important part of each boy's daily routine in the Boys Town dormitories of the 1920s.

BELOW: Boys Town's original chapel was located in the basement of the Omaha Building from 1923 to 1940, where Father Flanagan said Mass and delivered his Sunday sermons to the boys.

Boys Town has always sought to meet the spiritual needs of its youth, regardless of their denomination or beliefs. Dowd Chapel (below) became the spiritual center of the Village for Catholic youth after its construction in 1941. Protestant youth worshipped at the Nativity Chapel (left and bottom left) in the Boys Town Field House.

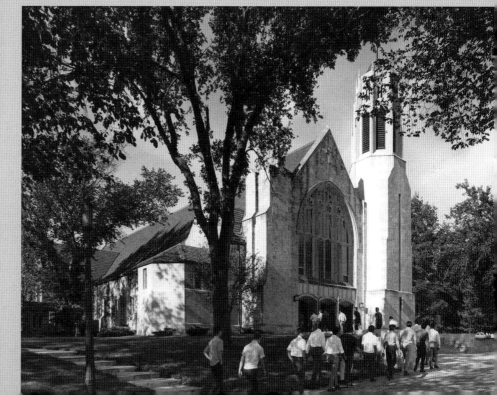

Chapel Facts

Chambers Chapel's majestic spire rises seventy-one feet above the ground

Chambers Chapel seats four hundred.

The aisle windows in Chambers Chapel depict stories of the Old and New Testaments, with special emphasis on issues important to children.

Despite its bronze-clad doors and heavy wood timber hammerbeam trusses, Chambers Chapel feels open and airy due to the beautifully crafted stained-glass windows.

Dowd Chapel was inspired by fifteenth-century Gothic churches of rural England. It was dedicated in 1941, with the entire cost being just under $200,000.

Dowd Chapel seats seven hundred.

The Carillonic Tower in Dowd Chapel consists of twenty-five notes in two full octaves. The notes may be played by hand from a keyboard or be automatically operated by a clock.

The largest and most spectacular stained-glass window dominates the building façade above Dowd's main entrance. The church's Reuter organ is unique and has 3,892 pipes in the choir loft.

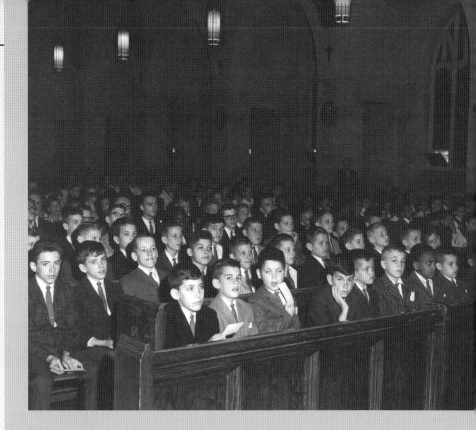

ABOVE: Younger youth in their Sunday best filled the pews during a Sunday Mass at Dowd Chapel in 1966.

BELOW: Two boys pray at the tomb of Father Flanagan. The tomb is housed in an enclosure attached to Dowd Chapel and is a popular place of reflection for Boys Town youth and visitors to the Village.

A group of older boys hold candles and wear stoles bearing their names during their Confirmation service in the 1970s.

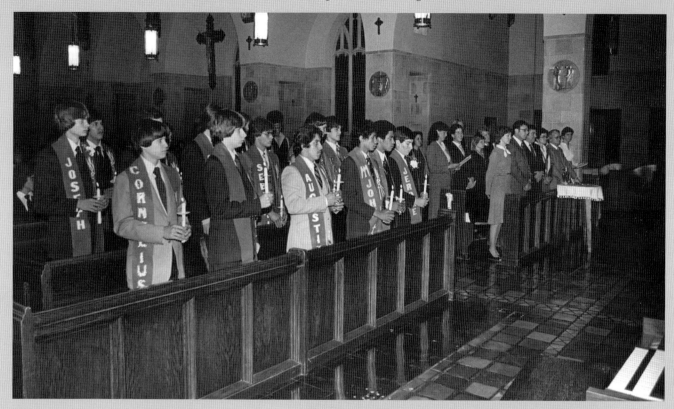

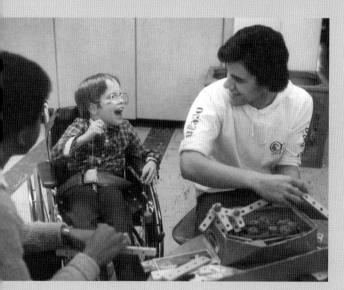

Providing opportunities for Boys Town youth to learn the importance of serving the community is another essential element of helping them build their spiritual lives. Whether it is volunteering to play a game with handicapped youth, spending time with senior citizens at a retirement home, or picking up trash at a lakeside park, youth learn the value of giving back and sharing their blessings with others.

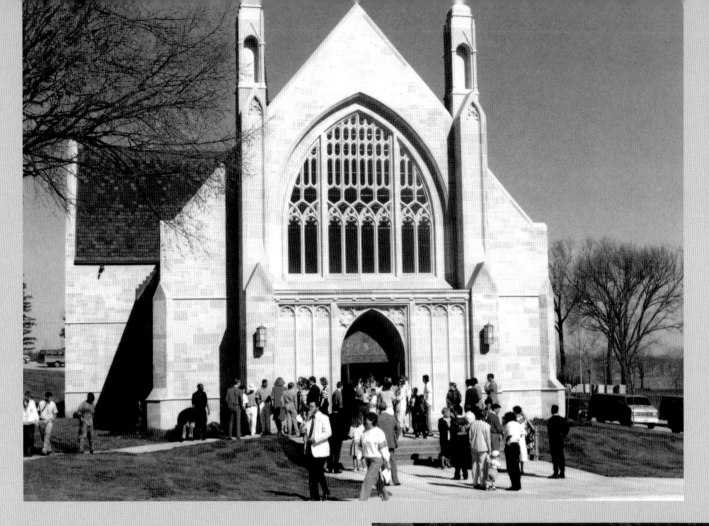

Protestant youth at Boys Town rejoiced at having their own church in the Village with the dedication of Chambers Chapel (above and right) in 1991. The chapel boasts unique flooring around the altar made up of hundreds of handmade tiles, each bearing a design created by a Boys Town youth. The youth also helped put the tiles in place (bottom right). The spacious sanctuary receives natural light through unique rosepoint stained-glass windows (below).

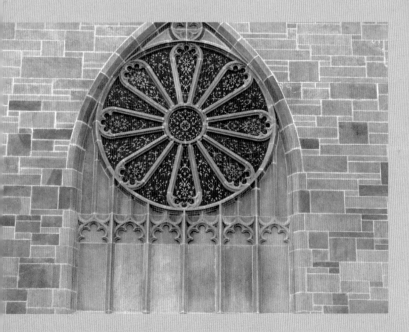

LEFT: Many former Boys Town boys have become priests and ministers, often following a calling that began during their time at the Home. Twin brothers George (left) and Benjamin Markwell, who graduated from Boys Town in 1956, both were ordained priests in the mid-1960s and celebrated their first Mass at Dowd Chapel. In 2015, the brothers led a celebratory Mass during a Boys Town Alumni Association Convention to mark their golden jubilee in the priesthood.

BELOW: A Confirmation class of Boys Town boys and girls gathered with Archbishop Eldon Curtiss at Dowd Chapel in 2000

In 2006, Father Steven Boes, the newly appointed executive director of Boys Town, participated in a religious ceremony in a Boys Town Family Home for Native American youth. Father Boes had served as the director of the St. Augustine Indian Mission in Winnebago, Nebraska, before accepting the Boys Town position.

The Next Person You Meet... Might Be from Boys Town

Over the past century, nearly 40,000 boys and girls have called the Village of Boys Town or one of Boys Town's national sites their home. Each one of these children brought to Boys Town a very personal, very real story of heartache, pain, loneliness, trouble, or loss. Most went on to write new, uplifting chapters for their lives that might never have happened without Boys Town's help and guidance.

So many young lives have been positively influenced by Boys Town that it is a common occurrence to meet someone working in a restaurant or a bank or a business office who proudly says, "I lived at Boys Town" or "I'm a Boys Town grad." That's where the title of this section originated, because the next person one meets **might** have grown up at Boys Town.

Boys Town is extremely proud of its alumni and their accomplishments. Former youth have become doctors, lawyers, business owners, musicians, skilled craftsman, construction workers, teachers, soldiers, administrators, photographers, chefs, and just about any other profession or occupation one can think of. Many entered the childcare field, and some returned to Boys Town to "give back" by helping youth who are struggling with life's challenges, just as they once did.

In the early 1950s, the Boys Town Alumni Association was formed to champion the dream and values of Father Flanagan through leadership and to unite and grow Boys Town's alumni family. Every two years, alums of all ages—from their twenties to their nineties—gather at the Village of Boys Town, Nebraska, for a biennial convention. They renew old friendships, relive the memories they made as Boys Town citizens, and work on ways to further support Boys Town's mission for future generations of youth. On in-between years, the alumni association organizes a mini-convention in a selected city—often where Boys Town has a national site.

Each year, the Boys Town Alumni Association provides thousands of dollars in scholarships to graduating seniors of Boys Town High School. Scholarships also are available to help alumni finish their college education or enhance their career-related skills.

This section features a number of Boys Town alumni who have proudly represented Boys Town as productive citizens and who are living proof of Father Flanagan's declaration, "When you help a child today, you write the history of tomorrow."

LEFT: Father Flanagan welcomes back a trio of former boys who visited Boys Town while on leave from military duty during World War II. Boys Town was a common destination for servicemen who had grown up at Boys Town and wanted to see their "home" again before going overseas.

BELOW: In July 1955, Monsignor Wegner (left) addresses a gathering of former boys at one of the first Boys Town Alumni Association Conventions. Early on, the wives of alums solidified their connection to the Home by forming the Boys Town Alumni Auxiliary (right). Today, the auxiliary remains active in organizing and supporting convention events.

Besides reuniting old classmates and bringing former residents back to the Home, alumni association conventions were meant to be fun. Dances (like this one in 1961), socials, dinners, church services, golf outings, and tours of Boys Town are among the many activities that have entertained alumni and their spouses over the years.

Alum Renteria Links Boys Town's Past to Present

As one of Boys Town's oldest alumni, ninety-three-year-old Joe Renteria is Boys Town's link to its past and a witness to its present and future. Looking back, Renteria says Boys Town showed him where family life begins. "Being in a family setting is good," Renteria said. "The way things are set up now here at Boys Town is the way it should be. A hug feels so good. That little sign shows that someone genuinely cares about you. That is the way it should be, and I hope that is the way it will continue forever."

When Renteria arrived at Father Flanagan's Home for Boys in October 1933, his options were running out. Renteria had bounced around from orphanage to orphanage. He was in one in Leavenworth, Kansas, when he decided he couldn't take it anymore. So he ran away. While he doesn't recall exactly how he got to Omaha, he had heard enough about Father Edward Flanagan and his home for boys there to believe it might be a good place for him.

A lot has changed at Boys Town since Renteria left in 1935. But one thing Renteria says remains the same is how Boys Town cares for youth and families.

Renteria returned to the Village of Boys Town to visit what he considers his only real home growing up. He spent time at the Hall of History reminiscing and looking through items from his time as a Boys Town citizen. As one of Boys Town's oldest living alumni, he says he feels honored to talk about his time there and to know Father Flanagan himself influenced his life. "I was one of the older boys here at the time," Renteria said. "Father Flanagan left a lot of decisions up to me when it came time to decide what I was going to make of my life. I think some of the simple things I learned were some of the most important. He taught me to follow the rules. He also taught me that we all have choices. The key is that we have to take responsibility when we make a choice. I never did forget that and it has stayed with me my entire life."

Renteria was one of the first candidates to run for mayor at Boys Town. While he didn't win the election, his picture is prominently displayed in the Hall of History along with the eventual mayoral winner. Renteria was able to serve his fellow students as a member of the Boys Town City Council.

Upon leaving Boys Town in 1935, Renteria lived with a foster family and graduated high school in 1936. He joined the U.S. Army and served three years and then moved to the U.S. Navy. As a navy photographer for the next seventeen years, he took on numerous projects while moving from ship to ship. He also spent time at a number of famous bases, including Pearl Harbor in Hawaii and the Bikini Islands when testing of the atomic bomb was underway.

After military service, Renteria found a new home in Southern California. He spent the next thirty years as a photographer for San Diego State University. He and his beloved wife, Jill, were married for seventy-one years and had seven children. Jill passed away in 2009.

Over the years, Renteria, a Native American, found time to work with numerous groups serving his people. He was a chairperson for American Indian Human Resources, American Indian Health Services, and American Indian Child and Family Services.

Through a life of dignity and service, Renteria has proudly represented Boys Town and carried on Father Flanagan's legacy.

LEFT: In 1976, the Boys Town Alumni Association spearheaded an effort to fund the renovation of the Father Flanagan House, creating a museum where visitors could learn more about this extraordinary priest and his mission to help America's children. This was the United States' bicentennial year, and Omaha Mayor Ed Zorinsky presented a proclamation to Monsignor Hupp and association members recognizing the campaign.

BELOW: Alumni convention attendees gathered outside the Great Hall during a Friday night social in the 1980s.

Several former residents who played football at Boys Town later excelled at the college level and went on to play in the NFL. Ken Geddes (left), a 1963 graduate, played at the University of Nebraska and enjoyed an eight-year career with the Los Angeles Rams and the Seattle Seahawks. He later became a middle school counselor. Shaquil Barrett (right), who graduated in 2010, was a two-year starter at Colorado State University and was drafted by the Denver Broncos. In 2016, he earned a championship ring as the Broncos defeated the Carolina Panthers in Super Bowl 50.

ABOVE: William Maddux came to Boys Town in 1948 from a two-room, dirt-floor shanty on the banks of the Mississippi River. He would later graduate from Notre Dame and Georgetown University, become a prominent Chicago attorney, and serve as a Cook County judge of the circuit court. In 1986, Maddux visited Boys Town after donating money to help build a new girls' home in the Village.

BELOW: Counting his time as one of the first boys taken in by Father Flanagan and his service as a long-time employee, Al Witcofski (left) spent nearly eighty years of his life at Boys Town. Witcofski's father left him and his two brothers at the Home in 1919. After graduating, Witcofski stayed on, living on campus and initially driving Father Flanagan's car and the Boys Town bus. He later worked on the farm and in the repair shop. Witcofski, who married in 1938, was still living at Boys Town when he passed away in 2000. An alumni association vocational scholarship is named in his honor.

Two Boys Town alums strike a famous pose in front of one of Boys Town's most famous icons during the 1987 alumni convention.

Regardless of how many years they've been separated, Boys Town alums still warmly greet each other as brothers bound by their common experiences at the Home when they meet during alumni association conventions.

RIGHT: Capturing history became Cecil Stoughton's life after leaving Boys Town in 1932 following a two-year stay. He joined the U.S. Army Air Corps at the outbreak of World War II, first serving in a unit that made army training films in Hollywood and then as a combat photographer aboard a bomber in the Pacific Theater. In 1961, Stoughton's photographs of President John F. Kennedy's inauguration led to his appointment as Kennedy's official White House photographer. On November 22, 1963, Stoughton was in the motorcade carrying Kennedy through downtown Dallas when the president was assassinated. Hours later, he would take one of the most famous photographs in American history—Lyndon Johnson being sworn in as president aboard *Air Force One* as Kennedy's widow, Jacqueline, looks on. Stoughton served as Johnson's White House photographer for two years and later served as the chief photographer for the National Park Service. Stoughton died in 2008.

LEFT: After her parents passed away, Carley Kaufman (left) bounced from one group home to another before coming to the Village of Boys Town. As a resident of a Family Home, the teen became part of a new "family," receiving guidance and support from her Family-Teachers and learning life skills. Kaufman graduated from Boys Town High School and then earned a degree in nursing at Methodist Nursing College in Omaha. She works as a nurse in a hospital in Colorado.

RIGHT: Pat Garcia has a long history with Boys Town. He came to the Home from New Mexico when he was eight and graduated nine years later, in 1985. After going to college, he was hired as an Assistant Family-Teacher at Boys Town, working with youth in a Family Home. Most recently, he accepted a position as the community engagement developer for Boys Town Iowa Family Services.

LEFT: Tony Jones came to Boys Town from the tough streets of Detroit, graduating in 1988 and later earning a bachelor's degree. In 1996, he and his wife, Simone, were hired as Boys Town Family-Teachers. Since then, the couple has touched the lives of nearly two hundred youth who have lived in their Family Home at Boys Town.

RIGHT: Diana Lauritson graduated from Boys Town High School in 2001. She attended Creighton University on a full scholarship and later went to law school there, earning double master's degrees. She later joined a law firm in Arizona, heading business development and marketing for a national company. She also started her own consulting company. "I think Boys Town works long-term for people because they don't give up on you," she said. "It's not just like you're there and then you leave. They teach to build healthier relationships and they care about you. It shows you that there are better things out there."

Making Boys Town a Household Name

As Boys Town's popularity and public awareness grew over the decades, its name became synonymous with a place where troubled youth could get a second chance and make a new start.

This is why references to Boys Town in popular culture and the media abound, from comic strips to television to movies to hit records.

Perhaps Boys Town's biggest splash in the entertainment area was the 1938 Academy Award-winning motion picture *Boys Town*. Starring Spencer Tracy as Father Edward Flanagan and Mickey Rooney as the tough street kid Whitey Marsh, the movie was a huge success and garnered the Best Actor Oscar for Tracy. Tracy later presented the Oscar to Father Flanagan, who proudly displayed it on his desk in his Boys Town office. Today, the statuette is prominently featured in Boys Town's Hall of History.

Several years later, a sequel called *Men of Boys Town* was made with Tracy reprising his role as Father Flanagan. While it didn't match the success of the original, the second film did highlight the abuses of the reform school system and again increased public awareness of America's homeless and troubled children. (Rooney would visit Boys Town several times in later years to commemorate the original movie's anniversaries. Another cast member, Bobs Watson, who played Pee Wee, became a minister and returned to the Village in 1991 to deliver the homily at the dedication of Chambers Chapel, Boys Town's Protestant church.)

In 1985, a made-for-TV movie, *Miracle of the Heart: A Boys Town Story*, starring Art Carney, was filmed in the Village, giving viewing audiences a modern-day look at Boys Town and its work. As in the original *Boys Town* movie, citizens of the Village and staff members served as extras in many scenes.

The success of the original movie and subsequent films helped make Boys Town a household name around the world. References to Boys Town appeared in comic strips (*Joe Palooka*) of the 1930s and 1940s and later in television programs such as *Cheers*, *Night Court*, and *The Simpsons* and in movies like *Caddyshack* and *Superman IV*. There were also two versions of the Top 40 hit song, "He Ain't Heavy . . . He's My Brother," titled after the famous Boys Town saying, released in 1970—one by the Hollies and one by Neil Diamond.

This section highlights some of the moments when Boys Town and popular culture crossed paths and helped keep Father Flanagan's vision in the public eye.

In 1939, the popular *Joe Palooka* comic strip devoted a series to Father Flanagan and his message about caring for kids. The nationally syndicated strip was read by millions and further publicized the priest's efforts and Boys Town's reputation as a haven for children.

The 1938 movie *Boys Town* was undoubtedly one of the biggest publicity triumphs in the history of the Home. On-location shooting took place over ten sweltering summer days in July, and many of the actual Boys Town youth were featured in the film as extras. At the Oscars, the movie was nominated for five Academy Awards, including Best Picture and Best Director (Norman Taurog). Spencer Tracy won the Best Actor Oscar for his portrayal of Father Flanagan, and Eleanore Griffin and Dore Schary won the Academy Award for Best Writing, Original Story. Here, the cast and crew prepare for a scene outside the Old Main building. (Photo Courtesy of the Academy of Motion Picture Arts and Sciences)

While shooting the *Boys Town* movie, a few of the actors took the stage with Father Flanagan to talk to and entertain the boys. Here, Bobs Watson, who played Pee Wee, gets a lift from Father Flanagan so he can speak into the microphone as (left to right) Sidney Miller, Gene Reynolds, and Frankie Thomas look on.

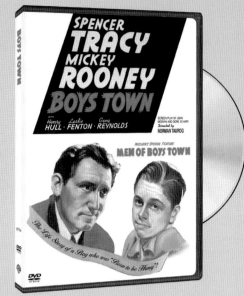

ABOVE: In 1941, *Men of Boys Town* was released as a sequel to the original *Boys Town* movie. The sequel was directed by Norman Taurog and also starred Spencer Tracy, Mickey Rooney, Bobs Watson, and several other stars from the first film. The second movie again helped keep Boys Town and its mission to care for wayward boys in the public eye. On the seventieth anniversary of *Boys Town* in 2008, the AFI Dallas International Film Festival held a special screening of the movie.

LEFT: Hailed as the "World's Largest Ball of Stamps," the ball has been a prominent feature of the Leon Myers Stamp Center in the Boys Town Visitors Center since the early 1950s. The sphere is thirty-two inches in diameter, weighs six hundred pounds, and contains a reported 4,655,000 canceled stamps, all stuck together, layer upon layer, by the Boys Town Stamp Collecting Club starting in 1953. By 1955, the ball had nearly reached its current size and was featured in the syndicated newspaper column of *Ripley's Believe It Or Not.* "The next day," according to a sign next to the ball, "crowds of people came to view the unique artifact, some traveling over one hundred miles."

Live Christmas Eve broadcasts of Midnight Mass from Boys Town's Dowd Chapel brought the Home's spiritual message into millions of American homes from the 1940s through the 1960s. For many families, the broadcast, featuring the music of the Boys Town Acapella Choir, was the highlight of their Christmas celebration.

Hollywood revisited Boys Town in 1986 to produce *Miracle of the Heart, A Boys Town Story*. Much of the made-for-TV movie was shot on location in the Village, with Boys Town youth serving as extras in a number of scenes. The plot revolves around a youth named Andy Grainger, portrayed by actor Casey Siemaszko (left), who gets into troubled after stealing a car and is sent to Boys Town. Academy Award winner Art Carney (right) plays Father Michael O'Halloran, a Boys Town priest who helps Andy find a positive direction in his life. The movie provided the public with a modern look at Boys Town and how it had evolved since the days of the original Boys Town movie.

The U.S. Postal Service commemorated the anniversary of Father Flanagan's one-hundredth birthday in 1986 with the release of a new four-cent stamp. The stamp was issued as part of the definitive series of Great Americans, helping to refocus attention on Boys Town and the important work begun by its founder.

The *Thata Baby* cartoon strip by Paul Trap recently described Boys Town as a popular tourist stop in Omaha, Nebraska. Trap, a Boys Town supporter, was an Omaha resident when this strip ran in the *Omaha World-Herald* newspaper in 2016. (Cartoon artwork provided courtesy of Paul Trap and used with his permission.)

The Clue Crew (above) of the popular TV game show *Jeopardy!* visited the Boys Town Hall of History in 2006 to research material for the program's answer-question board. During their stop, the crew also played a game of *Jeopardy!* with Boys Town youth (left). On a January 22, 2007, episode of the show, contestants were given this answer during their game: "He sent his 'Boys Town' Oscar to Father Flanagan, saying his 'great human qualities were strong enough to shine through my humble efforts.'" The correct response: "Who is Spencer Tracy?"

1917–2017
BOYS TOWN TIMELINE

-December 12, 1917-

Father Edward Flanagan borrows $90 to rent a boarding house at 25th and Dodge Streets in downtown Omaha, Nebraska, and officially opens Father Flanagan's Home for Boys.

-1932-

Boys Town is on the verge of closing as the Great Depression and Dust Bowl ravage the country.

-1925-

Two local businesses donate a new gateway arch for the Home's entrance.

-1922-

The Home breaks ground for a new five-story main building.

-1920-

The Mothers' Guild provides the boys with gifts and food for their Christmas dinner.

-1927-

New York Yankee sluggers Babe Ruth and Lou Gehrig tour Boys Town.

-1921-

Boys Town youth Reuben Granger is photographed carrying fellow youth Howard Loomis on his back. The photograph would later become the inspiration for Boys Town's famous "Two Brothers" symbol.

-1921-

Boys Town youth Father Flanagan moves the Home to Overlook Farm, ten miles west of Omaha.

-1923-

The Father Flanagan's Boys' Show, which put on shows to raise money and awareness of the Home, travels for the first time in its own Pullman railroad car named the "Overlook."

-1928-

The "Johnny the Gloom Killer" Club is formed and humorist Will Rogers is elected the club's first president. Johnny Rushing became known to thousands of radio listeners as "Johnny the Gloom Killer" as Boys Town sought to spread its positive message to a larger audience.

-1918-

To accommodate the growing number of boys, the Home for Boys moves to the abandoned German-American Home in South Omaha.

-1926-

The boys vote to officially change the name of Overlook Farm to Boys Town.

-1926-

Father Flanagan begins broadcasting his national radio program.

-1933-

The boys formed water brigades to save the vegetable gardens, but a drought destroys the crops.

-1938-

A cast and crew from MGM Studios begin filming the movie *Boys Town* in the Village.

-1934-

Boys Town's U.S. Post Office opens.

-1941-

CBS Radio airs the first of several national broadcasts featuring the Boys Town Choir.

-1941-

The Dowd Chapel of the Immaculate Conception, built through a donation from Marie Dowd, is dedicated.

-1946-

Boys Town announces a $30 million expansion that will double the size of the Home, adding an administration building, a high school, twenty-five cottages, a visitors center, a dining hall, a field house, a music hall, and a vocational career center.

-1948-

During a child welfare mission to Europe, Father Flanagan passes away in Berlin, Germany, at age sixty-one.

-1948-

Monsignor Nicholas Wegner is named the new executive director of Boys Town.

-1936-

Boys Town becomes an incorporated village of the State of Nebraska.

-1936-

The Boys Town Choir makes its debut in a concert at Joslyn Memorial in downtown Omaha.

-1944-

A crowd of over 43,000 attends the Boys Town vs. Detroit Catholic football game in Detroit. The game ends in a 14-14 tie.

-1950-

A major expansion of the Village is completed and its population swells to more than nine hundred boys.

-1939-

Spencer Tracy wins the Academy Award for Best Actor for his portrayal of Father Flanagan in *Boys Town*. He later gives the Oscar to Father Flanagan.

-1947-

At the invitation of the War Department, Father Flanagan tours Asia to investigate the need for aid for war orphans. He later presents his final report to President Truman at a White House meeting.

-1951-

The Boys Town National Alumni Association is organized and holds its first convention the following year.

-1967-
Vice President Hubert Humphrey delivers the commencement address to graduates during Boys Town's fiftieth anniversary.

-1974-
Boys Town hires the first Family-Teaching Couple for its new Family Home Program, which will provide care for the youth in individual, family-style residences.

-1965-
Boys Town High School joins the newly organized Metropolitan Athletic League.

-1972-
The *Omaha Sun* newspaper reports Boys Town has a large endowment fund. Boys Town and others defend the fund, saying it ensures the Home will be able to continue its work far into the future.

-1977-
The Boys Town Institute for Communication Disorders in Children (later renamed Boys Town National Research Hospital) opens near downtown Omaha.

-1956-
Boys Town graduate Charles "Deacon" Jones competes in the 1956 Olympic Games in Melbourne, Australia, finishing ninth in the 3,000-meter steeplechase. Four years later, he would finish seventh in the same event in the Rome Olympics.

-1962-
Indira Gandhi, the future prime minister of India, visits Boys Town.

-1962-
The Boys Town Choir records an album with the Everly Brothers.

-1966-
The Cowboys basketball team wins its second straight state basketball championship.

-1973-
Monsignor Nicholas Wegner retires as executive director.

-1973-
Monsignor Robert Hupp is named Boys Town's third executive director.

-1954-
World heavyweight boxing champion Rocky Marciano visits the Home.

-1968-
Boys Town alumnus Lloyd Bucher, commander of the USS *Pueblo*, and his crew are captured by North Korean naval forces. They are released in 1969 after almost a year of imprisonment and torture.

-1976-
Monsignor Wegner passes away.

-1976-
Mother Teresa of Calcutta receives the Father Flanagan Award for Service to Youth during a visit to Boys Town.

-1976-
Boys Town completes its transition to the Family Home Program as the last of the boys move into seventy family-style homes in the Village.

-1986-
The Boys Town Hall of History museum opens.

-1986-
Nancy Reagan receives the Father Flanagan Award for Service to Youth during a visit to Boys Town.

-1986-
The U.S. Postal Service issues a new four-cent Father Flanagan stamp.

-1986-
A second affiliate site, Boys Town Central Florida, opens in Orlando.

-1983-
The first five girls graduate from Boys Town High School.

-1983-
Boys Town North Florida, the organization's first national site, opens in Tallahassee.

-1993-
Boys Town Washington DC opens in the nation's capital.

-1993-
A national database is established to provide an informational storage and distribution link between all of Boys Town's programs.

-1993-
The Youth Care Administration building in the Village is renovated to centralize all of Boys Town's youth care programs.

-1993-
Boys Town National Training Center programs for educators impact more than 250,000 students nationwide.

-1997-
Boys Town's Common Sense Parenting program provides training for parents at bases around the world as part of the U.S. Air Force's Family Advocacy program.

-1997-
Boys Town launches its Reading Is FAME program.

-1997-
Boys Town celebrates its eightieth anniversary.

-1995-
A new Residential Treatment Center opens at Boys Town National Research Hospital to serve children with serious behavioral issues.

-1995-
A Continuum of Care is created to more closely connect Boys Town programs.

-1990-
The Boys Town New York site opens in New York City.

-1979-
The first girls are admitted to Boys Town.

-1989-
A new Boys Town Texas site opens in San Antonio.

-1989-
Three Family Homes open at a new Boys Town Louisiana site in New Orleans.

-1989-
The Boys Town National Hotline, a toll-free crisis telephone service, begins taking calls from all fifty states.

-1994-
A strategic plan to disseminate Boys Town's childcare technology is launched.

-1985-
Monsignor Hupp retires as Boys Town's executive director.

-1985-
Father Val J. Peter is appointed as the Home's fourth executive director.

-1985-
The U.S. Department of the Interior names Boys Town a National Historic Landmark.

-1991-
New affiliate sites open in Portsmouth, Rhode Island (Boys Town New England); Orange County, California (Boys Town California); West Palm Beach, Florida (Boys Town South Florida); and Las Vegas (Boys Town Nevada).

-1991-
Boys Town celebrates its seventy-fifth anniversary and Faberge unveils its commemorative Two Brothers Egg.

-1991-
The Herbert B. Chambers Jr. Protestant Chapel, a gift from the Chambers family of New Jersey, is dedicated in the Village.

-1998-
The hospital announces its researchers have located the gene responsible for Usher syndrome, Type IIa, which causes combined blindness and deafness.

-2006-
First Lady Laura Bush visits Boys Town to receive the Father Flanagan Award for Service to Youth.

-2006-
President George W. Bush presents the President's Volunteer Service Award to Boys Town volunteer John "Buzz" Garlock.

-2006-
The Boys Town boys' basketball team wins its first state championship in forty years.

-2002-
The hospital dedicates its National Center for the Study and Treatment of Usher Syndrome.

-2002-
A new life-size statue of Father Flanagan is unveiled in front of the Father Flanagan House on campus.

-2002-
Boys Town Mayor Amanda Martinez carries the Olympic Torch through Boys Town as it heads to the Winter Olympic Games in Salt Lake City, Utah.

-2002-
The Boys Town National Hotline answers its five millionth call.

-2002-
The hospital breaks ground for its new Lied Learning and Technology Center for Childhood Deafness and Vision Disorders.

-2004-
Godfather's Pizza becomes Boys Town's first corporate sponsor.

-2004-
The Lied Learning and Technology Center for Childhood Deafness and Vision Disorders opens.

-2006-
Boys Town opens an office in Council Bluffs, Iowa, to begin providing family-based services.

-2006-
The "Clue Crew" for the popular television game show *Jeopardy!* comes to Boys Town to research information for a future broadcast.

-2006-
The hospital hosts the first international symposium on Usher syndrome and related disorders.

-2006-
Boys Town National Research Hospital-West opens to provide patient services.

-2000-
Boys Town serves a record number of children through its youth care and health care programs.

-2000-
Boys Town hosts the national conference "Creating a Safe Environment and Safe Schools."

-2003-
Former Boys Town Executive Director Monsignor Hupp passes away.

-2005-
Staff and residents of Boys Town Louisiana are evacuated to Boys Town in Nebraska to escape Hurricane Katrina.

-2005-
The Village of Boys Town is named one of the "100 Best Communities for Young People" by the America's Promise Alliance.

-2005-
Construction begins on Boys Town National Research Hospital-West in the Village.

-2005-
Father Steven Boes is appointed as the Home's fifth executive director upon the retirement of Father Val Peter.

-2007-
Boys Town further develops its Integrated Continuum of Care to have an even greater impact with children and families through its services across America.

-2007-
The newly renovated Palrang Memorial Field House is dedicated.

-2007-
Father Boes travels to Father Flanagan's home in Ireland to commemorate the ninetieth anniversary of Boys Town's founding.

-2007-
Boys Town celebrates its ninetieth anniversary by unveiling a new logo and branding.

-2001-
A life-size bronze statue of Father Flanagan is unveiled in his hometown of Ballymoe, Ireland.

-2011-
The Archdiocese of Omaha announces the cause for canonization of Father Flanagan, declaring him a Servant of God.

-2011-
Boys Town Nebraska/Iowa expands its In-Home Family Services in Iowa.

-2011-
Construction begins on the new Boys Town Center for Behavioral Health and the Residential Treatment Center.

-2013-
All Boys Town national sites now offer In-Home Family Services.

-2013-
The new Center for Behavioral Health opens its doors to provide specialized care for children and adults.

-2013-
Boys Town takes a national leadership role in advocating for quality residential care for children who require more intensive interventions to overcome serious behavioral problems.

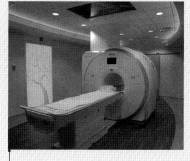

-2008-
Boys Town kicks off its first five-year strategic plan for youth care and health care services with the goal of expanding its Integrated Continuum of Care and helping more children and families.

-2008-
A new biography about Father Flanagan, entitled *Father Flanagan of Boys Town: A Man of Vision*, is released.

-2015-
Boys Town National Research Hospital adds 3T fMRI technology to its Center for Neurobehavioral Research on the west medical campus.

-2015-
Boys Town youth, health, family, and community services touch the lives of over two million people nationwide every year.

-2009-
The Boys Town Day School opens.

-2009-
Boys Town Washington DC youth march in the presidential inauguration parade.

-2009-
The Boys Town National Hotline creates its "Your Life, Your Voice" website, giving teens a safe place to share their concerns and seek assistance.

-2009-
Boys Town joins the Nebraska Families Collaborative, a private, nonprofit partnership that contracts with the State of Nebraska to provide child welfare support to families.

-2014-
The National Institutes of Health awards the hospital a $11.3 million, five-year Centers of Biological Research Excellence (COBRE) grant to study and better understand the consequences of childhood hearing loss.

-2012-
The first five-year strategic plan is completed; one outcome is a dramatic increase in the number of children receiving life-changing Boys Town services. A second five-year strategic plan is launched, focusing on community initiatives that will help children and families where the need is the greatest.

-2012-
The hospital's west campus is named the Patrick E. Brookhouser, MD, Medical Campus.

-2012-
Boys Town launches its Center for Neurobehavioral Research in Children, a collaborative effort between Boys Town National Research Hospital and Boys Town youth care services to study and improve methods for intervening early in the lives of children with behavioral and mental health problems.

-December 12, 2017-
Boys Town will celebrate its one hundredth anniversary.

Credits for Photos/Illustrations from Boys Town Archives

All photos are the property of Boys Town. Many people contributed to the archives from which the photos in this book were selected. Every effort was made to identify individual photographers. Listed below are identified photographers whose photos were used.

Al Bates

Ernest Bihler

Don Bindyke

Louis R. Bostwick

Michael Buckley

John Copack

Walter S. Craig

Christine Dirkschneider

Don Doll

Skip Kennedy

Tim McCormick

Robert McFarland

Metro News Photos

Paul Otero

George Skadding

St. Augustine Indian Mission

Henry V. Straka

James Tomczak

U.S. Army

U.S. Army Signal Corps

White House

Index

About the Authors

Thomas Lynch has worked at Boys Town for thirty years and currently serves as the director of the Boys Town Hall of History and Community Programs. Lynch, who earned his degree in history from the University of Nebraska-Omaha, also heads the organization's volunteer program and was responsible for gathering documentation in support of the cause for canonization of Boys Town's founder, Father Edward Flanagan.

Terry Hyland is the director of Boys Town's writing team, which is part of the organization's Marketing and Communications Department. With a degree in journalism from the University of Nebraska-Lincoln, Hyland has authored or co-authored numerous books and publications during his twenty-six years as a Boys Town writer.